It's GLOBAL

Unlimited scope

'All of us are surging through the most profound revolution in human history. Its impact is personal, national, global—and, in many ways unlimited. At its core are seven catalysts, now converging and fusing to change the way we live, work, play, learn, teach, think and create—at any age. They keys to unlock that future are simple but revolutionary. Once unlocked, that revolution has the power to unleash the combined talents of millions.' **Introduction, Page 22.**

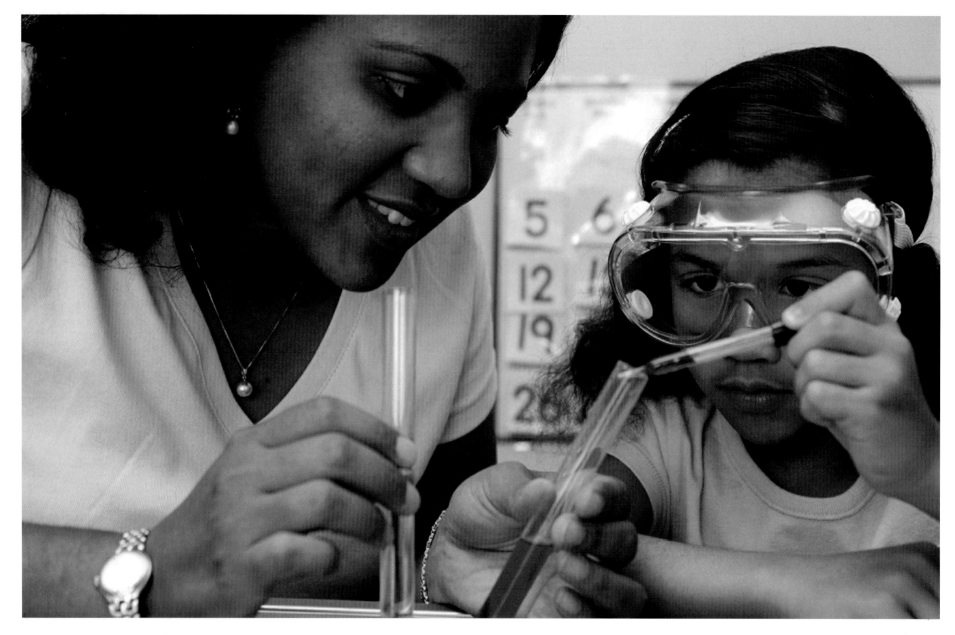

It's INTERACTIVE
Unlimited discovery

For decades most school students have learned **about** subjects such as history, space travel and science. Now they can actually **rebuild** ancient Rome and Athens (with SimCity); **create** their "own universe" (with Spore); and actually **become** a scientist. Brigham Young University's Virtual ChemLab provides a working classroom of the future, for some 150,000 online science students. Now: the new cyberspace university. **From Chapter ten, The co-creative revolution.**

It's EASILY SHARED

Unlimited partnerships

Amazingly, 59 million school teachers around the planet work in isolation, mostly in chalkboard classrooms—as if the Web didn't exist. But at Singapore's Overseas Family School (in photo) 3,500 students from over seventy countries not only co-create their vision of the future—they help their teachers digitize lesson plans with Macromedia Flash and computer animations. Now those brilliant lesson-models can be shared free. **Chapter thirteen, The global revolution.**

It's PERSONAL

Unlimited future

*'Everyone has the potential to become talented and successful, but in different ways. Every healthy baby is born with 100 billion active brain cells. Each has the ability to sprout at least 10,000 learning-branches. That learning ability soars most from birth to four.' And that is why, at Mexico's world-leading Thomas Jefferson Institute (in photo), psychologists help parents to work out a specific learning plan for every child. **Chapter three: The talent revolution.***

It's CO-CREATIVE

Unlimited innovation

When tens of thousands of passionate people who have never met can write ten million articles and together co-create the planet's biggest-ever encyclopedia, something magic is stirring in the world. When Wikipedia is available instantly and free to 1.4 billion people, the magic glows. When four billion will soon have that encyclopedia in their pocket, the world is surging into a new Renaissance: the one we will co-create. **In Chapter one: the Wikinomics revolution.**

It's INSTANT
Unlimited mobility

Even by 2000 half the people on earth had never placed a phone call. Only 12 percent owned mobile phones. Now over half own them: 3.3 billion. By late 2009, 4 billion will be in use, for the planet's 6.6 billion people. But now they are becoming 'teleputers' more than phones. And soon you'll be able to have Google on tap in your pocket, too. Google's new Android software platform will be available to use in any manufacturer's mobile phones. **Preface, page 18.**

It's OFTEN FREE
Unlimited choice

In China, students can now buy low-cost computers without an operating system—and download that free from the Web. Then they can use it for free international phone calls with Skype. Many teachers use the same tools to teach Mandarin each day around the world. Google's climb to several fortunes has been spurred by the simple idea: give away information free and "make a billion one 5-cent click at a time". **Chapter ten, The co-creative revolution.**

China TV apologized: only 10 million would be watching

But that interview launched the world's fastest-selling book

In photo: Gordon Dryden with one of the giant souvenir copies of the Chinese version of The Learning Revolution, printed to mark sales of 10 million copies in under seven months: a global non-fiction record. The book was launched on a late-night national TV show with apologies that "only 10 million people would be watching", but 260,000 copies were sold the next day, when thousands attended Learning Revolution exhibitions in China's thirty largest cities: 44,000 in Beijing alone.

Author biography: Gordon Dryden

How to quit school at age 14 and end up writing the top-selling book on learning

How Gordon Dryden and Jeannette Vos became the world's biggest and fastest-selling non-fiction authors is almost a fiction story in itself:

One: the New Zealander who left high school illegally at age fourteen. Yet he went on to become an award-winning newspaper journalist, top radio and television talkshow host and specialist in interactive multimedia communications.

The other: the Dutch-born wartime refugee, later United States school teacher who became so frustrated at the education system she decided to change it. That decision was to result in a seven-year research program into new methods of learning, and a doctorate in education.

When they met, by accident, sitting next to each other at a 1991 international conference on learning, their backgrounds could not have been more diverse:

Dryden's self-taught career up to then had mainly been in mass communications: in print journalism, advertising creative director, public relations. Later as marketing director for a major corporation; then a long stint in radio and television, as a producer-presenter and on international assignments that ranged from the revolution in Iran to the counter-revolution in Czechoslovakia.

In 1990—New Zealand's 150th anniversary—he persuaded that country's largest charitable trust to donate $2 million to set up the Pacific Foundation, to pioneer new methods of parenting and schooling. His chance meeting with Jeannette Vos happened while editing six one-hour television documentaries as part of that project.

Later, when the two swapped their research—TV programs for a thick doctoral dissertation on the same subject—the idea emerged for a joint book. That was to lead, late in 1993, to the first edition of *The Learning Revolution*—and later its world success: published in twenty different languages in twenty-six countries. This included world-record non-fiction sales of 10 million copies in one seven-month burst in China: 44,000 in one day in Beijing alone.

But what has struck them most: how their own backgrounds have provided completely different perspectives. Now these have converged to produce a complete new theory of learning, schooling, teaching and education.

Between researching and writing, Gordon Dryden mainly helps schools, businesses and other learning organizations put this research into practice:

❏   As seminar coordinator and presenter for a wide range of programs to marry the world's finest new interactive technology with the world's best teaching and learning methods: for the Singapore Ministry of Education's program to "teach less, learn more"; the New Zealand Ministry of Education's current five-year program on the use of interactive technology in schools; the British Government's program to teach business enterprise and innovation at high schools; the Swedish giant IKEA's management program to introduce new staff training methods in Scandinavia, Poland and Western China; and New Zealand's Southland Innovator Program to retrain teachers for the new century.

❏   As consultant to some of the world's most visionary schools, including: Mexico's Thomas Jefferson Institute (the supreme school-of-the-year for innovation and vision among all schools in the Spanish-speaking world); Singapore's Overseas Family School (the first in South-East Asia to introduce the International Baccalaureate Curriculum for all age groups, from pre-kindergarten to senior high school); and the Beijing Academy of Educational Sciences in Beijing.

❏ As a consultant to Arizona's University of Advancing Technology, which has awarded him an honorary Doctor of Computer Science for his contribution to creative thinking in using interactive technology as the catalyst to reinvent education.

Now six-year-olds make their own television shows

For almost twenty years, Gordon Dryden has been recording and promoting the way in which his home country, New Zealand, is using interactive technology in schools. He regularly takes international visitors to public schools such as Sherwood Primary, in the Auckland area, where six-year-olds, from their first day in grade one (above), learn to use video cameras. Within two days they are using Apple iMovie software to edit what they have shot, before adding their own computer animations.

From the freezing cold of northern Sweden to Canada and South Africa

The book that's been translated into twenty languages

In photo: Co-author Jeannette Vos with some of the twenty-six editions of The Learning Revolution sold around the world in twenty languages since her doctoral research and Gordon Dryden's television programs came together to produce the first edition in 1993, and five updates since then. At one stage she spent months doing up to six seminars a week in Sweden.

Author biography: Jeannette Vos

The frustrated teacher who spent seven years researching a better way

When Jeannette Vos arrived in Canada as a World War II refugee from Nazi-occupied Holland, she never dreamed her life in the Americas would take her to a career in teaching, research, authoring and consulting around the world.

Nor did she conceive that her later frustration with the education system would lead to designing a better one—and take her back to Europe and around the world to promote it.

When she first started teaching in the United States and Canada, her enthusiasm was high—and so was her success as she rose through the ranks of teachers, working with all age groups. But soon her frustration became so strong she almost gave up teaching—until she discovered the difference with the then-new SuperCamp, and its ten-day program to replace the boredom of school with confidence-building learning-to-learn courses.

Determined to prove that it worked, she embarked on a seven-year research study, not only into SuperCamp's programs but going beyond into other new methods of learning. It was to earn her a doctorate in education and the opportunity to put those methods into practice around the globe.

But her chance 1991 meeting with Gordon Dryden at an international learning conference was to produce an even greater coincidence. He was searching for a musical theme for the television series he was working on—and music is one of the Vos specialties. But when they swapped experiences, the coincidence was even more remarkable.

The television series showed how the new methods were transforming schools and teaching methods around the planet. The doctoral research confirmed the TV programs' other international findings.

When they met again the following year at a similar international conference, the ideas was born for the first of their new series of co-authored books on *The Learning Revolution*.

The first was written by fax machine across the Pacific—the first year's bills totalled $6,000—and then others by email as they toured the world promoting the results and adding more.

At one stage, Jeannette Vos was presenting at least six seminars a week over the length and breadth of five continents: Europe, the Americas, Asia, Africa, Australia and New Zealand.

She is also a well-known international keynote conference presenter and seminar leader with a "whole person" approach to learning – and practical applications to show how "true learning" works wonders. Her specialities encompass boosting the genius and achievement in people through "selling" and teaching to the full potential of the brain, which includes the use of music, the arts, movement, nutrition, and overall accelerated learning methods to help people become destiny-makers for a better world.

In her workshops, representatives have come from many countries and institutions: schools, hospitals, churches, and many companies such as Telenor of Norway, Ericsson, IKEA and SAAB of Sweden, Pipsa Paper Mill of Mexico, the Pysslingen and Lemshaga Schools of Sweden and The Master's Academy of Alberta, Canada.

When Vos and co-author Dryden had concluded the last update of *The Learning Revolution* in late 2005—with the core of a completely new theory of learning—both realized the world of education was about to undergo even bigger changes.

The latest in brain-mind-body research and the new breakthroughs in instant communications and digital technology were challenging the world to reinvent education in all its forms. This book takes up that challenge, to present a total new approach to lifelong learning—based on practical models that are already working.

New ways to make the most of your mind, brain and body

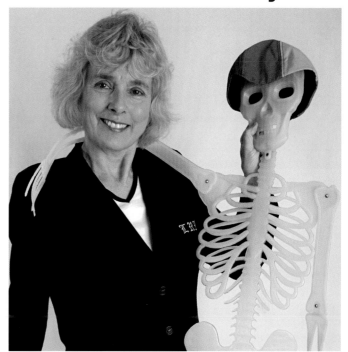

*When not co-authoring books, Jeannette Vos spends her working life these days touring the world, keynoting conferences and running workshops on two of her passions: new methods of learning and how to make the most of your mind through sensible nutrition and exercise. Apart from her doctorate in education, she is a Certified Natural Health Professional from the US National Association of Certified National Health Professionals. Generally she manages to combine both interests: like using "accelerated learning" methods to demonstrate the best ways to link good nutrition, good health with fun and good humor (in photo). **See Chapter three, The Talent Revolution.**

Also by Gordon Dryden and Jeannette Vos
Book, video, audiotape and CD-rom series:
The Learning Revolution
The New Learning Revolution

Also by Gordon Dryden
Books:
Out Of The Red
The Reading Revolution (with Denise Ford)

Parenting program:
FUNdamentals (with Colin Rose)

Television series:
New Zealand: Where To Now?
The Vicious Cycle
Right From The Start
The Vital Years
Back To Real 'Basics'
The Chance To Be Equal
The Future: Does It Work?
16-part United States series:
The Learning Revolution

Also by Jeannette Vos
Doctoral dissertation:
An Accelerated/Integrative Learning Model Program

Authors' websites and email addresses: Page 320.

UNLIMITED

The new learning revolution and the seven keys to unlock it

Copyright © 2008 Gordon Dryden and Jeannette Vos

Published internationally by The The Learning Web Ltd., P.O. Box 87209, Meadowbank, Auckland, New Zealand 1742. See page 320 for international agency address details.

In association with David Bateman Ltd, 30 Tarndale Grove, Albany, P.O. Box 100-242, NSMC, Auckland, New Zealand 1330. Phone (64 9) 415-7664. Fax (64 9) 415-8892. Email: bateman@bateman.co.nz

Pre press and international print management by Trends Media Services. www.trendsmediaservices.com

Casebound, published November 2008.

ISBN 978-0-9583701-5-8

Contents

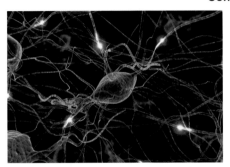   

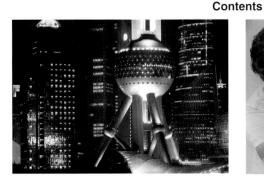

Guide to reading this book

The spelling used: For the English-language version of the book, the authors have chosen to use their own selection of "International English". Mainly the book uses the simpler American words: "program" not "programme". But it uses the English preference of "s" in verbs such a "practise", and "c" in nouns as in "practice". We have also chosen to hyphenate some words such as co-creative where the meaning, without the hyphen, may be unclear to readers in some countries.

Currency, and measurement: All currency is in US dollars. A billion is 1,000 million and a trillion is a million million. Generally international metric measurement is used.

Now more than half the world's people have mobile phones

And the online choice is virtually unlimited: from 83 million videos to English lessons

Preface by Gordon Dryden ▬▬▬▬▬▬▬

Welcome to the new world, with unlimited access to unlimited opportunities

Even by the year 2000 half the people on earth had never placed a phone call.

Now more than half own mobile phones: 3.3 billion of them by early 2008. Four billion phones will be in use by the end of 2009—for the planet's 6.6 billion people.

For more than twenty years the Sony *Walkman* personalized the world of portable music. Now the new era of Nokia, Apple *iPod* and *iPhone* will soon make almost any information available instantly on a multimedia computer in your pocket. And with its newest product, *Android,* all Google's services will be free on most cellphones.

Well over 550 million cellphones are now used in China. And more Chinese are learning English than the entire population of North America. They're learning it best by mobile-phone lessons and singing to karaoke machines in cyber-cafes.

By early 2005 no one had ever heard of *YouTube.* Now anyone with a computer—or broadband access through their cellphone-screen—can view from a choice of more than 83 million free videos on this one site: twenty-first-century literacy in practice.

Six years ago long international phone calls cost far too much for most. Now more than 300 million people make free international calls—or join in free video conference calls—anywhere on earth through *Skype*. Teachers can gain degrees in educational technology almost entirely online.[1] They are on campus only three weeks a year. And they can apply their lessons immediately in their own school classrooms.

Welcome to the new world of interactive, global and personalized learning. If these trends, and dozens of similar ones, changed only the world's technology and computer industries, they would be important enough. But they also form the catalysts to reinvent education, schooling and learning—even new global cyber-universities.

In the four-fifths of their time they spend outside school, students from Mumbai to Mexico are leading this new learning revolution. But most schools are struggling to use the new transforming tools—simply because they are trying to patch twenty-first century technology on to a system designed for a bygone age.

Yet in pockets around the globe brilliant teachers are doing it right. They are using new tools to turn "education" on its head: to start with individual passions, talents and interests and unleash each person's almost unlimited ability to flower.

Bright young students are reinventing a new society: of unlimited choices, unlimited options, and unlimited personal potential.

The brand names of this new era are passwords to the future: *Google, Yahoo, You-Tube, Wikipedia, MySpace, Facebook, Bebo, eBay, Skype, iPod, iPhone, iTunes, Sim City, PlayStation* and *Nintendo.* In South Korea, the phenomena of *CyWorld,* an online co-creative network, is shared by more than 90 percent of its fifteen-to-thirty-year-olds. In Japan, *DoCoMo*—the multilevel cellphone service that invented texting—is used by over fifty million people for everything from learning and portable video-conferencing to shopping and banking, from email to online games. And the DoCoMo company is worth more on the Stock Exchange than Google in America.

Some call it Web 2.0: the completely new interactive phase of the World Wide Web. Others call it the New Renaissance. Still others: the new era of mass innovation, mass participation, mass co-creativity, mass personalization.

At the base of the revolution is the ability to stack millions of transistors on to a chip of silicon, and to double the number on a circuit board every eighteen months. When five transistors doubled to ten, it launched the digital age. But when five billion now double to ten billion in eighteen months, the potential is almost limitless.

For the first time in history, everyone has the opportunity to turn individual personal passion and talent into a successful life and career. And to keep on adding new skills throughout life—with almost unlimited access to the world's best new retraining and relearning methods . . . to make the future itself almost without limits.

Gordon Dryden, co-author and editor

When five transistors on a chip rose to 10 the revolution began

When five billion soars to 10 billion the potential is unlimited

Real learning starts with a happy, healthy, secure child in a loving home

Foreword by Jeannette Vos

The more the new technology soars, the more the need for holistic balance

Even thirty years ago, most teachers were taught that intelligence was fixed—and could be measured from early childhood by standardized I.Q. tests.

Even today, in the country where I have spent most of my adult life, almost the entire American schooling system is based around standardized tests of standardized knowledge—as if all children were the same. They are not.

Some of the world's best neuroscientists have proved for over two decades that all of us are smart in different ways. We each have a different learning style, a different thinking style, and different ways of studying and working. So the school of the future will be personalized for every individual learning style.

We also learn best in a happy, safe environment, with good diet and nutrition, in caring, loving families, and in schools where lifeskills and holistic learning are even more important than learning to master the new tools of high technology.

So capitalizing on the new world of instant information and interactive technology is only one side of the path to a potentially unlimited future. Every good parent and teacher knows the other side involves the whole person, in a caring home and a caring community—with brain, mind and body acting together in balance.

At its simplest, you cannot learn well if you're hungry or fearful. You cannot learn well if your brain has been stunted from birth because you're under-nourished. You cannot benefit from a world of potential plenty if you live in a country with polluted water, unsanitary sewerage, without adequate food, clothing and security; in world where sometimes obscene wealth is surrounded by overwhelming poverty.

An over-riding message of this book is that all of us can also learn best when we use the whole world as a classroom . . . especially when that world is a welcoming, caring, sharing one. But even in the world's most affluent countries—in North America, western Europe, Australia and New Zealand—many are handicapped by poverty, emotional stress, bad nutrition and poor family environments.

We also all live in a series of interlocking eco-systems, where pollution, environmental degradation and climate change are crying out for new solutions. We live, too, in a world where a $600-billion-a-year pharmaceutical drugs industry is mistaken for a real health policy. Often where inadequate schooling is mistaken for real-life education. Where inefficient bureaucracy is mistaken for social innovation.

As we two co-authors have travelled to many parts of the world, we have seen the positive, holistic alternatives that can match the new digital wealth-producing revolution with an equal balance of social, emotional, mental and cultural enrichment.

❏ Children of poor parents in developing countries, like India, have filled schools whenever daily meal programs have been introduced.

❏ Entire school-age populations have prospered—as in Finland—when the government provides high-quality teachers and teacher training programs.

❏ The soaring world population, in over-crowded poor countries, is matched by a growing environmental crisis—and equally successful sustainable technologies.

❏ Small nations like Singapore, Ireland, Finland, Sweden, Norway, Denmark and New Zealand have shown that size is not important for national success.

❏ The enormous cost of the war in Iraq proves that money is not the problem. Nobel prize-winning economist Joseph Stiglitz estimates that war will end up costing at least $3 trillion.[1] So even a tiny fraction of that, invested in the right way, would more than solve the world's problems of poverty, malnutrition, poor health—and provide a decent basic education for all.

❏ Ideally, too, we now know that well-prepared parents are the world's best first teachers. A happy, healthy home is the world's best school. A healthy, caring community is the world's best playground. A secure, ecologically balanced world is the planet's best classroom—that unlimited global classroom we all share together.

Jeannette Vos, co-author

Sound nutrition and exercise are as much 'food for the mind' as for the body

Will students study tomorrow as the iPod works today?

Asked to predict the future, Google CEO Eric Schmidt admits "we don't know what's coming." But he adds: "I personally believe the right model is to think of all the world's information in the equivalent of an Apple iPod. What does it do to teaching when every student can do the answer quicker than any professor can get it out of her mouth?" But now Google's own Android software will soon put Google in your pocket too.

History's newest revolution and the seven keys to unlock it

All of us, together, are surging through the most profound revolution in human history. Its impact is personal, national, global—and, in many ways, unlimited.

At its core are seven catalysts, now converging and fusing to change the way we live, work, play, learn, teach, think and create—at any age.

This new networked age makes it urgent to rethink entirely what we mean by education, learning, teaching and schooling. For education is changing more than it has since the invention of the printing press over 500 years ago and compulsory classroom schooling 300 years ago. Now the world is your classroom and learning is lifelong.

Already two billion students spend four-fifths of their waking hours outside school, in an *iPod, YouTube, Google, Bebo, Facebook, MySpace, Wikipedia, Skype* and *SimCity* world so different from yesterday's deskbound classrooms.

Business Week magazine says lifelong learning will soon be the world's greatest growth industry, with $370 billion a year in sales as millions learn online. And Google CEO Eric Schmidt predicts that before long all the world's information will be instantly available on pocket computers like the Apple iPod. Then students will be able to find answers quicker than professors can ask questions.[1]

The keys to unlock the future are simple but revolutionary. Once unlocked, that revolution has the power to unleash the combined talents of millions:

1. It's PERSONAL: where information and learning programs can be personalized and tailored to your own passions, talents, interests and needs. And where you can share your own talents and skills with millions—for both fun and income.

2.   **It's INTERACTIVE:** with new digital platforms and templates to make it easy, simple and fun to learn by doing, playing, creating, producing and interacting—a new world of creative experiences.

3.   **It's GLOBAL:** the ever-expanding world-wide Internet owned by no one, used by everyone; where the combined knowledge of humankind is now available to virtually all at the tap of a digital keyboard or a touch screen.

4.   **It's INSTANT:** for the first time in history, the ability to learn anything "just in time", when you need it, as you need it, at your request, and in your own way.

5.   **It's MAINLY FREE:** or nearly so—one low-cost click-at-a-time. The World Wide Web, browsers, search engines and digital platforms make it easy to access much information free, and to download other information for a few cents. Even free international phonecalls.

6.   **It's EASILY SHARED:** the new world of collaborative networks to share your abilities with anyone, anywhere. To store—free online and on community websites—your family photographs, videos, music and even your digital multimedia portfolios to demonstrate what you know and what you can do.

7.   **It's CO-CREATIVE:** if we can dream it, we can now do it—together with millions around the world. Now we can merge our own talents into multi-talented global teams, to produce new innovative answers to major global problems.

These seven keys have already unlocked new doors to transform industries, countries, communities, commerce, communications and companies. They have the power to reinvent every aspect of lifelong learning, teaching and schooling. But when these "tipping points" link with other sweeping changes, the impact will be even greater:

❏   **The neuroscience revolution:** our new-found abilities to unlock the incredible potential of the human brain and mind, and shatter many of the myths on which much of "education" is based. That research shows that everyone can learn anything faster and more efficiently. That learning starts in the womb and flowers through life.

Latest neuroscience research is opening up new ways to reinvent education

How infants learn thousands of words before they can speak even one

Neuroscientists have learned more about the human brain in recent years than in all the rest of recorded history. Like the research which shows how babies can learn thousands of words even before they start speaking, around age one. The way parents talk to their babies and what they say is even more vital. ***See chapter three for an introduction to Your Future.***

Not long ago parents left their child's education to schools

Now real-life adult experience balances the hi-tech of youth

❏ **The genetic revolution:** the knowledge that "all life is one": that all living things are made from the same genetic code—where we'll soon have access to our own.

❏ **The demographic revolution:** in which, of all people who have ever lived longer than sixty-five years, two-thirds are alive today—while two billion, mainly in the poor world, are under age twenty. But now the wisdom of age and experience can link, in new ways, with the soaring hi-tech skills of children and grandchildren.

❏ **Above all, the new Open Revolution:** at long last the chance to find a genuine new way to reinvent society. Not only a choice between free-enterprise capitalism and state-controlled socialism. But a new unlimited choice of cooperative enterprise and collaborative co-creativity.

For global education the need has never has been greater.

❏ As Philippe Legrain summarizes it in *Open World: The truth about globalization:* "One in five of the world's 6.6 billion people live on less than a dollar a day—almost half on less than two dollars a day. More than 850 million cannot read or write. Nearly a billion do not have access to clean water, 2.4 billion to basic sanitation. Eleven million children under five die each year from preventable diseases."

But already the tools exist to share some of the world's best and simplest learning and health programs with billions of poor people: to provide them with most of the unlimited opportunities that today only rich countries and people enjoy.

❏ Those wealthy countries are already spending billions on these new tools that have the power to reinvent education. But most are "doing it wrong".

Very simply, they are trying to patch the technology of the twenty-first century on to a classroom system invented for a bygone age: a school system gradually conceived after the invention of the printing press in Europe more than 500 years ago.

❏ Where kindergartens, schools, colleges, universities and organizations are "doing it right", the results are remarkable. This book abounds with them. They start with individual brainpower and the seven keys to unlock the future that are already transforming nearly every other aspect of society. Together they provide the catalyst to reinvent education itself: personally, locally, nationally and globally.

1. It's PERSONAL

For everyone, everywhere, any time, in your own way

Two years ago, *Time* magazine named its Person of the Year simply: YOU.

Its cover subtitle puts it succinctly: "Yes, you. You control the Information Age. Welcome to your world."[2] That cover story simplifies its main message: "This was the year that the people took control of the media. Silicon Valley consultants call it Web 2.0, as if it were a new version of some old software. But it's really a revolution. It's a tool for bringing together the small contributions of millions of people and making them matter."

Time calls it a massive social experiment: "an opportunity to build a new kind of international understanding, not politician to politician, great man to great man, but citizen to citizen, person to person."   In some ways it's a "new digital democracy":

❏ **Blogs or Web-logs:** More than 100 million of personally-written websites flooding the Internet for anyone to share—not counting 72 million in China alone.

❏ **Mobile phones:** soaring to 3.3 billion in use around the world in 2008, predicted to rocket to at least four billion before the end of 2009.

❏ **eBay.com:** the world's biggest online auction site—where 200 million registered users each day trade goods and services worth $100 million: a new global community "flea market" where anyone can sell to anyone anywhere.

❏ **MySpace.com:** a new online community of over 100 million active users.

❏ **Fickr.com**: which hosts two billion photos in the world's biggest album.

❏ **Facebook.com**—also with more than 100 million registered users by mid-2008, growing by 25,000 a day, and 65 billion "page views" a month as friends share their experiences, videos and photographs.

❏ **YouTube.com**—the video-sharing phenomena where visitors to the site can choose from 83.4 million video-clips. *YouTube* is the forerunner to a completely new form of international online television. Only a few years back such videos would have been shot by professionals on expensive cameras and edited by other experts. Today

Now you can share your family photo album with millions on flickr.com . . .

and co-create your own global TV channel on YouTube

Five-year-olds used to learn from illustrated books

Now they can also create their own 3-D digital artwork on home computers

Even children as young as three or four find it easy to create simple computer animations with KidPix and KidPix Deluxe. And children as young as five are ready to do three-dimensional animations with free Web software such as 3D Blender. **See more details, chapter eleven.**

they're even shot by young children, edited on home computers and viewed on a new breed of digital pocket-phone-computers the size of a pack of playing cards.

No longer is education a one-way presentation process, with students as passive receivers. Now you can co-create your own lifelong learning plan—and keep on expanding your individual talent with new skills throughout life.

2. It's INTERACTIVE

Easy-to-use templates make it simple at any age

In yesterday's world, one-year-olds loved to see and hear their parents read colorful nursery-rhyme books.

Today's one-year-olds still do. *With the help of their parents, they can now also flop their tiny hands anywhere on to a computer keyboard, and see shapes, numbers and colors—and hear them in eight languages: on BabyWow software, invented by a parent for his new baby.*

Yesterday, four- and five-year-olds loved to color-in scrapbooks, with crayons and finger-painting. They still do. *They can also now create brilliant and colorful digitized artwork on such programs as Kid Pix Deluxe.*

Yesterday, children went to the movies. They still go. *They can also use Microsoft Movie Maker and Apple iMovie software to professionally edit videos they have shot themselves or in teams.*

In many New Zealand public schools, six-year-olds, from their first day in grade one, start using video cameras to explore their world and record it. They quickly learn to edit video and compose music.

In yesterday's world, seven-year-olds lucky enough to live near the sea loved to swim and build magic sand castles. They still do. *They can also now download free software from the Web to make their own three-dimensional animations.*

Great teachers have always involved their students in interactive learning. Now we can each use twenty-first-century tools to create an entire new world of interactive experiences: our own Disneylands if we wish.

3. It's GLOBAL

The Web owned by no one, but used by almost everyone

Better still, we can go on learning and sharing new skills throughout life: we can co-create the future together.

Says Canadian researcher and author Don Tapscott in *The Digital Economy:* "We are at the dawn of a new Age of Networked Intelligence—an age that is giving birth to a new economy, a new politics and a new society."

Says British scientist and author Matt Ridley, in his book, *Genome: The autobiography of a species:* "I genuinely believe we are living through the greatest intellectual moment in history. Bar none."

Says Dee Hock, the founder of Visa International and author of *Birth of the Chaordic Age:* "The undeniable fact is that we have created the greatest explosion of capacity to receive, store, utilize and transform information in history. There is no way to turn back. Whether we recognize it or not, whether we will it or not, whether we welcome it or not, whether it is constructive or not, we are caught up together—all of us and the earth as well—in the most sudden, the most profound, the most diverse and complex change in the history of civilization. Perhaps in the history of earth itself."[3]

Says Professor Michio Kaku, author of *Visions:* "Since the 1950s, the power of our computers has advanced by a factor of roughly ten billion. By 2020, microprocessors will likely be as cheap and plentiful as scrap paper, scattered by the millions into the environment, allowing us to place intelligent systems everywhere."[4]

Says Tim Berners-Lee, creator of the Web: "The vision I still have of the Web is about anything being potentially connected with anything."[5]

And from Google's Sergey Brin and Larry Page, on its mission: "To organize the world's information and make it available to anyone."

But the new co-creative learning revolution will be equally astounding.

❏   The Hewlett Foundation, inspired by the life of Silicon Valley pioneer Bill Hewlett, has invested $68 million charting precisely how it will come about: led by some of our best universities in North America, Europe, Asia, Africa and South America.[6]

59 million teachers still work mainly by themselves in isolated schools classrooms

Now fiber optics, low orbiting satellites and wireless make global classrooms possible

See globalizing the revolution, chapters ten and thirteen.

Imagine computer lessons instantly at your fingertips . . .

and access to 35,000 online video tutorials for $1 to $2 per student a year*

* www.atomiclearning.com

❏   The International Baccalaureate movement already provides a global curriculum to 539,000 students, aged from three to nineteen, in 2,051 schools in 125 countries.[7]

❏   SUN Microsystems' co-founder Scott McNealy has set up Curriki as The Global Education and Learning Network, to work towards a worldwide online curriculum for K-12 schools.[8]

❏   John Seely Brown, former head of the Silicon Valley Palo Alto Research Center that invented the personal-computer age, has spelled out how young students themselves are already leading that revolution.[9]

And brilliant schools, like Singapore's Overseas Family School, Britain's Cramlington Community High School, Mexico's Thomas Jefferson Institute, and The Master's Academy in Canada, are pioneering new ways to globalize lessons.

4. It's INSTANT
Just in time, when you need it, as you need it

For most of the last century, the assembly lines of Ford and General Motors typified the mass-production revolution.

Then Japan's Toyota introduced just-in-time mass-production, with all the hundreds of car-parts delivered each day as needed, where needed. Soon Japan and its methods dominated the world's car industry.

Then in the early 1990s a small band of computer-science students and graduates started to use online digital and interactive technology to reinvent the entire world:

❏   Tim Berners-Lee invented the tools for the World Wide Web.

❏   Mark Andreessen and his fellow Illinois students linked with financier Jim Clark to produce Netscape, the world's first real browser—to instantly surf the Web.

❏   Then students Sergey Brin and Larry Page invented Google, with the incredible ability to soon scan billions of Web sites and find answers in under half a second. Now with more than 300 million visitors every day.

❏   Atomic Learning,[10] a company set up by ex-teachers, offers 35,000 instant, on-demand personalized video tutorials to provide any subscriber with easy-to-follow graphic instructions to learn more than 100 computer programs: from editing video to making three-dimensional animations.

But probably the greatest early impact has been with music: and the power to allow fans anywhere in the world to download their favorite tracks, instantly and on demand, from a variety of online libraries, generally for under $1 a track.

The most popular service is Apple's *iTunes,* which by early 2008 offered a library of more than six million tracks. That links directly to Apple's other major twenty-first century innovation, the *iPod.* A brilliantly-designed personal music library, it's also only the size of a pack of playing cards, yet able to hold up to 15,000 personally-chosen tracks on the most expensive *iPod.*

And if students can download their choice of music instantly on demand, why not the same access to instant learning programs?

5. It's MAINLY FREE
Or nearly free: often one low-cost click at a time

Imagine any sales manager twenty years ago deciding to give away millions of copies of his company's main product absolutely free. The result: probably instant dismissal or referral to a psychiatrist. But that's what Netscape did in 1994 when it launched its first *Navigator* browser. Within a few weeks forty million computer buffs around the globe had downloaded it free. Soon Netscape was selling other advanced copies to business. And when their company "went public" in 1995 it turned financier Jim Clark into an instant billionaire. It also made multimillionaires out of Marc Andreessen and his fellow young Illinois college developers. Since then that's been one of the keys to the Web-based revolution: give away instant service free—and sell the extras.

But the new ingredient: sell those extras "one low-cost click at a time"—on some sites as low as 5 cents a click—just like Google does with its sponsored advertising links. Millions of people can now turn their own highly-specialized talents into saleable products or services. They can give away millions of free summaries on Google, and then sell the extras for a few cents or dollars on every click.

Now an entirely new marketing concept has soared into prominence. Chris Ander-

Not only instant access to information but much of it free

Google scans billions of Web pages 300 million times daily: answers in seconds

Three-dimensional science lesson plans take time to prepare

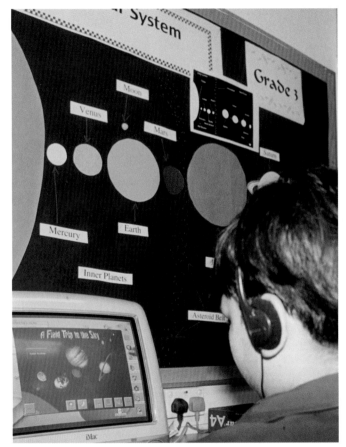

But they can be stored digitally and shared

Photo courtesy Overseas Family School, Singapore: see its remarkable story, chapters twelve and thirteen.

son, the Editor in Chief of *Wired* magazine, calls it "the long tail".[11] Up till recently, he says, we lived in "the age of the blockbuster". Only the world's top-selling books or long-playing records featured in most bookstores or radio-station play-lists.

Now, as Apple has proved, if only ten copies each of five million songs are sold, on average, at under $1 each, that would achieve sales of $50 million. Apple has made big profits from that.

But Apple has made even bigger ones by selling more than 140 million *iPods* in six years. In that time *iTunes* has sold over four billion songs, 50 million TV shows and 1.3 million movies. That's the kind of impact that Google's Schmidt is talking about when he says "we should think of all the world's information being available in the equivalent of an *iPod*".

And Harvard Business Professor Clayton M. Christensen—an expert on "disruptive innovation"—predicts this revolution will go further. No later than 2014, he says, 25 percent of all high school courses will also be available online—later personalized to each student's preferred learning style. By 2019 that will be 50 per cent.[12]

6. It's EASILY SHARED
The new world of collaborative networks

All seven "keys" are of vital importance for education. But none more so than the new world of cooperative networks of teachers and students.

Wikipedia is the ideal example.[13] Ten years ago it didn't exist. Other encyclopedias, such as *Britannica* and *World Book,* sold for $1,000 or more. Microsoft's *Encarta* soon surpassed them in popularity, given away free or sold cheaply on a CD-rom to encourage sales of *Windows.* But *Encarta* was based on an inferior printed encyclopedia, with only 4,500 articles.

Now *Wikipedia* is by far the world's largest encyclopedia. It has around 2.5 million English entries, with over ten million in all its 252 languages: instantly available, free, on the Web. All are contributed free by more than 75,000 volunteers.

Wikipedia founder Jimmy Wales states his aim succinctly: to give "every single person free access to the sum of all human knowledge".[14] Now apply that same principle to learning and schooling. The world currently has around 59 million K-12 (kindergarten to twelfth-grade) teachers, with about 1.5 billion students.

Silicon Valley researchers say around 2 percent of adults are innovators and another 13 percent "early adopters". Simple arithmetic shows 15 per cent of 59 million equals 8,850,000 teachers. Imagine each of those contributing only one favorite teaching or learning idea in a year, and sharing it with teachers around the world. Now imagine one each a month!

Britain's Promethean company already provides a model. It makes some of the world's best interactive digital whiteboards (at right), with built-in touch-screen software to teach mathematics, science, geography and other subjects. Promethean also coordinates collaborative online classrooms. In them, science and other teachers at every level can share their best lesson plans online with teachers around the world.

7. It's CO-CREATIVE

To link your unique talents with multi-talented teams

As we'll explore in later chapters, everyone has a talent to be good and probably great at something. The trick is to find that something, and now to blend it together with the talents of others—anywhere.

Most people—if provided with the opportunities—probably have a passion for something. And when both passion and talent are unleashed, those opportunities are virtually limitless. Great schools are already achieving this by enthusing students to set up their own personalized learning plans. And to keep on upgrading them, and their skills, throughout life": to be self-directed, self-motivated lifelong learners.

Many brain researchers, such as Harvard's Professor Howard Gardner, have argued for more than twenty years that intelligence is not fixed and that each of us is smart in different ways. Many schools now include Gardner's theory of "multiple intelligences" into their daily program—so that students can build on their own strengths and learn from the strengths of others.

But the new twenty-first century world of digital multimedia means that students, even from early elementary-school age, can blend their own talent into semi-profes-

After three centuries, the era of chalkboard and passive listening is finally ending

Now school can be fun and involving with interactive electronic screens* and global lesson-plan sharing

* Photo shows a Promethean Activboard in action.

Once children could only go to the movies at the cinema

Now they can create their own in digital classrooms and multi-talented teams

In photo: *Twelve-year-old students in a "digital classroom" at New Zealand's Gulf Harbor public primary school use the world as their classroom. On outdoor adventure camps (on screen) and field trips, they capture their discoveries with video cameras, then edit them on Apple iMovie video software. In this way they learn to blend their own individual talent into multi-talented teams.* **See The Digital Revolution, chapter twelve.**

sional multi-talented teams. Scripting, shooting, editing and providing music and props for school videotape, for example, requires many different talents: technical, visual, musical, graphic, linguistic and animation.

Wikipedia provides a brilliant one-dimensional model for cooperative sharing and co-creation. But leading American digital games producer Marc Prensky has an even better idea.[15]

Like the co-authors of this book, he wants the world's students to reinvent education, reinvent schooling, reinvent the way the world learns and teaches.

And he wants them to do it by cooperatively building digital learning games with the same appeal that Sony *PlayStation 3,* Nintendo and Microsoft interactive games already have for tens of millions of children in every continent. Kids love them because they're interactive fun.

Now imagine tens of thousands of individual colleges, schools or millions of classrooms each taking responsibility for becoming the expert on one "subject" or aspect of each subject. The goal: the best learning software, produced by the students of the world, and shared freely with all other students around the world—on every aspect of every "subject". Welcome to the real Free World. Linux, the open-source computer operating system inspired by Finnish student Linus Torvalds, was co-created by thousands of computer-science students around the world. You can now download it free from the Web, like you can download low-cost or free software or music.

"Linux," says Eric Raymond, "was the first project to make a conscious, successful effort to use the entire world as a talent pool."[16] A small group of students on the new Web first proved this by together co-designing a complete computer operating system. Now one million are working together on other digital projects—and a new business model: instead of the winner-takes-all—all can be winners.

In pockets around the planet, talented school teachers have also started the reinvention. All great teachers involve their students in challenging, interactive projects.

Some of their interactive classroom innovations are brilliant, but serve only twenty to forty students. We've called that *The Learning Revolution 1.0.*

Now the overwhelming need is to "scale up" their efforts—to make them available to hundreds of millions—to use the whole world as this new talent pool. And this is *The Learning Revolution 2.0.*

Just as genius students like Google's Brin and Page can turn their combined talents into a company valued at $170 billion—so too can the world's greatest teachers and other bright students share their talents with millions—some free and others as income-earners.

❏ At Singapore's Overseas Family School, with international students from seventy-four countries, teachers and students have digitized most of their lesson plans, for sharing with others. And they've also used their own excellent computer network to provide individual learning programs for all 3,500 students.

❏ At Mexico's K-12 Thomas Jefferson Institute, highly creative students from its high schools and middle schools each produce one Broadway musical a year to professional standards: from *The Disney High School Musical* to *Cats* and *Wicked.* And the Institute has ongoing global relationships with MIT's MediaLab, NASA, Apple, Microsoft and top-tier schools and universities around the world. Their high school students even take the Harvard Business School's business courses.

❏ In New Zealand, the Government abolished its national Education Department almost twenty years ago and replaced it with a much smaller policy-recommending Ministry. Since then all schools, public and private, have been charter schools, run by local boards. Innovation has soared.

At two new special-designation schools in Christchurch, students use the entire city as a classroom. Each student has a personalized learning plan, worked out in partnership with parents and learning advisers. Each plan starts with the student's own passions, talents, interests, vision and drive. The very names of the schools—Discovery One (for primary students) and Unlimited (for high school)—echo the emphasis.

New Zealand's new national curriculum guidelines are also being hailed as an international model for K-12 education.[17] The vision is for young people who are confident, connected and enthusiastic lifelong learners, with goals to achieve excellence,

At many schools students perform in annual musicals

Now their videos of Broadway hits are good enough for the Disney Channel

*Broadway musicals produced each year by the students at Mexico's Thomas Jefferson Institute are so professional that the Disney Channel screened the video of their production of The Disney High School Musical. To produce the Broadway hit Wicked (above), the challenge was even harder: to translate and rhyme the English script in Spanish. For two years in a row the Institute has been voted Latin America's school of the year for vision and innovation. **See full story, chapter twelve.***

But the real power to reinvent everything: the human brain

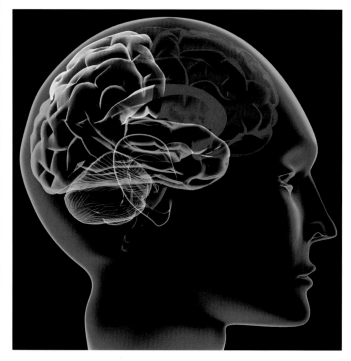

❏ # A trillion brain cells
❏ # 100 billion neurons
❏ # 900 billion others
❏ # 100 trillion 'files'

❏ *For a new theory of learning:* **chapter two.**
❏ *For the latest brain research:* **chapter three.**

innovation and diversity as well as twenty-first century literacy and numeracy.

A completely new approach is also about to revolutionize university life. A group of educational leaders have used a $68 million fund from the Hewlett Foundation to show how the world can build a new online Global Cyberspace Learning Web. This will be co-created by all, shared by all, expanded by all.

But we stress that this is not a book that recommends interactive technology and the Internet as new all-embracing "magic bullets" to transform education. Only a fool worships his tools. But over centuries dramatic new *disruptive technologies*—from the wheel to the plow, sail-power to steam-engines, printed books to electric power, automobiles to television—have ushered in great *social* changes.

Those changes transcend the technologies themselves. And this new revolution is more about the social and personal changes than the technologies that spur them.

Link those new innovations with the incredible powers of the human brain—and the new breakthroughs to unleash the unique power of the human mind—and the scope of the new revolution is truly unlimited.

As Gary Hamel summarizes it in *Leading The Revolution:* "We are now standing on the threshold of a new age—an age of revolution. Change has changed. No longer is it additive. No longer does it move in a straight line. In the twenty-first century, change is discontinuous, abrupt, seditious. In a single generation, the cost of decoding the human gene has dropped from millions to less than a hundred bucks. The cost of storing a megabyte of data has dropped from hundreds of dollars to essentially nothing. The Web is rapidly becoming a dense global matrix of connections between people, their ideas and their resources."[18]

In this new world, says Hamel, the future is not something that happens to you, but something you create.

And now we can co-create that future together, wherever we live.

Part one
The future

Even ten years ago the digital-divide was a global chasm

Now billions can plug themselves into the new Renaissance

The seven ways Web 2.0 is changing the future of everything, everywhere

Five hundred years ago the first Renaissance transformed Europe. Now a new one plugs everyone into a new Renaissance that has the power to co-create a new world.

"What happened in the western half of Europe just before 1500 was one of the most remarkable convergences of influential events in the known history of the world to that time," says historian Professor Geoffrey Blainey, in *A Short History of the World*.

"It was like a crossroads where, almost by chance, extraordinary meetings took place between navigators and painters, priests and teachers and scientists.

"There emerged a new way of painting and sculpting and a fresh perspective in architecture which, seen as a whole, was called the Renaissance or rebirth. A religious awakening, the Reformation, swept across northern Europe.

"The technique of printing, a wonderful way of disseminating new and old knowledge, leaped from town to town. An entirely new world emerged with the discovery in quick succession of the American continent and the all-sea route from Europe to eastern Asia."

The late Peter Drucker summarized that Renaissance impact on education succinctly: "The printed book in the West triggered a surge in the love of learning such as the world had never seen before, and has never seen since.

"It made it possible for people in all walks of life to learn at their own speed, in the privacy of their own home, or in the congenial company of like-minded readers."[1]

But for almost two centuries, says Peter Drucker, that message was largely lost on schooling. "The printed book, fiercely resisted by schoolteachers in the fifteenth and sixteenth centuries, did not triumph until the Jesuits and Comenius created schools based on it in the seventeenth century. The printed book forced schools to change drastically how they were teaching. Before then, the only way to learn was either by laboriously copying manuscripts, or by listening to lectures or recitations. Suddenly people could learn by reading."

But an even more important learning revolution is exploding today. Its early stages became the theme of our earlier *Learning Revolution* books: new ways to learn anything easier, faster and more effectively, even in existing schools. Its next stage came with the World Wide Web in the 1990s—and its ability to supply instant information and synthesized knowledge direct to those with personal computers. Some call that Web 1.0: the first phase of the global Internet revolution.

But the components of the new twenty-first-century learning revolution now blaze around the planet in new symbols dubbed *Google, Wikipedia, Skype, iPod, YouTube, Facebook, Nokia, Yahoo, eBay, Flickr* and *MySpace*. Some now label it Web 2.0: the fusion of technologies that make the soaring changes global, instant, free and open, personal and mobile, interactive, co-creative and easily shared—by billions.

Canadian Don Tapscott, who has written eleven books on the new digital age, describes Web 1.0 as similar to a global digital newspaper. "You could open its pages and observe its information, but you couldn't modify it or interact with it. And rarely could you communicate meaningfully with its authors, apart from sending an email to the editor.

"The new Web is fundamentally different in both its architecture and applications. Instead of a digital newspaper, think of a shared canvas where every splash of paint contributed by one user provides a richer tapestry for the next user to modify or build on. Whether people are creating, sharing or socializing, the new Web is principally about participating rather than about passively receiving information."[2]

More than 1.4 billion Web-networked personal computers are now in use. Over 3.3

Everyone can be a movie maker in this Renaissance

YouTube videos fill more Web space than total Internet in 2000

The first Renaissance unleashed the creative power of brilliant individual artists. The new one unleashes the power of all, starting at elementary school and before. **In photo:** *students at the Key School in Indianapolis, USA, re-create the exploration of the planet Mars—and video their research and discoveries. Other amateur movie-makers have contributed 83 million videos to YouTube in its first three years of life. And those take up more space on the World Wide Web than the contents of the entire Internet in 2000.* **For more details of the Key School's "multiple-intelligence classrooms", see chapter four.**

Forty years ago 30 transistors powered a pocket calculator

Now 200 million transistors can fit on the head of a pin

billion people have wireless mobile phones—powerful multimedia computers in their pockets: more than half the people on earth. By 2010 there will be over two billion (PC) Internet users. Around 30 percent of all households in the world will have them. And well over four billion people will each have a hand-held mobile computer much more powerful than all the computing power that existed only a few years ago.

But Web 2.0 is much, much more than personal computers and information on demand. Now everyone, individually and together, can program the future. And self-organizing, self-governing communities are replacing monopoly central control. In the 1990s, we built passive websites. Now we co-create vibrant, interactive, sharing, global, social-networking communities, from MySpace to Facebook.

If you think that won't write a new agenda for education, think again. We're moving rapidly from a world of isolated school classrooms—used for only twenty-five to thirty hours a week—to an always-in-use global learning network: a second-phase Web of interactive, co-creative lifelong learners, explorers and discoverers.

Moore's Law and Metcalfe's Law

Two of the main catalysts for the new era have been obvious for years.

❏ **Moore's Law:** which carries the name of Gordon Moore, co-founder of Intel, the giant Californian corporation and the world's biggest maker of silicon chips that have given the planet's best-known valley its name.

In 1965 Moore predicted that the number of tiny transistors that could be crammed on to each silicon chip would keep doubling every year, with no increase in price. Later Intel changed that to eighteen months. That prediction has proved true ever since. When Moore made the original forecast Intel had succeeded in placing thirty integrated circuits on a chip. And Intel's laboratory was about to increase this to sixty. Then came the impact of redoubling.

By 1971, the number of transistors on a chip had climbed to 2,300. By 2004: 592 million. Eighteen months later: over a billion. Eighteen months more: over two billion. Now four. By 2010: ten billion. And at the same price that once bought thirty.

Forty-odd years ago those thirty transistors could power a pocket calculator. Now 200 million of them can fit on the head of a pin. Says Intel: "In 1978, a commercial flight between New York and Paris cost around $900 and took seven hours. If the principles of Moore's Law had been applied to the airline industry, in the way they have to the semi-conductor industry since 1978, that flight would now cost about a cent and take less than one second."[3]

As Don Tapscott says in *The Digital Economy:* "Today's greeting card that sings 'Happy Birthday' contains more computer power than existed on earth before 1950."

❏ **Metcalfe's Law**: Robert Metcalfe, founder of networking company 3Com, first talked in 1980 about the explosive power of networks. And in 1993 journalist George Gilder dubbed it "Metcalfe's Law". Simply put: connect one phone to another and only two people can speak. But connect more cellphones to millions of others, and every extra one multiplies the entire network. Gilder maintained that Metcalfe's Law would amplify Moore's Law, and together that combination would remake the world. It has.

The converging revolutions

But those two laws are not the only drivers of the new economy. Michio Kaku, Professor of Theoretical Physics at the City College of New York, in his far-sighted book *Visions* (subtitled: *How science will revolutionize the twenty-first century*), says we are now living through the convergence of three revolutions:

❏ *The biomolecular revolution;*

❏ *The computer revolution: and*

❏ *The quantum revolution.*

Says Kaku: "In the past, scientific revolutions, such as the introduction of gunpowder, machines, steam power, electricity and the atomic bomb, all changed civilization beyond recognition. How will the biomolecular, computer and quantum revolutions similarly reshape the twenty-first century?

"The biomolecular revolution will give us a complete genetic description of all living things, giving us the possibility of becoming the choreographers of life on earth. The

Facebook started out in 2004 for students to share photos

Now 100 million have made it a vibrant social network, linking global friends

'Three billion more can now plug and play with everyone else'

And a call center in India can cover the globe at a fraction of the price

computer revolution will give us computer power that is virtually free and unlimited, eventually placing artificial intelligence within reach. And the quantum revolution will give us new materials, new energy sources, and perhaps the ability to create new forms of matter."   Scientist Kaku looks forward to a global society that is not "haunted by brutal sectarian, fundamentalist, nationalist and racial hatred of the past millennia".

He envisages a new era in which:

❑ **The computer revolution** will link all peoples with a powerful global telecommunications and economic network;

❑ **The biomolecular revolution** will give them the knowledge to cure disease and feed their expanding population; and

❑ **The quantum revolution** will provide the power to build a planetary society.

All require new ways of looking at everything. In *The World is Flat,* author and newspaper columnist Thomas Friedman sees a slightly different three-way convergence powering many of the new changes:

❑ **Convergence 1:** The same tipping point listed among our "seven keys": "The creation of a global, Web-enabled playing field that allows for multiple forms of collaboration—the sharing of knowledge and work—in real time, without regard to geography, distance or, in the near future, language."

❑ **Convergence 2:** Friedman says dramatic changes come when a new technology is merged with new ways of doing business. He says this marriage of new technology and new business methods has now been consummated.

❑ **Convergence 3:** Since 1990—and the collapse of the Berlin Wall—"three billion people who had been frozen out of the field suddenly found themselves liberated to plug and play with everybody else." Hundreds of millions more have joined the new global community: in China, India, Latin America and central Asia.

The systems revolution

Margaret Wheatley, Dee Hock and Ervin Laszlo are among many challenging the dominant old-style model of the Industrial Age. All stress the new world model provided by the quantum revolution. They say the old command-and-control model is completely outdated.

Wheatley, an American leader in "systems thinking", says the quantum worldview stresses that "there are no independent entities anywhere at the quantum level; it's all relationships". She says most systems should now be seen as "webs of relationships".[4]

Hock, the inspirer of Visa International, stresses the new word *chaordic*—a combination of chaos and order—to show how institutions should now organize themselves along the lines of nature: as self-organizing organic entities.

The Internet itself is a "chaordic" organization: like nature, an ordered web of networked information, but with seemingly no one in charge. Hock says this principle will now be a major shaper of the next society.

And Hungarian Professor of Philosophy Ervin Laszlo, in *The Chaos Point,* says we are now at a critical junction in history: with the choice between "breakdown or breakthrough".

But these are not the only coalescing forces. We have simplified them into seven main keys to unlock that "breakthrough future". Those keys apply to virtually every aspect of that future. They interlock. They merge. They coalesce. And they unlock entirely different doors to lifelong learning.

1. It's GLOBAL, national and local at the same time

The world has developed an amazing ability to store information and make it available instantly in different forms to almost anyone, anywhere. That ability is revolutionizing business, education, home life, employment, management and virtually everything else we take for granted.

Our homes are re-emerging as vital centers of learning, work and entertainment. The impact of that sentence alone will transform our schools, our businesses, our shopping centers, our offices, our cities—in many ways our entire concept of work.

Our ability to communicate is one of our key human traits. Many historians agree that

Now Discovery is more than an online television network

It also provides interactive global lesson plans for schools worldwide

From Central American Aztec art and history to the latest in math and science, the Discovery TV Channel's online 'Discovery Education Streaming' provides 87,000 videoclips and 8,700 full-length videos as part of its global service. All are linked specifically to United States K-12 curriculum goals, but are used internationally by leading schools such as in this photo courtesy of Mexico's Thomas Jefferson Institute.

By 1988 a single fiber optic cable could carry 3,000 messages

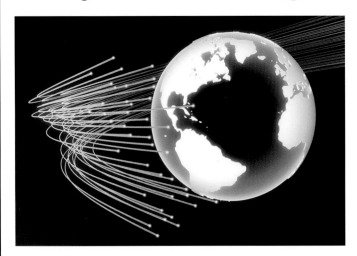

Now 300 million miles of multi-strand optics can send millions of messages a second

For over a century after the invention of the telegraph and telephone, telegraphy messages were sent over wires, often made of copper. But now the world can send millions of messages in a second over 300 million miles of multi-strand fiber-optic "cable". And by linking with laser and satellite technology, they carry billions of emails, radio and television programs—and an increasing volume of educational programs: "streamed" on demand just like airline passengers access movies and videos.

spoken language, thinking and writing are probably the three main abilities separating the human species from others. Yet our ancestors did not invent any form of writing until between 5,500 and 6,000 years ago: first by drawing symbols instead of words.

It took another 2,000 years before they created the first alphabet. That unique concept eventually enabled all knowledge to be recorded by rearranging only twenty-six symbols.

But not until the eleventh century did the Chinese start printing books. And it was not until 1451-53 that German inventor Johannes Gutenburg machine-printed the first European book. This transformed our ability to store and communicate knowledge by making books available to millions. Before Gutenberg, there were only about thirty thousand books on the entire continent of Europe—all hand-written. By 1500, there were more than nine million. That led two hundred years later to printed textbooks, classroom-based schools, blackboards, chalk and slates. Incredibly, that is how millions still operate. Only the slates have gone. And the blackboards are green.

Not until the mid-1800s did we begin to speed up the process, starting with Samuel Morse's telegraph in 1835. The first typewriter appeared in 1872, the first telephone message in 1876, the first typesetting machine in 1884, silent movies in 1894, the first radio signals in 1895, talking movies in 1922, infant television in 1926, and the computer microprocessor and pocket calculator in 1971. Since then the communications revolution has exploded.

The world is now one gigantic information exchange network. By 1988 a single fiber optic "cable" could carry three thousand electronic messages at once. By 1996: 1.5 million. By 2000: ten million. But now, says George Gilder, more information can be sent over a single cable in a second than was sent over the entire Internet in 1997 in a month. Gilder predicts that, over the next decade, "new technologies of sand, glass and air will form a web with a total carrying power, from household to global crossing, at least a million times larger than the networks of today".[5]

Wired magazine's co-founder Kevin Kelly calls the new economy a tectonic upheaval. "The irony of our times is that the era of computers is over. All the major consequences of stand-alone computers have already taken place. All the most promising technologies making their debut now are chiefly due to communication between computers—that is, connections rather than computations."[6]

Kelly says the network economy is "fed by the resonance of two stellar bangs: the collapsing microcosm of chips and the exploding telecosm of connections. These sudden shifts are tearing the old laws of wealth apart and preparing territory for the emerging economy.

"As the size of silicon chips shrinks to the microscopic, their costs shrink to the microscopic as well. They become cheap and tiny enough to slip into every—and the key word here is 'every'—object we make."

Peter Drucker says the "enormous" psychological impact of the Information Revolution is just about to arrive. "It has perhaps been greatest on the way in which young children learn. Beginning at age four (and often earlier), children now rapidly develop computer skills, soon surpassing their elders; computers are their toys and their learning tools. Fifty years hence we may well conclude that there was no 'crisis in American education' in the closing years of the twentieth century—there was only a growing incongruence between the way twentieth-century schools taught and the way late-twentieth-century children learned."[7]

But now that new learning revolution becomes global: a new, mainly borderless world. While international finance has spurred the growth of the one-world economy, there are at least five national ways to a better future:

1. The continued role of America in the vital field of electronic innovation and hi-tech investment, and the model to link universities, innovators and investors.

2. The rebirth of Europe as a single economic entity—a working example of how many countries can form integrated communities.

3. The rise of dynamic "Tiger economies"—particularly in Asia—as models for small countries and examples for the world's giants.

4. The resurgence of China, the world's most populous country, as the planet's fastest-growing manufacturing dynamo.

Education's
as seen by
management

44

'From age four or earlier, computers are already their toys and learning tools'

When he made that statement in 2001,* America's foremost management thinker of the past century, Peter Drucker, predicted that within twenty years the Internet would have its greatest future impact on education and health. And this, he predicted, would entail redesigning everything about the way we teach and learn. Like the authors of this book, Drucker's forecast of The Next Society stressed that the social changes brought about by the new technologies are much more important than the tools.

* Managing In The Next Society. See fuller quotation at left.

Silicon Valley's six innovation secrets*

1. Major research institute
Like Stanford University

2. One big success story
Like Hewlett Packard, Nokia, Acer

3. High-tech talent
And the ability to attract it

4. Venture capital
Bangalore, Taiwan, Shanghai

5. Infrastructure
Singapore the government model

6. The right attitude
Risk-taking confidence

* Steven Levy: The Hot New Tech Cities, Newsweek, Nov. 9, 1998.

5.   The rise of India, to start joining America as a new poor-country model on how to become an information technology powerhouse and online service center.

The first route: the American flair for quickly turning hi-tech research into breakthrough products, services and experiences. In spite of short-term Government deficit and finance-lending problems, the resilience and productivity of the American economy remains a strong base for growth through innovation. Despite some setbacks, California's Silicon Valley is still the model for the future. Even fifty years ago the area south of San Francisco Bay was a county of orange groves and vineyards. Now it has given birth to more than 240 publicly-listed technology companies with a market worth of over $500 billion, annual sales of $170 billion and 377,000 employees—plus at least 4,000 small non-public companies.

But its lesson for the future is probably even more important: a unique series of university-business partnerships. Today half of Silicon Valley's revenues come from companies seeded by Stanford University. And this kind of education-business partnership will continue to provide some of the twenty-first century's greatest growth models. America's emerging new catalyst is the way several of its ground-breaking industries are now converging: computers, television, entertainment and instant communications. That convergence, too, has tremendous implications for education: and the potential to bypass the school system if it stays locked into an outdated model.

The second route to a one-world economy is modelled by the European Union. It now links twenty-seven countries, 500 million people and creates 30 percent of the world's gross domestic product. Long in the shadow of the United States, Europe is once again re-emerging as the second global anchor for prosperity and stability.

Europe's single currency, the Euro, links most of its members. And, in spite of high unemployment in some traditional manufacturing industries, Europe's software and telecom companies have been pumping out jobs. Finland's Nokia, Sweden's Ericsson and Britain's Vodafone have shown how the new technologies can revitalize the new century's economies when backed by equally dynamic educational policies.

The third alternative is the new model of the internationally-minded small country or state: Taiwan, Ireland, South Korea, Finland, New Zealand, Singapore and Dubai, with pockets elsewhere such as Bangalore, Hyderabad and Madras in India, Tel Aviv in Israel, Kyoto in Japan, and the five coastal cities that house 80 percent of the population of the giant Australian continent: Sydney, Melbourne, Brisbane, Perth and Adelaide.

When co-author Dryden first visited Taipei in 1964, the capital of **Taiwan** had only one set of traffic lights: turned on only when a visiting dignitary entered town. Now Taiwan, with 23 million people, boasts 14,000 electronic companies with total sales of $75 billion, mostly exported, including 120 hi-tech public companies, with a market worth of $100 billion, sales of $27 billion and 72,000 employees. It also graduates 10,000 engineers and scientists a year and attracts back thousands from Silicon Valley. And it is now a major investor in hi-tech industries on the Chinese mainland.

Singapore provides equally important lessons. Forty years ago it was a poverty-stricken island. Over twenty years ago the Government began a campaign to attract hi-tech multinationals—with tax incentives, an educated workforce, and an amazing infrastructure program. Fired by an enormous Government-investment policy from compulsory superannuation savings, the island state's biggest infrastructure project, Singapore One—worth hundreds of millions of dollars—has been built to connect every household, school and office to the Internet.

Ireland, with about four million people, tells a similar story. Twenty-five years ago it was a poor farming country. But by 2001 it had surpassed the United States as the world's biggest software exporter: Silicon Valley's English-language, Euro-currency gateway to the European Community. It has attracted 1,100 international companies to the republic, and these now have 107,000 employees. The country's annual exports have soared to $102 billion. Its average incomes per person are the seventh highest in the world. Ireland's tax incentives to attract hi-tech companies are matched by extensive policies to develop the skilled people to staff them.

Finland has even a more amazing story to tell—and in many ways it is the story of one company: Nokia. Back in the 1980s, Finland's major industry was paper and pulp. Helsinki-based Nokia, the country's largest company, was known more for its

Singapore: from sleepy slum to world-class city

$2 billion for computers in schools and every home and school linked to the Internet

How tiny Finland became the world's cellphone capital

From $82 billion in mobile phones to 400 hi-tech firms, and top school system

rubber boots and lumber than tiny phones. But when the economy took a nosedive in the early 1990s, Finland turned to hi-tech for salvation. The Government decided to put 2.9 percent of the gross domestic product into technology research and development. Companies turned to international partners to start electronic ventures, and Nokia discovered a seemingly endless market for cellphones. It now produces almost 40 percent of the world's output: 1.4 million sets a day. That's half a billion a year, with $82 billion a year in sales. Nokia has also invested in university science parks—mainly funded by government. Today Finland has 400 hi-tech firms. And also a great education system, with one of the world's best teacher-training programs.

South Korea leads the world in fast, broadband Internet use: more than 75 percent of its homes are connected. And South Korea also aims to dominate the rapidly increasing market for digital home theaters.

Dubai, in the United Arab Emirates, has also proven how a small city-state can provide the dynamic leadership model for its larger neighbors. Like Singapore, it has used its own modern airline, Emirates, and one of the world's most modern airports, to turn itself into a tourist and business hub. Its Internet City houses regional offices of such companies as Microsoft, Dell, Siemens, HP, Oracle and IBM. Its Media City is home to the regional bureaus of several TV networks. It has also added a new Knowledge Village, as a Middle Eastern educational center.

And now nearby Qatar is replanning its entire education system with the aim of becoming a world leader. Both are working models for the future of a new Arab Renaissance: turning oil wealth into a modern society.

New Zealand has become a world leader in using the new interactive technologies as the catalyst to reinvent schooling, especially in the primary years. Its leadership in film-making, through *Lord of the Rings* and *King Kong* creator Peter Jackson and partner Fran Walsh, has turned Wellington into one of the world's movie capitals. And tourism, New Zealand's biggest foreign-exchange earner, is a magnet for international students to learn English on working holidays.

Australia's main wealth still comes from its enormous mineral deposits, but it abounds in other advances—from sports-development academies to a new billion-dollar Federally-funded $1-billion "Digital Education Revolution".

Significantly, advanced democratic countries with small populations lead the world with Internet connections: from top-ranking Norway—where 88 percent of its population is online—through the Netherlands, Iceland, New Zealand, Sweden and Antigua-Barbuda to Australia, at 76 percent.

But the biggest awakening giant is China. After the stagnating years of Mao's Cultural Revolution, since 1979 it has released more people from poverty than any other society in history. In the past twenty-five years it has increased its economy more than 400 percent. Many coastal "special economic areas" have grown even faster. Sure: the country still has big problems, but it is now racing to apply the lessons of Japan, Singapore, Hong Kong, Taiwan and South Korea.

In the past eight years its soaring production has made it the world's new manufacturing powerhouse. And an educational one, too. More than 2.8 million students graduate each year from its institutions of higher learning. That is twice as many as America. Its other educational demands are enormous: with 100 million children under six, 120 million at elementary school and 80 million at high school. And, with the national policy of one child per family, the average city family spends 35 percent of its annual income on the education of that child. The overall family dream is three-fold:

❏ To obtain a university degree, preferably from a leading Western university.

❏ To speak fluent English. And

❏ To become an expert in digital technology and the Web.

China, too, has an extra "secret weapon": the 51 million Chinese who live outside its mainland borders. Together they own liquid assets worth two trillion dollars. Their over-riding ethic is educational achievement. Most of their historic family links are with major areas of growth along China's eastern seaboard. With their investment in those areas, and the country's own internal growth policies, the Chinese economy is set to become the world's largest no later than the 2030s, maybe much earlier.

Already by the end of 2004 China had between 35 million and 45 million households

China's stagg growth: ecor increases 400% in twenty-five years

Shanghai—China's leading commercial center—by night: regarded as the model for China's other emerging cities.

❏ **4 million graduates a year**

❏ **253 million on Internet**

❏ **550 million cellphones**

❏ **100 million middle class**

❏ **$1.6 trillion reserves**

❏ **$200 billion investments**

India: the world's new low-cost high-tech center

with the equivalent purchasing power of a U.S. household earning $25,000 to $30,000 a year. At least 100 million Chinese are now living the middle-class life. Economists forecast that number to double or triple over the next ten years. Already China's leading personal-computer company, Legend, has acquired IBM's PC division and renamed itself Lenova to pave the way for international expansion. In a reverse drive, Amazon has bought Joyo.com—China's biggest online retailer of books and music—to add to the American giant's millions of existing online customers in China.

In only a few years China has amassed $1.6 trillion in foreign-exchange reserves, the largest such reservoir in history. With Japan, it funds most of the United States' Government's gap between spending and income from taxes. It has now earmarked $200 billion of its current savings to fund new investments in its own country, through the China Investment Corporation.

Then there is India. What China has started to achieve in manufacturing, India is doing with information technology.

By the end of 2003, there were more IT engineers in the Indian city of Bangalore (150,000) than in Silicon Valley (120,000). And India is graduating 260,000 more engineers every year. McKinsey, the giant consulting company, estimates that by the end of 2008 IT services and IT outsourcing work in India will have reached $57 billion in annual exports and four million employees.

India's second richest man, 57-year-old Azim H. Premji—with a net worth of $5.3 billion—has set up a foundation focused on achieving universal elementary education for India. But the Premji Foundation doesn't donate money direct to schools. Instead, it works in with UNESCO to develop models for better teaching methods.

To date, India's rapid rise to IT power has rested almost entirely on its preoccupation with higher education. But as *Business Week* reports: "The real problem is with primary education. When they were at the same stage of development as India is now, South Korea, Taiwan and China focused on elementary and secondary schools. As a result, they achieved nearly universal literacy among youth—the educated workforce that fuelled economic takeoffs." Significantly, in the 2004 election, India's Congress

Party swept to power on a policy to double the country's educational spending, and to concentrate this on primary education.

As the positive surge of globalization circles the planet, soaring challenges remain. More than two billion people exist on under $2 a day. More than 26,000 children die each day due to poverty. In India almost half its villages do not even have a school. At least 100 million children, mainly in Africa and India, never get to school. Nearly a billion people entered the twenty-first century unable to read a book or sign their names. "Less than 1 percent of what the world spent every year on weapons was needed to put every child into school by the year 2000, and yet it didn't happen."[8]

While more than 50 percent of the people in forty-three countries have Internet access, in Latin America—with 550 million people—it's under 9 percent. And in Africa, with almost one billion people, it's under 6 percent.[9] Around 1.6 billion—a quarter of humanity—still live without electricity.[10]

Yet simple answers to many of these challenges are also emerging, as we explore in Part Four of this book. One of the most exciting is the 50 x 15 Initiative, pioneered by Mexican-born, Silicon Valley IT leader Hector Ruiz, CEO of AMD Corporation, the No. 2 manufacturer of computer chips. This initiative aims to have 50 percent of the world's population connected to the Web by 2015—as part of the United Nations goal to cut world poverty in half and provide primary education to all children by that date. Already this initiative is equipping schools in Africa with computer labs and other new tools to learn, including low-cost portable laptop computers that can run without wired electricity.

2. It's INSTANT: anywhere, any time

As the combined impact of 1.4 billion online computers merges with 3.3 billion mobile phones and the soaring power of broadband access, the new world of instant communications changes everything, including education.

Not only can we communicate globally and instantly; we can trade instantly and learn instantly.

Peter Drucker picks the "revolutionary" impact of Web-based e-commerce as being

Now it's instant: design your own PC online, order by card; overnight delivery

600,000 students in 160 countries learn networking online

39 Cisco Academies in Morocco, with 31% of students female

In photo: A Morocco student on graduation. Over 600,000 students are now enrolled every year in Cisco Networking Academies in 160 countries. Around 31 percent of the 7,000 students in Islamic Morocco are female. And 54 percent of all university students in Islamic Iran are also female.

a dominant change-driver in the early part of this century: "the explosive emergence of the Internet as a major, perhaps eventually the major world-wide distribution channel for goods, for services, and, surprisingly, for managerial and professional jobs". He says e-commerce is to the Information Revolution what the railroad was to the Industrial Revolution: "a totally unprecedented, unexpected development".[11]

By mid-1997, Dell was selling computers through the Internet at a rate of $1 million a day. By 2007: $50 million a day. And nearly all of those computers are being "configured" by the users themselves on the Internet, selecting from individual modules. The orders are then emailed to FedEx depots, quickly assembled and delivered overnight or within two days to more isolated areas.

The Dell model for education is obvious: soon everyone will be able to type individual learning goals on to the Web, and select personalized modules of interactive courses to make those goals possible.

Similar moves are revolutionizing commerce in other fields. By 2003 at least thirty million people a year were buying and selling $20 billion in merchandise through e-Bay online auctions: more than the gross domestic product of all but seventy of the world's countries. Now 200 million people make sales on eBay of $100 million a day.

Total retail online sales now exceed $136 billion a year, and are still soaring.[12]

But non-retail sales are even higher. The giant Cisco Systems corporation, for example, is the world's largest integrator of routers and switches—vital links that connect computers around the world. Its sales have risen from $1.5 million in 1987 to $40 billion in 2008. Its Internet-generated sales have been as high as $40 million a day. And because its digital network automatically links all its customers—who create and share answers to hi-tech queries—this saves Cisco from employing thousands of customer-answering engineers.

Similarly, it is now possible and desirable for all the world's best teachers to share the world's best lesson plans online. Already, in a world where corporations are desperately short of skilled information technology specialists, giant IT companies like Oracle, Microsoft and Cisco are running their own training programs around the world.

Cisco Systems has Networking Academies in 160 countries. They offer a four-semester course that trains students to design, build and maintain networks. The total Cisco program links hands-on, practical training with Internet back-up, and guarantees high-paid jobs. So far its Academies have taught critical IT skills to more than 1.2 million students—in partnership with high schools and colleges.

One of the Academies' big achievements: the large percentage of young women taking their courses in countries where females have often been under-represented in education. In the small Middle Eastern country of Jordan, for example, ten Cisco Academies have been opened. More than 600 students have entered their IT courses, 65 percent of them women.

But to glimpse a big part of the future of lifelong learning, click on virtually any one of YouTube's 83 million free view-on-demand short videos. Now imagine the world's 59 million school teachers, and their millions of students, providing similar video lessons on demand—instantly available to anyone, anywhere, at any time.

Another model for the future is the Atomic Learning online service, with its 35,000 instant video tutorials on more than 100 of the most-used software programs, from *Powerpoint* to *Photoshop*. Software companies and designers are notoriously poor in writing instruction manuals, either hard-copy or online. And even after a half-day or one-day course on an updated system, most users quickly forget one or two vital steps—until they have embedded them, by frequent use, in their memory-banks. Atomic Learning answers this need instantly and cheaply, with a low-cost annual bulk-fee per student for schools and a higher one for individual users. The importance of this cannot be over-rated. If you forget how to insert video-clips, animations or music into a *Powerpoint* presentation, Atomic Learning instantly shows you how.

3. It's OPEN, free or almost free

Even better, it is now possible to get free access—or very cheap access—to instant information. And even to get free computer software and PC operating systems. The seven new free building blocks for a world wide learning web are already in place:

1. The World Wide Web itself: conceived by Tim Berners-Lee in 1989 and operating

Students everywhere now have free access to MIT courses

Anyone in world can access lecture notes

*In photo: An Asian student online to the Massachusetts Institute of Technology where free lecture notes and background information for almost 2,000 courses are now available in its Open CourseWare program. **Fuller details, chapter ten.***

Over 300 million now use Skype for free world phonecalls

With free online video conferencing

by 1991. Berners-Lee invented Hyper-Text Markup Language (HTML). This enabled millions of Internet-users to create automatic click-through links to thousands of other websites.

2. **Linux open-source operating systems.** In 1991, too, Finnish computer-science student Linus Torvalds couldn't afford to buy a Microsoft *Windows* operating system for his personal computer. So he designed the kernel of a new system, and "posted" its "source-code" on the Internet, seeking suggestions and improvements. They started to roll in, and soon gave birth to the Linux open-source movement (named after its founder who in turn was named after double Nobel Laureate Linus Pauling).

3. **Open-source software, too.** Now 100,000 collaborative groups (http://source-forge.net) are working round the world to produce open-source software, and share the source-code freely with all others. The result: a burst of collective innovation that will send the cost of much computer software down to zero or near zero.

4. **Free browsers:** the innovation, started by Marc Andreessen's University of Illinois Mosaic team—and later his Netscape *Navigator*—to add graphics to the World Wide Web through free browsers. Mozilla's free *Firefox* browser was launched in 2004, and by early 2008 more than seventy million Web users had downloaded it.

5. **Free search engines:** starting off with Yahoo but then booming with the development of Google, and its ability to deliver, in under half a second, the answers to almost any query.

6. **Free social networking**—with hundreds of millions sharing videotape, photos and personal friendships.

7. **Free international phone calls:** starting with *Skype* and its free video phone service between individual computers around the world. Now, at a tiny fraction of standard charges, *Skype*-users can also call any landline phone anywhere. By mid-2008, more than 300 million subscribers were using the service.

"Open source" does not mean stealing inventors' patent rights. It firstly means sharing the "source code" for computer operating systems. That's very much like everyone sharing the "source code" for writing: the various alphabets, grammar and syntax. But "open source" also means a philosophy of cooperative collaboration: a new type of mass innovation.

If these new developments affected the Internet alone, they would be highly important. But "open source isn't just about better software," writes Thomas Goetz. "It's about better everything." He says it is doing for mass innovation what the assembly line did for mass production. We are at a convergent moment when a philosophy, a strategy and a technology have aligned to unleash great innovation."[13]

"Open source" means those signing a licensing agreement can download software free of charge, including its source-code. But they guarantee to pass on, free to others in the movement, any improvements they add to that source-code. Developers can still brand and sell their own products.

This has major ramifications for the future of a new world society. Traditionally universities existed to share knowledge without restriction. The Internet itself grew out of the same desire. And the open-source movement works on the principle that all of us are more intelligent than one of us, so let's share that collective intelligence.

More importantly, this "free pass-on principle" has the power to enable the world's poor countries to benefit, free of charge or at much lower prices, from the collective contributions of thousands of researchers, teachers and other students. Some are already doing that. And they are doing it fast. In the third quarter of 2003, sales of laptop computers in China increased by 56 percent. Their price dropped by up to 90 percent as China officially adopted open-source computer systems. Students can thus buy laptops without operating systems, and download those free from the Web.

OpenOffice (a free competitor to Microsoft *Office,* the world's biggest-selling software suite) is available in eighty languages, including many non-alphabet ones, such as Japanese and Chinese. It includes *Write* (for word processing), *Calc* (for spreadsheets), and *Impress* (for slide and multimedia presentations similar to Microsoft *Powerpoint* and Apple's *Keynote).* By 2008, the standard Microsoft *Office* suite was available online from the company at between $239 and $399. But *OpenOffice* can be downloaded off the Web—free (openoffice.org). And Microsoft has responded by reducing the price of

China slashes laptop prices 90% with open-source system

Operating systems downloaded free

More than half the world's population have cellphones

Now Africa, with 280 million subscribers, surpasses USA

its *Office* suite, in poorer markets like China, to $3—but only when used on *Windows* computers.

OpenOffice is a partnership between SUN Microsystems and thousands of volunteers working through the International Open Source Network (iosn.net). Many of the developers, particularly in education, are also members of the Creative Commons network (http://creativecommons.org).

When the Hungarian translation of *OpenOffice* was moving slowly, more than a hundred volunteers completed it in three days. And the entire Creative Commons movement has the power to transform education, with the free sharing of lesson plans and digital "learning tools".

Its impact is already about to be felt in an American K-12 education system dominated by the multi-billion-dollar textbook industry. Here the two giant states of California and Texas are key players, because of their state-wide public university systems. And the California Department of Education has already launched its California Open Source Textbook Project (COSTP). This is designed to harness the abilities of its own teachers to produce digital textbooks at a saving estimated to be $400 million a year.

A similar world-wide movement, now well underway, is about to transform global education, including university level, as we cover in the part four of this book.

4. It's MOBILE as well as personalized

The new Web 2.0 revolution is also personal, portable and mobile: for everyone, everywhere, anytime.

Its growth is summed up by the mobile wireless phone. By 2000 only 12 percent of the world's people owned one. Now it's more than 50 percent, and climbing faster than any electric or electronic appliance in history. In thirty countries, including most of western Europe, Australia and Hong Kong, there are more mobile phones than people, as many carry two devices: often one for personal use and one for business.

The biggest increase of all is in countries with low access to wired phones: China, with over 550 million users by mid-2008, India climbing towards 300 million, and even Africa now has 280 million cellphone subscribers, more than the United States and Canada combined. Finland's Nokia is by far the world's biggest producer. It and other manufacturers are racing to provide low-cost links to the other 3.3 million global citizens who still don't have cellphones, especially those living in poverty in Asia, Africa and Latin America.

But the new soaring demand is for multimedia versions: the combined handheld computer, cellphone, video-camera, music-player and video-phone in your pocket—with instant links to the Web. Link it with free open-source technologies, and the opportunities for lifelong learning are almost limitless.

Already language-learning is a major use. More people in China are learning English than the entire population of the United States: well over 300 million. Yet China's in-school language-teaching methods are often extremely poor.

Most good foreign-language teachers will summarize the eight most effective stages to learning English or any other second-language:

1. Hear it— spoken clearly.

2. Say it—so you can practise what you hear.

3. See it—so you can see the words while you hear them: like singing to a karaoke machine, a favorite pastime in China, Japan and South Korea.

4. Type it—so you can reinforce your learning with "muscle memory", just as great golfers or tennis players grove their swing or their serve.

5. Enjoy it—because learning is much more effective when it's fun.

6. Embed it—by repeating typical phrases, sentences, questions and answers.

7. Tailor it—so that learners become fluent in ways that are of most practical and meaningful use to them, like studying a specific subject. And, above all . . .

8. Use it constantly—what teachers call "total immersion".

And here the new "multimedia computer in the pocket" provides constant personalized tools for learning. Nokia, for example, has signed joint-venture language-teaching deals with the British Broadcasting Corporation, China's MobileEdu group and Wid-Sets, China's first mobile Internet service to empower mobile phones with Web 2.0

Learning English is major use for new technology in Asia

Karaoke joins mobile phones as favorite ways to learn

With 375,000 travellers a day packed into world's fastest trains

Japanese invent texting to avoid the voice clutter

In photo: One of Japan's famed bullet trains that have so far whisked more than 4.5 billion passengers around that crowded country at speeds of up to 300 kilometers (188 miles) an hour. With up to 375,000 passengers crowded aboard each day, and thousands more on city commutes, the railways have banned spoken mobile phone calls. So—in the country that has given birth to Sony and Nintendo digital games, karaoke and sudoku—the Japanese have invented the new language of cellphone texting.

services. China's 550-million-plus mobile phone users can easily download the WidSets software free. The software uses mini-applications called widgets to deliver real-time Internet content to mobile phones. That enables users to read news, blogs, emails, browse photos and video clips and play games. And Chinese students, in particular, can use some of the 1.5 billion text messages they exchange with friends each day to "embed" English phrases as games.

Japanese are probably the world's most sophisticated and varied cellphone users. Crammed into mass-transit commuter trains, millions use their personal touch-pad keyboards and flip-screens to play games, learn English, watch television, take photos, exchange email and text messages. They now even use mobile phones to bypass credit and debit cards—swiping phones across vending machines and in-store computer terminals to pay for virtually anything by direct bank debit.

But, like Web 2.0 itself, billions of cellphone and computer Internet connections do more than provide personalized information from central databanks. They mean any expert on any subject can also now become a global teacher. And each teacher and potential learner can easily be connected.

As we explore in the next two chapters, everyone has a potential talent to be good at something. Most people have passionate interests. And when talent and passion combine, the opportunity exists to be great at something—and to keep on upgrading personal skills. That passion, talent and skills can be in sport, hobbies or careers from bookkeeping to beekeeping, public speaking to photography. The Google concept of "building a global business one 5-cent click at a time" can now apply to anyone with any talent.

Selling homework, new skills or second-language training to a few locals might not earn a great living. But find a way to sell those services online to millions—and your entire future changes. Better still, we now know how to teach and learn anything more effectively, using what some call "accelerated learning" techniques, like those eight stages to learn a second language. We also now know how to link those methods with the world's best interactive digital technologies. But marry both those methods—brain-friendly fast learning techniques and interactive technology—with 3.3 billion mobile phones and 1.4 billion online computers, then highly personalized and specific and learning-on-demand becomes possible: anywhere, any place, any time.

Then link the wisdom, knowledge and specific skills of today's grandparent generation with the multimedia IT skills of new-age students, and the opportunity exists to share one's wisdom and skills with millions—for pleasure or profit. So just as anyone, anywhere can now sell products to anyone else through eBay, so too anyone can sell talents and learning services instantly online.

But the "personalization revolution" has much wider ramifications.

❏ Virtually any service can now be personalized on the Web: from learning and health plans to personalized daily news on any subject.

❏ As we explore in more depth later, everyone has a personal learning style, thinking style and working style almost as unique as one's fingerprints. And just as virtually any skills can now be taught online in sequence, from beginner level to world master, good teachers and multimedia experts can tailor such instant learning programs to individual learning styles and in individual modules.

5. It's INTERACTIVE and enjoyable

But the new Web 2.0 revolution involves much more than education. It has completely revolutionized entertainment and music—and these, too, can be major aids to learning.

Already interactive video games have climbed past movies in global sales, with the fastest rise by far in Asia. In the year to March 2008, global digital games sales totalled $26.5 billion, only slightly behind the film industry's $26.7 billion.

But in April 2008, the biggest new video game of the first half of the year, *Grand Theft Auto IV,* took only one week to shatter two Guinness world records: the biggest-ever sales on its first-day release ($310 million) and for the first week ($500 million). That soared past the previous first-day games record of $170 million, achieved by Microsoft's *Xbox 360* game, *Halo 3,* in 2007.

For centuries Asian children have learned math on the abacus*

Now interactive games are building world industries on the same principles

* In China, the abacus is known as the suanpan.

Digital games sales now climb past Hollywood movies

$310 million sold in a day and $500 million in a week for new record-holder

In photo: Interactive games are ideal for family enjoyment. One of the most popular of all times: SimCity, which has sold more than 100 million copies. With it, families can design entire cities. And in the newest game by SimCity designer Will Wright—Spore, being launched in late 2008—players can design an entire new universe.

It helped boost U.S. games sales by 47 percent in the month. The compound growth of the digital games sales is now well ahead of both movies and music.

By 2008, *The Sims*—one of several "simulation" games created by American designer Will Wright—had sold 100 million units. And more than 90 percent of the games' content has been produced by the players themselves. Wright's original *Sim-City* has long been the model for many more educational games. As its name implies, the objective of *SimCity* is to simulate the design of a city, and everything in it from a transport system to its electric power grid. But, like all such games, interactive action is the key, as a player may face flooding, tornadoes, fires and earthquakes.

The original *SimCity,* released in 1989, kicked off a tradition of goal-centered games that could be won or lost depending on the performance of the player. Many scenarios were based on real world cities and disasters that had struck them—from the 1906 San Francisco Earthquake to the rebuilding of the bombed German city of Hamburg after the Second World War.

Now Will Wright is completing a new interactive game, *Spore,* in which players will create a unique universe as they explore the development of our own. While many of the latest online games allow dozens or thousands of players to interact at the same time, *Spore* is a completely different concept. Nearly everything in the game is created by players, from the early tribal societies to space exploration. Wright calls it a "massively single-player online game". It not only provides the "templates" for players to create their own characters; it lets the inventors upload those features on to a central global database. Other players can access to them, and add to them. Thus, if your new planet doesn't have a large predator, you can download one off the *Sporeopedia* global online server, use it and adapt it. Many games experts expect it to be the forerunner of a new type of creative learning game.

The most famous games character to date is Mario, a short pudgy Italian plumber who has appeared in more than 200 video games since his creation by Japan's Nintendo company. Games featuring Mario have sold a record 285 million units.

Nintendo was founded almost a century ago, and for most of its life sold playing cards. But in the 1970s, the founding family's heir, Hiroshi Yamauchi, decided to move into electronic games. When asked by his first games designer, "What should I make?" Yamauchi replied: "Something great". And that may just be the best job description for the new Web 2.0 age. The result has helped make Japan the world capital for interactive digital games, and Nintendo its third most valuable listed company. Its annual sales now exceed $16 billion. And Mario is now taking his fun-filled action message on to the 550 million mobile phones in China, especially those owned by students.

Equally big interactive achievements are now being created by Apple Inc., with its simple OS X computer operating system, *iPod, iTunes* and now *iPhone* innovations.

Since co-founder Steve Jobs has returned to lead Apple and turn it into a consumer products company, he has pioneered a key aspect of the Web 2.0 revolution: he has simplified it. And that, too, is a major challenge for the future of eLearning.

Apple's new computer operating system has allowed Jobs to condense its core function into a tiny computing kernel that requires only a million bytes (a megabyte) of data—a thousandth the size of Microsoft's new *Vista Windows*. That kernel can now be used in all Apple products, no matter how small. So suddenly the new Apple *iPhone* has become a mobile computer, as easy to use as the touch-pad *iPod* that makes it simple to download and play music. And the *iPhone* and the *iPod Touch* have become a true mobile computing platform.

Apple now provides a software developer's kit so any software designer can create new applications to run on the portable Apple kernel. And Silicon Valley's best-known venture capitalist, John Doerr, has kick-started the *iPhone* marketplace with a $100 million *iFund* to invest in companies developing *iPhone*-compatible products. "If you want to invent the future," said Doer in his launch announcement, "the *iFund* wants to help you build it."[14]

The response has been huge. More than 100,000 developers unloaded the new software developers' kit in the first week. And whatever new applications they develop can be shared across the Apple platform, from *iPhones* to *Mac* laptops.

Business Week says another Apple initiative may have finally broken the 20-year

Apple iPod and iPhone show how to simplify the Web 2.0 revolution

You can also play chess, bridge and many more games online

Yahoo alone has four million active groups of all types and 300 million users

grip that Microsoft has held on the core of computing: a dual-system computer. The magazine says that grip has been pried loose with just two fingers. "With one finger you press 'Control', and with the other you press 'Right arrow'. Instantly you switch from a *Macintosh* operating system to a Microsoft *Windows*. Then, with another two-finger press, you switch back again. So, as you edit family pictures, you might use *Mac's iPhoto* and when you want to access your corporate email, you can switch back instantly to Microsoft *Exchange*."[15]

The world is crying out for such simplicity. Consumers are fed up with paying for complex software features they don't need. And survey after survey shows twenty-first-century students are bored with old-style "drill and kill" lecture-based teaching methods. Simplify the future of Web 2.0 learning, and a new future beckons.

Already, around two-thirds of American K-12 students regularly play online games in the four-fifths of their waking time they spend outside school. On average they spend ten hours a week playing such games. Among teenagers that figure is much higher. Most of them would like to see educational games in schools, but only 19 per cent of parents and 15 percent of teachers agree. Yet where teachers do use such games, the learning results can be spectacular, particularly to learn difficult math concepts. New York-based Tapula Digita, for example, makes a series of immersive educational video games called *DimensionM*. These help students master math by completing missions, or lessons, in a game-based environment. Three Florida counties—Orange, Seminole and Volusia—have adopted this software in their middle school classrooms. The result? "A metamorphosis," says Melissa Young, district mathematics specialist for Orange County Public Schools. "Within the first few weeks we saw students seeking assistance from their teachers even before their scheduled time for math, so they could beat their friends."[16] And because students are playing the math games outside as well as inside class, their understanding rises sharply.

IBM has produced a free business innovation game, *Innov8*, designed to help university students and young professions develop a combination of business and information technology skills to succeed in a global economy. Says *Business Week:* "At least 100 of the global Fortune 500 will use gaming to educate their employees by 2012. The possibilities are huge—and not just for business. The application of serious gaming techniques in science, medicine and other industries could help solve some of the world's biggest challenges."[17]

Education is already a multi-billion-dollar-a-year market. Millions of today's students have mastered digital games and three-dimensional design technology, such as *Game Maker, Click & Play, Scratch, Stagecast Creator, Flash, Machinima, 3D-Blender* and Google's free *Sketchup*. So stand by for the next generation of entrepreneurial companies based on students' ability to reinvent the future around interactive games.

The total world digital games market is predicted to reach $49.9 billion by 2011. Almost $19 billion of that is forecast to be in the Asia-Pacific—around 50 per cent higher than America. So with Taiwan's leadership in low-cost computer production, China's $200 billion development fund and education-ethic, Japan's lead in digital games, South Korea's lead in fast broadband, and India's lead in Skype-based global call centers, prepare for an interactive Asian Renaissance.

6. It's CO-CREATIVE: the new era of mass innovation

American digital games designer Marc Prensky has already suggested a world-wide drive to involve the planet's two billion students and 59 million teachers in producing interactive digital learning games on every aspect of schooling and education.[18]

That follows what many regard as the most brilliant concept of the Web 2.0 revolution: how to co-create the future.

Wikipedia is the prime model: co-created since 2001 by thousands of experts in their subject, updated regularly by others to produce more than ten million articles in 252 languages. All are available free at the touch of 1.4 billion computer keyboards—and soon from the touch of a screen on four billion handheld multimedia pocket phone-computers.

Author Don Tapscott calls today's society the start of the new age of *Wikinomics*. His new book of the same name is subtitled: *How mass collaboration changes everything*. And it does. He says, *"MySpace, YouTube, Linux* and *Wikipedia*—today's examples of mass collaboration—are just the beginning: a few familiar characters in the opening

Computer games now outsell movies, and soar in use for interactive learning

Students to co-create to reinvent education?

Ten years ago giant US companies kept all research inhouse

Now some of the biggest are tapping the brains of the former Eastern bloc

pages of the first chapter in a long-running saga that will change many aspects of how the economy operates.

"Rather than just read a book," he says, "you can now write one. Just log on to *Wikipedia*—a collaboratively created encyclopedia, owned by no one and authored by tens of thousands of enthusiasts"—and only five full-time employees. It runs on a *wiki,* software that enables users to easily edit the content of Web pages, inside a simple, easy-to-follow template—like Microsoft *Powerpoint* is a similar, if costly, template.

"Or perhaps your thing is chemistry," says Tapscott. "Indeed, if you're a retired, unemployed or aspiring chemist, Procter & Gamble needs your help. The pace of innovation has doubled in its industry in the past five years alone, and now its army of 7,500 researchers is no longer enough to sustain its lead. Rather than hire more researchers, CEO A.G. Lafley instructed business unit leaders to source 50 percent of their new product and service ideas from outside the company. Now you can work for P&G without being on their payroll."

Or if you're a scientist in any field, just register on the InnoCentive network where you and 125,000 other scientists from 175 countries already help solve tough R&D problems for a cash reward. Some thirty-five Fortune 500 companies already use it to create new solutions—companies like Boeing, Dow, DuPont and Novartis. With funding from the Rockefeller Foundation, InnoCentive now runs a non-profit service to generate science and technology solutions for the developing world.

Or how about the mass media? "Rather than consume the TV news," says Tapscott, "you can now create it, along with thousands of independent citizen journalists who are turning the profession upside down. Tired of the familiar old faces and blather on network news? Turn off the TV, pick up a video camera and some cheap editing software, and make a news feature for Current TV, a new national U.S. national cable and satellite network created almost entirely by amateur contributors. Though the contributors are unpaid volunteers, the content is surprisingly good. Current TV provides online tutorials for camera operation and storytelling techniques, and their guidelines for creating stories help get participants started. Viewers vote on which stories go to air, so only the most engaging material makes prime time."

The Human Genome project is another great example of international co-creativity, with DNA scientists around the globe combining to unlock the secrets of life itself.

And if you don't think that concept will change the face of schooling and education, consider the example of New Zealand, with its four million people and 2,600 schools, many of them with small rolls in county farming areas. Ten years ago, New Zealand embarked on a nationwide program to co-create schooling in the twenty-first century. So far more than 1,600 schools, their teachers and students have become active co-inventors. They have done it in "school clusters", each with one school—more skilled than the others in new digital technology—training up to eight others.

Enter a first-grade classroom in one of those schools and you're likely to find six-year-olds starting the new year by videotaping their new classmates and interviewing them on their passions, strengths and hobbies.

One of the pioneers of New Zealand's digital classrooms in public primary schools, Warren Patterson, describes the video-camera and Apple *iMovie* editing software as "the best new combined learning tool" in decades. As the former Principal of Sherwood School, in the main Auckland urban area, he says learning to shoot and edit videotape turns even young students into multimedia journalists—"using twenty-first century tools to explore their environment and present their results". Learn digital-animation, digital music-composition and digital games-creation, and that's the basis for the new digital school.

But New Zealand's digital pace-setters do not see their example as "hi-tech"; more as catalysts to use the new interactive tools to replace the old classroom system. Visit Gulf Harbor, Tahatai Coast or Sherwood primary schools, Otumoetai or Somerville Intermediate (middle) schools, and you'll often find students back from a field trip or adventure camp and using simple Apple *iMovie* software to edit their videotape for the each school's own online television station. You will probably be interviewed for the same school's TV station—run by students. And most of the "cluster schools" share their lessons online through their own school Websites, the New Zealand Ministry of

Two-thirds of New Zealand schools now link in co-creative technology sharing

Model schools take lead to train others

In photo: Video training at Sherwood Primary School. See fuller New Zealand story, chapter twelve.

From photos to abstract art, Flickr online community shares two billion creative works

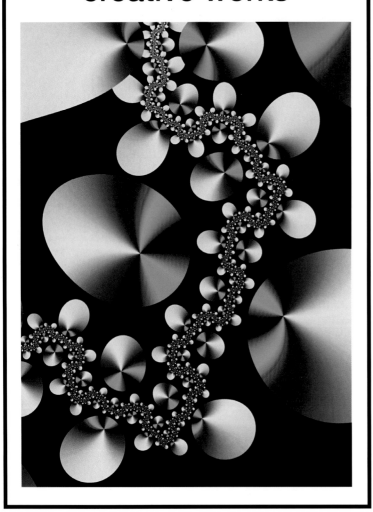

Education's online learning center's Website (tki.org.nz)—named in the indigenous Maori language, Te Kete Ipurangi (the three baskets of knowledge)—and through CORE Education (home.core-ed.net).

7. It's EASILY SHARED—with millions

That sharing is the last key. And to see the results in action, look no further than *YouTube, Flickr, MySpace* or *Facebook* internationally, or examples like South Korea's *CyWorld.*

YouTube, in less than three years, has reinvented the future of television: 83 millions often-brilliant videoclips, mainly shot by people under age twenty—then shared free with the millions who view them every day: when they want them. In practice, it is the world's biggest do-it-yourself global TV station. But with a big difference: anyone can watch any of its programs at any time of the day or night, anywhere. And it's a short step from there to all television on demand, and millions of lifelong-learning videos on demand—just as international airline travellers can now often choose from hundreds of movies to play on demand.

Flickr is the world's most popular photo-hosting sites. Launched in Canada only in 2004, it already hosts and shares more than two billion images. Each is tagged so viewers looking for a photo can find it under various categories. Each photo is also tagged so you know whether it is for sale or you can use it without paying.

MySpace, too, is one of the new age of American "social networking" websites: an online network where anyone can share music, photos, videos, blogs and personal profiles—and seek to meet other friends online. Rupert Murdoch's News Corporation bought *MySpace* in 2005 for $580 million—described by many news commentators as "the steal of the century". By late 2006, it claimed 110 million active members, mainly in the United States and Britain.

Facebook is one of the fastest-growing sites in America, with more than 100 million active users by mid-2008. While it started as a network for college students, more than half its users are now outside college and aged twenty-five years or older. It is particularly strong in storing and sharing photos between "friends of friends": thus introducing millions of people with shared interests around the globe.

CyWorld, the leading social networking site in South Korea, has 90 per cent of fifteen-to-thirty-year-old Koreans signed up and a quarter of the entire population. Proportionate to population, that makes it one of the most popular sites in the world. And, in the crowded main city of Seoul, with 23 million people in its metropolitan area, thousands of teenagers gather every night, in tiny apartments and crowed cybercafés, to create their own online make-believe homes and friends.

Among other specific social networking sites:

Friendster is a general friendship site, with 65 million people, mainly in south-east Asia.

Bebo has 40 million members, and is especially popular in America, Britain, Ireland, New Zealand and the Pacific Islands.

BlackPlanet links 20 million African-Americans.

Classmates has 50 million registered users, linking those who have previously attended the same schools, colleges or military units.

Flickster links 53 million movie buffs.

At *geni.com,* 15 million members can trace their family genealogy and contact previously-unknown relatives.

Hi5 is a site popular with 75 million teenagers, particularly strong in Latin America and parts of eastern Europe.

And at least 15 million passionate individuals create their own blogs—or Weblogs—every day with an online audiences of hundreds of millions. And almost another 100 million have created less-frequent blogs

Huffington Post—conceived and funded by millionaire socialite Arianna Huffington—emerged in early 2008, in the midst of the U.S. Presidential election campaign, as the English-speaking world's most influential blog.

Boing Boing—a "directory of wonderful things"—is one of the most popular, with an audience of 750,000 daily readers: more than the online readership of Business Week,

Brain-fitness now also a big new craze: for young and old

In photo: Students at Singapore's Overseas Family School regularly explore the human brain and body with software programs such as 3D Body Adventure, by Knowledge Adventure. But one of the latest world crazes is 'brain fitness', a $225-million annual market with such programs as Nintendo's Brain Age game and a spate of brain-fitness websites and blogs.

Watch videos 'to leverage the power of ideas to change the world'

go to: www.TED.com

. . . and see dozens of by innovators whose ideas are changing the world, like Virgin's Richard Branson (above). and one of our favorites: Kevin Kelly on the next 5,000 days of the Web.

Time and Forbes. Yet Boing Boing is all compiled by one enthusiast, science-fiction writer Cory Doctorow.

Daily Kos—"state of the nation"—attracts more than a million "page-views" a day: more than the online edition of the Chicago Tribune.

One of the most stimulating Web sites of all is that of TED (Technology Entertainment Design: www.TED.com) which feature twenty-minute video presentations by stimulating innovators, on "leveraging ides to change the world."

New ways, too, are emerging to share many of the world's best learning methods with the two billion people who live on less than $2 a day, as we explore in the last section of this book:

❏ China's recently-retired Vice-Premier in charge of education, Li Lanqing, in *Education for 1.3 Billion,* spells out how satellite and wireless networks, in particular, will be needed to retrain China's 10 million school teachers, and to provide quality education for all its 120 million primary school and 82 million high school students.

❏ Britain's BBC broadcasting service is also in the midst of transferring much of its seventy years of often-brilliant television programs to the Web, for not-for-profit use. Although BBC radio and TV programs in Britain carry no advertising, it is probably the world's best-known not-for-profit brand. So the Corporation is selling video footage and digital photos to global advertising agencies and video producers, while continuing to provide public schools and students with free access to one of the world's greatest educational and cultural libraries—to reuse in new ways. School-teacher Frances Hill and her Alpha Educational Consultancy in New Zealand are using these BBC resources extensively in the daily personalized lessons she runs on line for children who are gifted in many fields but face other learning problems from autism to dyslexia. And she is doing this from her home in the foothills of New Zealand's Southern Alps, which are themselves one center of that country's "outdoor classroom" tourist service industry.

❏ And as Don Tapscott summarizes it in *Wikinomics,* as he writes of any student in the world who can now tap into MIT's free online global university service: "She can engage with the content and faculty of one of the world's leading universities, studying everything from aeronautics to zoology. Download the readings and assignments for courses. Share her experiences in one of the community forums. Become part of MIT, participating in lifelong learning for the global knowledge economy."

Tapscott calls it *mass collaboration.* "It's a new way," he says, "for people to socialize, entertain, innovate and transact in self-organizing, peer-to-peer communities of their choosing. Companies can design and assemble products with their customers, and in some cases the customers can do the majority of the value creation. Scientists can reinvent science by open sourcing their data and methods to offer every budding and experienced scientist in the world an opportunity to participate in the discovery process. Even governments can get involved by using the new digital tools to transform public service delivery and engage their citizens in policy making."

In twenty years, he says, we will look back on the start of the twenty-first century as a turning point in economic and social history. "While the old Web was about website clicks and 'eyeballs' . . . the Internet is now evolving into a global, living, networked computer that anyone can program." It already "covers the planet like a skin".

Consider any of the major economic crises facing the world in the midst of the current decade—soaring oil prices, mortgage-bank collapses and sky-rocketing food prices—and the global mass-creativity models in *Wikinomics* suggest co-creative alternative and innovative answers, using the combined wisdom of humanity.

And in another book, Growing Up Digital, Tapscott says we are well into the first revolution in history where children know more about the dominant technology than most adults.

"I have become convinced," he says, " that the most revolutionary force for change is the students themselves. Give children the tools they need and they will be the single most important source of guidance on how to make the schools relevant and effective."

But that is only partly true. Teachers acting as learning guides and coordinators and a whole range of other networks will complete the new revolution.

Give children the tools and they will change the way the world learns

For three centuries chalkboard teaching has been equated with education

The same ritual continues: often only the blackboards have changed—to green

A new framework for education in the new networked world

Visit schools around the globe for more than fifteen years, as we authors have, and the stunning facts emerge:

❏ *Most schools are teaching students for a world that no longer exists.*

Prominent American educator Professor Seymour Papert says the world is currently entering "the most momentous mega-change that has ever come to the practice of learning and education".[1] But overwhelmingly, he says, most educational systems are failing to lead the change. Papert is a co-founder of the Massachusetts Institute of Technology's world-famous MediaLab.

He says the typical school-classroom system is still very much like the production line in the original 1907 Henry Ford Model T factory: "The car moved along and at each station an additional change was made, a piece added, something was checked, an exam was given." He concedes that this model for education might have been appropriate for an earlier age"—when we didn't know any other way to do it. But now we do. And much better ways are working brilliantly in pockets of excellence in many countries, many states or districts.

❏ *Most schools are still teaching in ways similar to the blackboard-and-chalk, desks-in-rows classroom model invented more than 300 years ago.*

Graham Nuthall, a New Zealand Emeritus Professor of Education, has spent forty years researching classroom practice around the world. And almost everywhere he's found what he calls the same "cultural ritual" of traditional classroom teaching. It's a ritual that has remained largely unchanged for decades—in many cases for more than three centuries.

"We're locked," he says, "into a system that inevitably produces failures and inequalities."[2] Nearly all adults have gone through this ten-year classroom ritual. Many thus automatically equate classroom teaching with real learning.

❏ *It's almost as if the biggest communications revolution in history has bypassed most education systems.*

Almost every school system in the world is investing big money in "information and communications technology". America has spent $60 billion on it in the last twenty years. But nearly all are doing it ineffectively. Locked into the old classroom model, they're slapping twenty-first-century technology on to an seventeenth-century design. But elsewhere a new teaching vanguard is linking the same technology with the latest neuroscience research as catalysts to rethink the entire system.

Even where governments have invested hundreds of millions or billions of dollars in IT, we still see classes of forty or more children sitting in rows, facing a teacher at a blackboard or static whiteboard while expensive computers lie unused at the back of the room or in nearby "computer laboratories".

William D. Pflaum confirms our experiences. As a designer of educational software, he took a year off to visit schools across America. And the story he tells in *The Technology Fix*[3] is sobering: "The average student spends only about an hour a week with a computer at school. Many spend far less." Just as many confuse traditional classrooms with real learning, many schools confuse computers with interactive digital technology in all its aspects: the tools that elsewhere are reshaping the next society.

❏ *But we're not talking only about a different world. We're talking about a different people. "Our students have changed radically. Today's students are no longer the people our educational system was designed to teach,"[4] says digital-games producer Marc Prensky. He says children's brains are now actually "wired" differently.*

And noted neuroscientist Dr. Richard Restak confirms this in his latest book, *The New Brain: How the modern age is rewiring your mind.*

Even in new schools with fine buildings, often classroom practice is similar

In America, with $60 billion spent on IT, the average student uses a school computer only one hour a day

In a new era of breathtaking digital simplicity . . .

most schools are still teaching for a world that doesn't exist

Prensky dubs today's youngsters *digital natives.* Just as natives of any country speak their own language naturally and in the local dialect, today's young people have grown up in a world that thinks and communicates differently to their parents. Prensky calls those parents *digital immigrants.* Like new migrants to any country, they often find it difficult to become fluent in the new language of interactive multimedia.

Those new digital natives, he says, are being socialized in a way that is vastly different from their parents. "The numbers are overwhelming: over 10,000 hours playing video games; over 200,000 emails and instant messages sent and received; over 10,000 hours talking on digital cell phones; over 20,000 hours watching TV; over 500,000 commercials seen—all before the kids leave college. And, maybe, at the very most, 5,000 hours of book reading."[5]

Prensky's inventions include brilliantly-created interactive games for learning. But that's only the start. He wants to see all the world's two billion students and 59 million teachers working together to co-create "the new tools" for learning. Says Prensky: "The idea is that the educational software we use (all of it—games, non-games and anything else—at all levels, preschool to adult) should be created by the 'world mind', should not belong to any of us, and should be available, free, to anybody, anywhere, who wants to use it."[6]

❑ *A working model already exists to achieve this: the 100,000-plus collaborative groups working online to produce open-source software, in exactly the same way that the Linux movement has created cheap, and often free, computer operating systems.*

That's how *Wikipedia,* the Internet's free encyclopedia, is compiled. It's the way students at some of the best schools on the planet are already learning: using the world as their classroom, and using the world's best interactive tools to explore it. It's just one of several ways that education needs to change.

Above all, it provides the blueprint to solve the problem of the two to three billion people left on the wrong side of "the digital divide". And we are not talking about how interactive technology, and new methods of networking, impact only on education. We're talking about the trends that are creating an entirely new type of society, and how "education" should be a key catalyst for that transformation.

Some lessons from history

But anyone searching for a new theory of human behavior and learning should recall the words of George Santayana: "Those who cannot remember the past are doomed to repeat it."[7] Most people have a natural tendency to remain locked in existing mental models. In education, that is specially so for teachers who have spent much of their life in classrooms—as students and then teachers.

That mental model of school began over three hundred years ago. It started with Jon Amos Comenius and the Gutenberg printing revolution. Mass printing made it possible for tens of thousands to study *The Bible*—if they could read. So Comenius, a Moravian-born Czech bishop, invented the modern textbook and a schoolroom system to teach reading. Comenius also created a new educational philosophy, called *pansophism,* or universal knowledge, designed to bring about worldwide understanding and peace. He advised teachers to help children learn through all their senses, as well as the printed word. Unfortunately, others distorted his wider vision. But the classroom stayed.

In 1717 Prussia became the first state to make primary schooling compulsory. This started with a schoolroom, blackboard and chalk, and students sitting at desks in rows—facing a teacher. This became the model for much of the world. And, as Professor Nuthall concludes, ever since then education has been enmeshed in a "web of supporting myths".

Between 1850 and the 1930s a whole raft of new educational and behavioral theories surfaced. These ranged from two extremes:

❏ **Francis Galton,** with his belief "that all genius and intelligence is inherited"— the forerunner of the IQ or intelligence quotient tests. And

❏ **John Broadus Watson,** who resurrected the Thomas Aquinas and John Locke *tabula rasa* (open slate) theory that everyone is born with a blank-slate mind, waiting to be filled with information and knowledge.

A challenge for two billion students and 59 million teachers:

To copy the Wikipedia model and together co-create and share new learning tools

An excellent resource on how to use interactive technology, and especially co-created digital learning games is: www.marcprensky. com and his articles filed under "Writing". Prensky is a well-known American games designer. Recommended articles include: Digital Natives, Digital Immigrants; Do They Really Think Differently?; and Students as Designers and Creators of Educational Computer Games. We return to this subject in detail in chapter ten.

Montessori proved 100 years ago that children learn with all their senses in stages

That's still true but we know much more about how to unlock the brain's secrets

And in between, the full spectrum of competing concepts, often enshrined in dogmatic practice:

❑ **Charles Darwin:** with his theory of the evolution by natural selection: what some others dubbed "survival of the fittest".

❑ **William James:** the champion of instinct as a dominant characteristic of all behavior, including human.

❑ **Hugo De Vriess,** who rediscovered Gregor Mendel's laws of heredity, including dominant and recessive genes.

❑ **Ivan Pavlov:** with his conditioned reflexes and salivating dogs.

❑ **Sigmund Freud** and **Emil Kraepelin,** with their theories of psychiatry based on each patient's memories of personal history.

❑ **Emile Durkheim:** the pioneer of sociology, and the overriding importance of social trends.

❑ **Franz Boas:** with his insistence that culture shapes nature, not the other way around.

❑ **Konrad Lorenz:** with his view on how the human brain is vitally influenced by "imprinting" from early experiences.

❑ **Maria Montessori,** and later **Jean Piaget,** presenting evidence that children develop through a period of critical stages—although still disagreeing, many years later, on the timing and nature of those stages.

Now, in *Nature Via Nurture,* British scientist Matt Ridley outlines the theories of these key shapers of twentieth-century behavioral and educational psychology. And he reaches a surprising conclusion: "They were right. Not right all the time, not even wholly right, and I do not mean morally right. But they were right in the sense that they all contributed an original idea with a germ of truth in it; they all placed a brick in the wall." Ridley says the Human Genome Project has proven that we are all a combination of both nature and nurture. Human behavior is, in fact, a combination of our genes, our instincts, our environment and our experiences—including our education.

We are also very much creatures of our culture. And the cultural gap between humans and other species is a gulf. Humans, says Ridley, have "nuclear weapons and money, gods and poetry, philosophy and fire. They got all these things through culture, through their ability to accumulate ideas and inventions generation by generation, transmit them to others and thereby pool the cognitive resources of many individuals alive and dead.

"An ordinary modern businessman, for instance, could not do without the help of Assyrian phonetic script, Chinese printing, Arabic algebra, Indian numerals, Italian double-entry bookkeeping, Dutch merchant law, Californian integrated circuits, and a host of other inventions spread over continents and centuries." And of course the incredible methods we have invented over the past two decades to change technology, change culture—and the way we transmit it.

One would think this common sense would make us all more than a little nervous about dogmatic theories of education and learning.

Yet entire education systems have been built on rival claims to be infallible dogma. Each of Ridley's "wise men" of behavioral science may have placed a brick in the wall of knowledge, but their followers turned each brick into the whole wall. Many teaching methods are still based on those rival part-truths—all claiming to be "evidence-based".

And probably the two most conflicting theories are those of the behaviorists—led by Watson and his disciple, Burrhus Frederick (B.F.) Skinner—and the rival school of John Dewey. Watson summarized the behaviorist theory, in part, in 1924: "Give me a dozen healthy infants, well-formed, and my own specified world to bring them up in, and I'll guarantee to take any one at random and train him to become any type of specialist I might select—doctor, lawyer, artist, merchant-chief, and, yes, even beggarman and thief, regardless of his talents, penchants, tendencies, abilities, vocations, and race of his ancestors."[8] He was only slightly exaggerating his beliefs.

This is the theory that drives many school systems today, especially in the United States. At its simplest: if each brain is an empty vessel to be filled in the same way,

Nature or nurture? Now we know how to combine both

Rival "schools" of educational psychology have battled each other for more than 150 years. But British neuroscientist Matt Ridley has proven that both are partly right: we are each a unique mixture of nature—our genetic and DNA inheritance—and nurture: what we absorb from our environment and culture. In photo: an infant learning from nature at the Lemshaga Barnakademi in Sweden. It's one of many new-type learning communities which blend the most effective educational psychology with practical real-life experiences: a "school without walls". And it also blends the world's best technology with hands-on experience: where "students from early childhood can learn from chickens and computers"—what Ridley calls Nature Via Nurture, in his book of the same name. We explore both concepts in depth in chapters three and twelve, as part of the new theory of lifelong learning.

Early last century John Dewey showed a major glimpse of the best way to learn

❏ **We learn by doing**

❏ **By experiencing**

❏ **In one's own way**

❏ **Meaningful projects**

❏ **By collaborating**

then "learning" can be measured in a similar way—by the same "standardized test". As Pflaum found on his recent one-year tour of American campuses: "The reality of schools today is that they are all about measurement." But critics would say they're measuring the "wrong thing".[9] As educator John Holt asked many years ago in *How Children Fail:* "How much of the sum of human knowledge can anyone know at the end of schooling? Perhaps a millionth. Are we then to believe that one of those millionths is so much more important than another?"[10]

But visit any major American "educational" conference today and you'll be amazed at the similarity of the commercial displays. The overwhelming majority sell textbooks, instructions to "teach to the test" and "guaranteed ways" to measure and achieve "standardized test results". And all based on a student's ability to memorize and regurgitate a limited selection of the world's knowledge-base. "Standardized test scores" have become the dogmatic mantra that has mesmerized a nation.

Significantly, the Watson-Skinner theories were based very strongly on that early standardized production-line industrial model that Ford introduced so successfully around the same time.

It's unfortunate that Professor Dewey's counter-theories have been placed under one of those academic labels, *constructivism,* that is generally not part of everyday lay language. Standardized testing is easier to understand, even in a country like the United States where non-standardized innovation has been the overwhelming wealth-creator. In real education, said Dewey, we should all:

❏   Learn by doing.

❏   Learn by experience.

❏   Learn by linking the mind, brain and body together.

❏   Learn by actually constructing your own mental storehouse of knowledge and creative ability.

❏   Learn by engaging in activities that "mean something to you".

❏   And learn by collaborating with other learners.

Now schools that have built on the Dewey methods for more than half a century are leading the world in using interactive technology and instant communications to successfully reinvent schooling. That's because the new tools enable the creative ability of children to flower in co-creative interactive ways.

This is not to deny that truly educated citizens should be familiar with a core body of knowledge, and be able to read, write, spell, count and understand the basics of history, geography and science. But we live in an era where around 10,000 new research papers or articles are published every day—in science alone. So it's much more important to learn how to find the new information, and to turn that combination into new knowledge, ideas and actions.

Fortunately new research provides us with associated new insights to transform learning, teaching, education and schooling. And to make it easier for students to prove what they know and can do.

❏ *Some of these breakthroughs come from genetic research, unlocking many of the secrets of life itself.*

Says Ridley, in his other book, *Genome: The autobiography of a species:* "I genuinely believe that we are living through the greatest intellectual moment in history. Bar none."

New genetic research, for example, confirms the worst doubts about the "blockbuster magic-bullet" drugs that have been the mainstay of the multi-billion-dollar pharmaceutical industry. And it's highlighting better paths to more personalized health:[11] wellness instead of sickness.

❏ *Some breakthroughs come from outstanding advances in neuroscience: new secrets of the human brain and the mind-body network.*

As American scientist Michio Kaku says: "The three and a half pounds sitting on our shoulders is perhaps the most complex object in the solar system, perhaps even in this sector of the galaxy."[12]

❏ *Some breakthroughs have come from organizational and management research.*

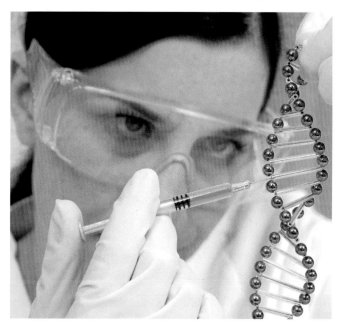

Now science and new technologies prove Dewey right but in new ways

Human Genome program and brain research provide 'greatest intellectual moment in history'

Some of the best new models come from business: everyone has a unique talent

So the trick is to find yours; then add the skills to keep learning more throughout life

Some of the most important come from extensive surveys by the Gallup polling group, into what makes organizations effective.

Among their main conclusions:

❏ Everyone has a potential talent to be good at something, but not good at everything—a complete contradiction of Watson and Skinner.

❏ The trick is "to find that something", and then to develop the skills and abilities so that talent can flourish.

❏ But talent is not merely a specific vocational skill. Rather it is a mixture of each person's personality, behavioral traits and passions.

❏ Great managers select for talent, and then train for skills. But that's also a great lesson for parents, teachers and students: learn how to identify talent, and then develop the skills and abilities to let it flower.

❏ *Some breakthroughs come from the continuing power of "Moore's Law": the doubling of computer power every eighteen months.*

That doubling is expected to continue until at least 2020. So a simple calculation provides the arithmetic: if Intel could fit only 30 transistors onto a tiny silicon chip in mid-seventies—and this has soared to 1 billion by the end of 2005—then by the mid-2007 the total had climbed to 2 billion. By 2010, it will be 8 billion; by 2013, 32 billion; by 2016, 128 billion; and by 2019, 256 billion. And that by the time today's six-year-olds turn seventeen. By then, those chips will be everywhere, in almost everything—and connected to everything.

❏ *Some breakthroughs continue to blossom from "Metcalfe's Law" of exploding networks.*

And not just of individual networks, but the convergence of so many different types: television, radio, movie-making, PCs, laptops, cellphones and those new "computers in your pocket".

As Mark Thompson, Director-General of the British Broadcasting Corporation, says: "We are all hurtling towards an on-demand, pan-media universe".[13] And he adds: the cost of versioning content—video, music, movies, and digital learning—for different kinds of devices "is collapsing and will tend to zero".

Already the BBC is well on the way to converting all its excellent television, radio, music and digital libraries into on-demand multimedia services, including interactive learning.

❏ *Other breakthroughs are rewriting the total manual for business as corporations discover the power of the "frictionless web": the ability to weave together new seamless digital networks that completely short-circuit outdated sales and distribution methods.*

The banking, insurance, computer sales, airline travel, publishing, book selling and entertainment industries are all being blown to bits and put together in new ways.

That's happening by the way in which industries are slashing *transaction costs,* largely by selling online. After recording music, for example, it now costs about 50 cents to mass-produce each CD. Sell it in through traditional chains and each transaction adds a cost. But make the same music available on the Web, through *iTunes,* and the transaction costs drop to zero, slashing music prices online.

Papert calls for a similar rethink to all aspects of education. That will probably also include new dynamic ways for "education" to interact with other disciplines—as physics, electronics, genetics, biotechnology and computer science are also converging.

The new framework for learning

That interaction will provide a new framework for a more holistic learning culture. The broad outlines of that framework, we believe, are already creating the scaffolding to build a new learning society:

1. *The diversity of talent:*

Everyone does have a talent to succeed at something. And a one-size-fits-all learning-model stops that.

2. *The new science of learning:*

Neuroscience is exploding: the combined research on how the brain, mind and body

World's best schools are now weaving the new findings into an action framework

From the pre-kindergarten years at Mexico's Thomas Jefferson Institute, highly-qualified educational psychologists (one at right in photo) work with parents to produce a "development profile" for each child. This identifies strengths, possible problem areas, personality and behavioral traits and temperaments. These profiles are then used as the basis for first-stage personalized learning plans, as the students proceed through to senior high school. But these plans do not aim for limited early specialization. The aim is to produce happy, balanced human beings, learning to develop their own talent, passion and interests but inside a nurturing, holistic environment. The institute operates three campuses, in separate cities, linked together with live video and computer networks. See following page for another photo.

The new model links unique individual potential with team collaboration

And it combines hands-on projects with digital learning

In photo: Elementary school students, at the Thomas Jefferson Institute's Mexico City campus, work in a hands-on team to produce a model when studying the geography of the world. But they also work together on computers to download information from web sites such as Discovery. They may shoot videos to combine global and local information; then create computer graphics and edit all together to produce digital portfolios.

work together to make learning easier, faster and more effective—to learn how to learn, learn how to think, learn how to create.

3. *The changing role of teaching:*

Teachers as coaches and stimulators—not instructors and information-purveyors. Each a guide on the side, not a sage on the stage.

4. *The new core of knowledge:*

Not as isolated facts to be remembered, recalled for exams and then often forgotten—but as the scaffolding and building blocks for an interconnected, integrated, more holistic learning experience.

5. *The common sense of doing:*

As Dewey said: to learn it, do it. And to absorb new knowledge faster, embed it with all your senses and in other effective ways.

6. *The new art of creativity:*

In a new creative age: the ability to combine mind-power and new interactive tools to create new solutions, products, ideas, services and experiences.

7. *The mastery of skills and abilities:*

"Select for talent, train for skills and abilities" is sensible "shorthand". But as all great sporting achievers demonstrate: great coaches develop mastery—both for individual strengths and to produce champion teams.

8. *The balance of lifeskills:*

The full mix of abilities that make us truly human, including better communications and relationship skills.

9. *The proof of performance:*

To move away from the narrow concept of "standardized recall tests"; instead to demonstrate living proof —to "show you know" though personal digital portfolios.

Your seven interlinked learning networks

That new scaffolding will change many things. But it will cause the biggest cultural earthquake in the current *structure* of schooling, where so many people have a stake in the status quo. While Amazon, Dell and other industry leaders are slashing their "transaction costs", university fees are soaring. And the traditional way to set fees, on an annual basis per student, does not encourage more efficient ways of learning.

The late Peter Drucker went much further in the years just before his death. Writing in the March 10, 1997, issue of *Fortune,* the most-respected management thinker of the century said: "Thirty years from now big university campuses will be relics . . . Already we are beginning to deliver more lectures and classes off campus via satellite or two-way video at a fraction of the cost. The college won't survive as a residential institution. Today's buildings are hopelessly unsuited and totally unneeded."

Papert urges us all to think of the quick collapse of the former Soviet Union: "It is a system, I think, that was becoming increasingly incompatible with the modern world for reasons not very different from those that operate in the education system. It tried to run a country as a production line, as a top-down command economy where what people made would be determined by a committee somewhere. We try in our school systems to decide what people will learn in this top-down centralized way and, for the same reason, it is not compatible with the modern world."[14]

We authors believe this modern world demands a new learning theory that links *the uniqueness of individual potential* with the developing world of *interlinked networks* and new models of efficient collaboration.

But we stress that many of these conclusions are tentative. Read any history of science and philosophy over the centuries, and some conclusions are obvious: Plato, Aristotle, Galen, Ptolemy, Newton, Copernicus and Galileo were all geniuses. But in every case major aspects of their theories were later proven to be wrong.

So, as Karl Popper puts it in his theory of knowledge: "We make progress not by adding new certainties to a body of existing ones but by perpetually replacing existing theories with better theories." [15]

This chapter summarizes our overall "rethink." These conclusions are then expanded throughout the book. But they will be improved as new and better models emerge:

But in a world where two billion live on under $2 a day . . .

much better methods are needed to bridge the digital divide

Incredibly, while Africa, India and China race to join the world's interlinked mobile phone, Internet and Web business worlds, tens of thousands of their schools are based on the old, old model. Yet the technology now exists to share lesson plans from the best schools and colleges in the world with others less fortunate. In India, almost half its villages don't even have a school while its global high-tech call-center business booms.

The new learning model starts with each person's unique neural network . . .

and a brain born with 100 billion active cells and unlimited scope

The importance of this is so all-embracing that the entire next chapter is devoted to it: How to develop your unique talent, through nature, nurture and neurons.

1. Your internal genetic and neural network
and the brain-mind-body talent that makes you unique

That network-model starts with you—and how you, and not schools or systems, are the most important component for lifelong learning.

The human species is unique. But so is every other species, although all are created from the same genetic building blocks or code. Says Ridley: "Trunks are unique to elephants. Spitting is unique to cobras. Forty years of field primatology have confirmed that we [humans] are a unique species, quite unlike any other." But there is nothing exceptional in being unique. "Every species is unique."[16]

So are you as an individual. For centuries, scientists could only speculate on some of the most intricate workings of this neural network. Now technologies like positron emission tomography (PET), magnetic resonance imaging (MRI), and functional MRI (fMRI) allow scientists to actually see the brain at work as it learns.

So they're providing new evidence of how each of us develops from the continual interaction of "nature and nurture". We are each born with inherited characteristics, and not just the color of our hair and eyes and the basic build of our bodies. We are all either born with or soon develop our own distinct personality and behavioral patterns. But these then interact with our experiences, our environments and our cultures.

"Armed with these and other tools, we have taken giant leaps in learning," say Marcus Buckingham and Curt Coffman in *First, Break All The Rules,* the summary of major Gallup surveys of effective business.

2. Your personal learning network
Linking home, school and the real world together

Traditionally, we've called learning organizations "schools'"—and kindergartens, colleges and universities.

Comenius is rightly regarded as the "father of modern schooling". Building on Europe's mass-printing innovation, he was the first to use pictures in textbooks: in *The Visible World in Pictures,* published in 1658. By the time he died in 1670, he had published 154 books, mostly dealing with educational philosophy. And his concepts of schooling were being taken up in various parts of Europe, though not all. But he was decades ahead of his time.

Unlike many religious leaders of his day, he contributed greatly to *The Enlightenment*. He was a strong advocate of what today would be called holistic education. He taught that education begins in the earliest days of childhood and continues throughout life. He encouraged learning by seeing, hearing, tasting, smelling, touching and doing. He advocated formal education for girls—an idea very revolutionary at that time.

His philosophy of *pansophism* attempted to incorporate theology, philosophy (effectively, the pre-scientific name for science) and education in one. He believed that learning, spiritual and emotional growth were all woven together.

This wasn't the model, however, adopted by the Prussian state in its first compulsory public schools. They set the pattern for the regimented, classroom that has continued, basically in the same form. Comenius's schools were established to teach religion along with reading, writing and arithmetic. But to this the Prussian Government added as a main component: to build disciplined "duty to the Prussian nation state".

Some governments—and textbooks—continue that emphasis today, with many history textbooks notoriously biased. But already talented school teachers are transforming even complex subjects into more interactive learning journeys. Many others are creating environments and networks from which everyone can emerge as a better learner. And here two research-results are vitally important:

❏ *Create the right environment, and even very young children "explode" into learning.*

Maria Montessori was proving this a century ago in the slums of Rome. Exposed to multisensory environments, even children considered "mentally retarded" were reading, writing and counting before starting school. But more important, they were also becoming confident, self-acting, enthusiastic learners. And doing that while enjoying themselves.

❏ *We also have different ways to take in, process, store and use information.*

We each have a learning style, thinking style, creative style and working style as

Step two is to link home, school and Web into a personal learning network

The vital importance of the early years mean parents are world's first teachers

We now know that every child's brain-development soars from birth. In the first few months, those 100 billion brain cells can sprout trillions of neural pathways. And all future learning will travel along the most-developed paths. Language development, in particular, has its biggest growth-spurt in those first few months, as we explore in depth in the next chapter.

Every child's brain is 'wired' differently, crafted from their total environment

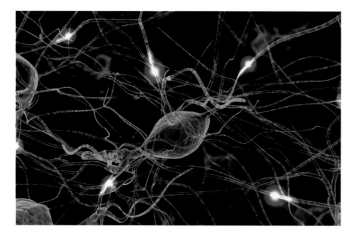

A stimulating, happy, safe environment = a stimulating, happy secure child

Not long ago, scientists could find out such basic research only by laboratory tests on rats. Now the latest fMRI (functional Magnetic Resonance Imaging) scans can take moving pictures of human brains (above). In the center is one of the brain's 100 billion neurons or active cells. All the learning branches (dendrites) sprouting from it are actually grown and then changed by everything a child experiences. See more details, next chapter.

unique as our fingerprints. So learning environments need to cater to that diversity, and build on it.

Some of the strongest examples of great learning environments come, surprisingly, from rats. For years, neuroscientists at the University of California at Berkeley have shown what happens to rats reared in both dull and interesting environments. Place baby rats in dull, boring cages — with bland, uninteresting food — and you produce dull, bored, unintelligent adult rats. But place young rats in bright, interesting, colorful environments—with plenty of games, color, movement and multisensory stimulation, plus a good diet—and they grow to be bright, interesting, intelligent rats.

Common sense should tell us that the same simple truths can turn all environments into more stimulating, interesting "learning places".

The family learning network

Our first environment, of course, is inside our own family. Home is our first school, and our family our first teachers. We also know that each one of us goes through distinct "ideal teachable moments" and "ideal learning moments". And for parents, those vital moments include five main periods: during pregnancy, from childbirth, from a child's first days at an early-learning center, when starting school and later at the onset of puberty and then on to high school.

All children also grow through very specific developmental stages, in sequence. Both Montessori and the Swiss psychologist Jean Piaget have identified such stages. Parents who study developmental-phases, during pregnancy and early childhood, probably learn more from that direct experience than they'll ever learn at school.

And you don't have to spend big money to develop an emotionally-safe and stimulating learning environment in your own home. Several in-home training programs are now available to help parents develop as their children's first teachers.

New school networks

Schools themselves will continue—but hopefully with a much more expanded role. Amazingly the big majority of primary and high schools around the world are used for only around 20 percent of total time. Any corporate leader underusing the main business capital resource to this extent would be fired. And the models already exist to use schools much more effectively:

❏ Brislington High School's new Digital Learning Center in Bristol, England, is used during school hours by its own students for learning interactive technology. Outside school hours, the center is used by other schools, parents, grandparents and community groups.

❏ At Brislington and many other United Kingdom classrooms, interactive, digital whiteboards have already replaced chalkboards. In this way, school lesson plans can be shared through the Internet to classrooms, for use on digital whiteboards—and on students' home computers.

❏ The University of Western Australia has developed a lesser program of online interactive "whiteboards"—directly to home computers in distance-learning programs.

❏ A major report on the importance of early-childhood education, prepared for the provincial government of Ontario in Canada, has recommended that good early-childhood learning centers be built in the grounds of all primary schools.

❏ Many schools in China have created their own natural history museums—with all the exhibits either collected outside school or made by the students.

❏ In Christchurch, New Zealand, Discovery One is a public primary school that uses the entire city as its classroom. Every child, in partnership with parents and school, works out a personal study plan. So biology study might start in the public botanical gardens, actually working with gardeners and botany researchers. The school's multimedia center adjoins the center-city bus terminal, and students return there to record their research in multimedia portfolios.

❏ Schools themselves also work more effectively if the total curriculum is based on how the human brain processes and stores new information, like branches on a tree.

Here the International Baccalaureate Organization provides a brilliant operating model—for students from age three to senior high school: All IB elementary-school study is based around global projects, so students can build each theme as a separate

If you want to study botany, use a civic botanical garden as your classroom

Teachers can now obtain quality degrees with mainly online study

Working school teachers can gain undergraduate, graduate and doctoral degrees in educational technology from Pepperdine University with only three weeks on campus, the rest on line. More importantly, they can put study into practice every day.

branch of that tree of knowledge, and explore its expanding patterns in interactive ways, as we'll explore in the last chapter of this book.

Community learning networks

Almost everyone will soon have in-home or community access to a wide variety of educational services. The trend is already there:

❏ Community libraries are becoming alternative learning centers, extending their normal book-lending role to provide digital training.

❏ Thousands of Microsoft, Cisco and Oracle specialists now achieve high-earning qualifications largely online, but generally combined with hands-on courses at community schools or colleges.

❏ More and more schools are building community-learning and development programs into their regular curriculum: like students doing project work in association with local industry and commerce.

Teacher networks

Probably nothing is more important than professional-development programs if teachers are to break out of the "cultural ritual" of traditional classroom practice. Trend-setting schools are now following the example of leading corporations—and building daily learning programs into their working life.

Online networks

For post-secondary education, online learning is growing:

❏ California's Pepperdine University offers undergraduate, masters and doctoral courses in educational technology—with only fifteen days a year on campus, in three separate weeks: the rest on line.

❏ In China thousands of students are studying for an online MBA degree from the Beijing Academy of Sciences.

❏ Other skills are also easily learned online or from interactive CD-roms—designed by some of the world's best "subject masters". To learn the bridge card game, for example, you can buy software or linkup online to actually "play against the computer".

❏ But bridge experts don't have to be software specialists to create games. They merely need to find software-design talents to match their own game-playing skills. Great teachers can do the same with any subject.

❏ Digital chess games provide even better examples. All players can select their level of competence: from beginner to world master. And then sequentially increase one's skill levels.

❏ Just as *Wikipedia* has provided a "template" for everyone to contribute to the world's biggest encyclopedia, so the best digital game to teach chess—from level 1 to level 10—could become a model to learn virtually every skill.

3. New interactive information networks

How to interact with the new pool of instant information

If you want to set up your own local bridge club, you can benefit from world champions who have joined with software designers to make that easy. The experts provide hundreds of sample hands, a system to grade results and computer printouts to show all players how they scored and how they could have done much better. So you combine the brilliance of the global instant-information network, the skill of world-master teachers, the talents of multimedia designers—and your local community.

It also bears repeating: for the first time, we now know how to store virtually all humanity's most vital information and to make it available, almost instantly, in almost any form, to almost anyone on earth. We also know how to do that in great new ways so that people can interact with it, and learn from it.

Since the fifteenth century in Europe, until the early 1990s, mass information for education was dominated by the mass-produced book. Gutenberg's invention not only revolutionized printing: it caused more important revolutions in religion and education—as the Protestant Reformation spurred the importance of reading. With it came the birth of the modern primary school.

By the early eighteenth century, the first British encyclopedia had been born. Then, from 1772, came the first books of the thirty-five-volume *French Encyclopedia:* up to that time the biggest publishing venture in any language.

Now teachers can use interactive online learning aids from global networks

BBC's online lesson plans call on over 70 years of the world's top TV experience

British-born school principal Frances Hill now runs an online school from her country home in New Zealand for students who are highly talented but have specific learning difficulties. She prepares personalized developmental profiles for each student— as the basis for individual learning programs. And she calls on the great online program service from the British Broadcasting Corporation for world-class interactive lessons (in photo).

Wikipedia now gives instant free access to 10 million articles in 252 languages

Other online services provide extra links

In 2001 no one had ever heard of Wikipedia. Now it is the biggest single encyclopedia in the world, providing more than 10 million articles, free on line, in mid-2008: 2.5 million of them in English, and others in 252 languages. The Oxford Reference Online data base allows teachers, students and anyone else to check information from 162 encyclopedias and encyclopedic dictionaries. Wikipedia's articles are contributed and added to by thousands of volunteers, generally specialists in each subject.

Most of France's outstanding writers and thinkers contributed to it. "But what made it intellectually and historically important was that it embodied the new attitude to knowledge that Voltaire had imported into France from England—a scientific approach that looked to Francis Bacon and Isaac Newton as its great forebears, married to a philosophical approach that looked, above all, to John Locke (the philosophical 'father' of democracy). Denis Diderot, its editor, admitted that his aim was to change the common way of thinking. And, to a very considerable extent, he did".[17]

Encyclopedism, in fact, became the core of what has since dominated much of Europe's school curriculum. But printed encyclopedias are soon out of date. So are most textbooks, yet they dominate most school systems.

❏ Now Google not only scans billions of pages in half a second to find answers on any subject.

❏ Google, Yahoo, Microsoft and other search engines also compete to personalize information: to tailor it to the specific needs of individuals. And more and more this information is available instantly through new wireless technology: not just on the new array of mobile phones but through wireless connections in homes, offices and those tiny appliances that started out as cellphones and are now pocket multimedia PCs.

❏ On Amazon, you can not only shop for any book you want—you can download summaries, read reviews, and contribute your own.

❏ Yahoo provides dozens of ways to play games and engage in other activities with like-minded people around the world. It also provides personalized touring maps; and, through Geo-Cities, helps you design your own website.

❏ And at Altavista you can use *Babelfish* technology to translate this paragraph, or any other text, from English into Spanish, Dutch or eleven other languages.

So the new emphasis is on personalizing the information. And then using that to actually *construct* knowledge: putting the information to practical and creative use.

Once you could only *read* about the adventures of such explorers and scientists as Vasco de Gama, James Cook or Albert Einstein. Now you can actually *become* an explorer or scientist.

High school students can even form a team with other countries to join Oracle's annual *ThinkQuest* competition to build a combined website on your findings. The rewards: a possible $25,000 college scholarship.

4. Your creative network

How to think for new ideas and innovate with others

Learning how to learn is now a core part of the challenge. The other is learning how to think—and learning how to create.

Here, too, new networking models are emerging strongly. Often these involve students working together in groups, using their own preferred learning, creative, thinking or working style—in partnership with others who have different talents and attributes. New digital "templates" make it even easier to share creative ability both around your own network and around the world.

Nearly every bit of "authoring" software is already designed to include *templates.* Microsoft *Powerpoint* and Apple *Keynote* slides are well-known simple examples. They make it easy for even young children to insert their own videos, computer animations and self-composed music into personal presentations. Apple *iMovie* and Microsoft *Movie-Maker* video-editing templates, *Kidspiration, Inspiration* and *MindManager* Mind Mapping software, and *Hyperstudio,* Macromedia *Director* and *Flash* animation tools are other templated products. And once such templates are available, then anyone else with the same software can use them. The idea is not to copy others' work but, like professional authors, TV producers or journalists, to work individually and collectively inside professionally-designed layouts.

The New City School in St. Louis, Missouri, produced its first "multiple-intelligence" book more than ten years ago: researched, tested and written collectively by the teachers at the school. It covers the entire Missouri state curriculum, in every "subject" at every grade level, using Howard Gardner's model of multiple intelligences.[18] And it provides hundreds of easy-to-use resources for parents, teachers and students: like lists of musical tracks so that "musical learners" can learn mathematics and science to music—as we will explore in Chapter eight. Many Chinese children effectively learn

On YouTube, Flick and Facebook, millions now share their creativity

Videoclips, photos and clipart all free

...ain research ...ing, every ...n can now ...hare talents in online communities

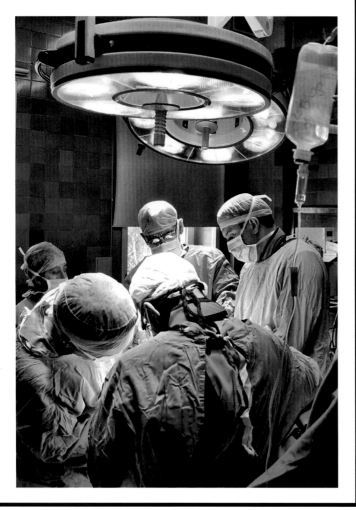

English by singing-along with musical templates on karaoke machines.

So what happens if we involve all fifty-nine million teachers in the world and their brightest students in producing not just a book but interactive, online "templates" so that all can share their knowledge?

Now imagine that done on "open source" software, and translated into every language of the world by the students of the world. That's what we mean by "mass innovation". And cooperative enterprise.

But it's also what we mean by the gap between those who shape much educational policy and today's twenty-first-century youngsters.

5. Your talent network
How to share your skills and professional knowhow

You can also use the same methods to share and expand your talents, skills and abilities: whatever your age or occupation. Already many university disciplines link through digital networks. Type "teachers learning networks" into Google, and it will give you a choice of 898,000. Among our favorites:

❏ **www.smartbrief.com/ascd:** the daily news summary, from newspapers and magazines around the world, on matters of interest to educators—compiled by the American Association for Supervision and Curriculum Development.

❏ ***www.theage.com.au:*** a daily summary of the world's best IT news, prepared by *The Age* newspaper in Melbourne, Australia.

❏ ***www.newhorizons.org:*** the website for New Horizons for Learning.

❏ ***www.bbc.co.uk:*** the website of the British Broadcasting Corporation, with its excellent links to other interactive learning sites around the world.

In almost every academic discipline we have looked at to research this book, we've found excellent websites operated by practitioners: from biology to brain research, Montessori to Comenius.

In a world where ten giant pharmaceutical companies dominate the $600-billion-a-year prescription-drug market, British universities are now regrouping around a policy of developing "ethical pharmaceuticals". When produced through cross-campus co-ordination, these will be offered to competing pharmaceutical companies to keep the cost down to developing countries, as India's Cipla group has done so well.

In the latest world-changing technology, the cost of international optic-fiber links has come down dramatically. For the first time ever, this enables China's 1.3 billion people, India's 1.1 billion and the hundreds of millions in eastern Europe and the former Soviet Union to join the global talent network.

Most of those countries have a strong core of educated talent. The new low-cost communications network enables competent mathematics teachers in India to coach students in Singapore. And it enables hundreds of English-speaking Indians to run American telephone call-centers from their own villages or homes. But the ramifications are even greater. Faced with low-cost competition from China and India in particular, the brightest companies in "the West" are already gearing up for what they are calling the switch from the Knowledge Economy to a new Creative Economy.

Says *Business Week:* "What was once central to corporations—price, quality, and much of the left-brain digitized analytical work associated with knowledge—is fast being shipped off to lower-paid, highly-trained Chinese and Indians, as well as Hungarians, Czechs and Russians. Increasingly the new core competence is creativity—the right-brain stuff that smart companies are now harnessing to generate top-line growth. The game is changing. It's not just about math and science any more. It's about creativity, imagination and, above all, innovation."[19]

And about setting up effective cross-border creative talent-sharing networks as among those most vital for building the Next Society.

6. New organization networks
New social movements linked to open partnerships

Digital networks are, of course, already transforming the corporate world—and several are now proving models for learning:

❑ Dell—the computer giant that pioneered the selling of personal computers on the Internet. Dell customers actually choose all their own PC-components on line, to

From buying baby books to airline travel, welcome to a networked world

You can even build a personal PC or share Sesame Street fun

Teachers can share their lessons through collaborative global classrooms

Interactive digital whiteboards make 3-D graphics easy to store and reuse

In countries like China (with 10 million teachers and often 60 students in a chalkboard class) and India (with 47 percent of villages without a school), low-cost computers and interactive whiteboards will soon make it easy to share lessons. And in subjects with a shortage of teachers, such as mathematics and science, sharing lessons between schools is already working well.

their specifications. And we see similar personalized online learning programs as a major wave of the future. Learners will be able to choose from just-in-time learning "modules", custom-designed for their own learning styles and level

❏ Eighty percent of BMW's customers now design their own new car online—by selecting from 350 model variations, 500 options, ninety exterior colors and 170 interior trims. When a BMW dealer enters a customer's chosen options into BMW's Web ordering service, he receives the precise date of delivery five seconds later. The information is then relayed to thousands of suppliers who ship the components in sequence. The cars arrive eleven to twelve days later, one-third of the time it took before the online system was in place.

❏ Apple Education in New Zealand—a subsidiary of the Apple Computer distributor in that country—has done one of the finest jobs in the world in training teachers for new concepts in interactive technology. It even runs regular bus-tours to model schools.

❏ From Britain, Promethean—the European leader in electronic interactive whiteboards—also hosts an online collaborative-classroom service. This lets successful subject-teachers around the planet share interactive lesson-plans and "digital flipcharts". By mid-2005 150,000 schools around the world had installed such interactive whiteboards, often linked up to students' own computers or "digital slates". The market has grown fastest in England, where the Government in 2005 announced plans to spend $2.8 billion putting electronic whiteboards into all its schools. And Mexico has also recently bought 30,000. So maybe the blackboard-and-chalk era is finally, slowly coming to an end.

❏ In China, Legend (now Lenova internationally) has become the biggest computer seller, largely because of its retail network of Legend computer-training centers, open to parents, teachers, students and lifelong learners.

But these are not isolated minor examples. We cannot restress too strongly the way in which nearly all successful businesses today are reinventing themselves around the concept of interactive electronic webs, and as "creative learning organizations". Generally these link suppliers, manufacturers, retailers and customers. They have major lessons for education:

❏ The Apollo Group's University of Phoenix is the biggest of America's for-profit universities, with 280,000 students enrolled in its physical campuses and almost 80,000 online. Nearly all students are learning new skills while in permanent jobs.

❏ *And* **Business Week** *forecasts that online study over the Web will soon have spawned a $370-billion-a-year industry: mainly through distance-learning and self-directed study.*

❏ Accenture, the world's biggest business consulting company, spends $425 million a year on staff training: much of it digitized. It spends another $100 million a year on its own digital intranet to make all its best business case studies available to its global consultants. FedEx spends $500 million on internal staff training; its training and software headquarters in Memphis, Tennessee, is a model for hi-tech universities everywhere. And GE's total staff-retraining budget is now $800 million.

7. New global learning networks

A new society based on shared "digital tools"

The inevitable end result of all this will—we suggest—be a new global learning web that will link thousands of networks where everyone can share individual talents, cultures and information. Already local, company, community, group, state, school and national digital networks are merging together with others around the world.

And like the Internet and the World Wide Web itself, the organization of the new global learning web will be chaordic: the same dynamic combination of the unity and diversity that underlies the planet's eco-system.

As Bill Bryson puts it in his brilliant book, *A Short History of Almost Everything,* in summing up the mystery of life itself:

"It cannot be said too often: all life is one. That is, and I suspect will for ever prove to be, the most profound true statement there is."

But inside that unity of all life is the uniqueness of each individual. And, in the challenge of Buckingham and Coffman: "Everyone can probably do at least one thing

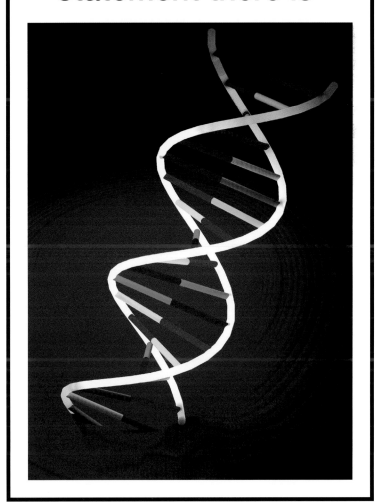

'It cannot be said too often: all life is one—the most profound true statement there is'

The Wikipedia dream: 'To give every single person on earth free access to the sum of all human knowledge'

better than ten thousand other people.   The trick is to find that something."[20]

Then to open-mindedly share and network that talent—and your culture—with the uniqueness and culture of others. Not only in your local networked teams, but with other talents around the globe. Many, of course, will continue to share their talents commercially. Others will do so freely through educational webs, like scientists have always done.

And yet others will link in with emerging organizations like *Wikipedia.* Says *Time* magazine, on the *Wiki* phenomena: *"Wikipedia* is a free open-source encyclopedia, which basically means that anyone can log on and add to or edit it. And they do."[21] By mid-2008, it had over ten million entries in 252 languages. But Jimmy Wales, the founder of the Internet's largest encyclopedia, says he is just getting started. He is expanding into *Wiktionary,* a dictionary and thesaurus; *Wikibooks,* textbooks and manuals; and *Wikiquote,* a book of quotations. His goal: to give "every single person free access to the sum of all human knowledge."[22]

Wasn't that once the main job of schools, colleges and universities? It still is, in part. But now they too are more and more locking into new networks.

New breakthroughs in neuroscience are also shattering the old myths of education: to make it easier, faster and more effective to learn how to learn, to learn how to create—and to learn how to lever your own unique talent, learning style, thinking style and working style into an enjoyable, worthwhile, creative future: your own personal learning revolution.

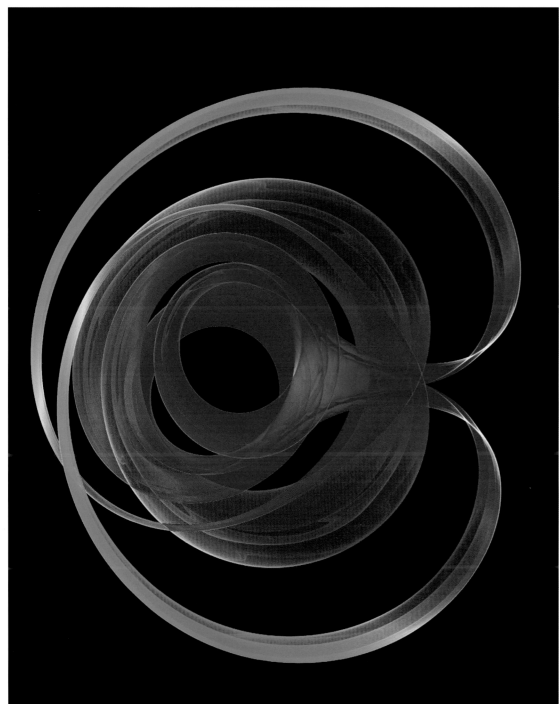

Part two
Your future

Every healthy baby is born with the world's most powerful learning tool, waiting to be switched on

How to develop your unique talent through nature, nurture and neurons

It is hard to believe that four hundred years ago Britain's Oxford University insisted that the human brain was unimportant, and that all intelligence resided only in the heart.

To teach otherwise was to risk excommunication and even death.

Now we know the unique power of the human brain as the world's greatest creative learning organ. Without that power, no Web 1.0 or Web 2.0 revolutions—or any other innovation—would be possible.

With it:

❑ Everyone has the potential to become talented and successful, but in different ways.

❑ Every healthy baby is born with 100 billion active brain cells or neurons—as many cells as there are "stars" or planets in the Milky Way.

❑ Each of those 100 billion cells has the ability to sprout at least 10,000 branches—to speed information around your brain and body faster than a racing car.

❑ From birth, the brain can create trillions of these neural pathways—which sift, store and link the array of interacting networks that combine to make each individual brain and person unique.

Says prominent British neuroscientist Professor Steven Rose: "With its 100 billion nerve cells, with their 100 trillion interconnections, the human brain is the most complex phenomenon in the known universe—always, of course, excepting the interaction of some six million such brains and their owners within the social-technological culture of our planetary eco-system."[1]

In his book, The 21st–Century Brain, he predicts more startling breakthroughs as "the complex interconnected web between the languages of brain and those of mind has come to be seen as science's final frontier".

Tens of thousand of scientists and researchers continue to unlock these secrets of the brain and mind—and the DNA building blocks of life:

❏   The multi-billion-dollar Human Genome Program has at last helped to resolve the long-running nature-versus-nurture debate. We now know that both play a big part in our personal development. Nurture builds on nature. They link together.

❏   Latest neuroscience research and new brain-scanning technology has revealed new insights into how the brain, mind and body together play a much more interconnected basis for learning.

❏   Many schools develop only a limited part of students' brainpower. But by moving beyond simple multiple-choice Scholastic Achievement Tests, we now know how to develop the much greater power of the whole brain.

❏   And the world's biggest survey of corporate employees and managers reveals that individual talent is much more important than any narrow definition of intelligence.

That finding comes from Gallup, the world's largest polling organization. And it summarizes two mammoth research studies over the final twenty-five years of the twentieth century.[2] In them, Gallup interviewed more than one million employees and 80,000 managers. We know of no other survey anywhere near that large in scope. And the results are startling in their simplicity:

❏   "Everyone has a talent to be good at something. The trick is to find that something."

❏   "Everyone can probably do at least one thing better than ten thousand other people."

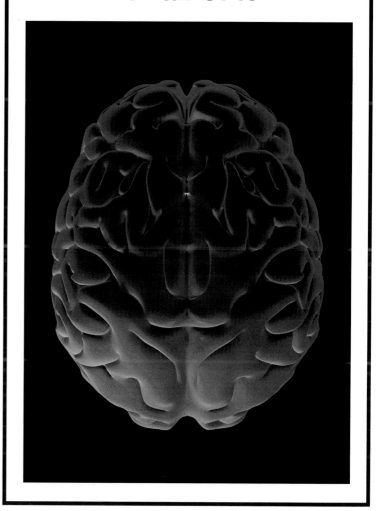

Many education systems concentrate mainly on only part of the brain instead of all of it

Every infant has the potential to be talented and successful—but in different ways

❏ *But talent is not the same as intelligence, knowledge, skills or specific abilities. "Talent" is your individual uniqueness: your recurring pattern of personality, drives, passions, temperament and almost automatic behavior that together makes you uniquely YOU.*

❏ By talent we are not referring only to world-acclaimed public champions like Tiger Woods and Michael Phelps. As Marcus Buckingham and Curt Coffman say in *First, Break All The Rules,* their book of the Gallup research: "Every role in life, performed at excellence, requires certain recurring patterns of thought, feelings and behavior. This means that great nurses have talent. So do great truck drivers, and great teachers, great housekeepers and great flight attendants."

❏ Successful managers identify specific talents and nurture them. They then make sure to create an environment in which each person develops the skills and abilities needed for those talents to flower.

❏ And so should good parents, schools and great teachers.

❏ "Don't waste time trying to put in what was left out. Try to draw out what was left in."

Which, incidentally, was the original Latin meaning of "education": *educare*—pronounced *educaray:* to draw out the unique qualities of the whole person.

From the late Peter Drucker, with his usual common sense: "We've known the secret of real learning for more than 2,000 years. "The first and wisest writer on raising small children, the great Greek biographer and historian Plutarch, spelled it out in a charming little book, *Paidea (Raising Children),* in the first century of the Christian era. All it requires is to focus on the strengths and talents of learners so that they excel in whatever it is they do well. Any teacher of young artists—musicians, actors, painters—knows that. So does every teacher of young athletes. But schools do not. They focus instead on a learner's weaknesses."[3]

Even worse, many schools concentrate so much on all students memorizing the same information that they neglect the unique potential of each individual student. Then they concentrate so much on a limited strength of only a part of the human brain that they neglect the incredible power of the whole brain. So, instead of "no child left behind", they program to leave millions behind.

Many schools already reverse this, of course. Some of the best focus on developing what Harvard University Professor of Education and Psychology Howard Gardner has dubbed "multiple intelligences" or different traits. Gallup favors "multiple talents" as a better description—because then it is much simpler to identify potential talent, and then develop the skills and abilities to ensure that talent flourishes. And to link it in with multi-talented teams and networks.

Former Stanford University Professor of Business Jim Collins has reached almost exactly the same conclusions in extensive research into what makes companies and organizations great, including schools. As he summarizes them in *Good To Great,* he says the business answers come from three "simple, simple, simple ideas":

❏ Start with what you are deeply passionate about—with each person's own deep-seated passions and talents.

❏ Define what you can be the best in the world at—and what you cannot be the best at.

❏ Fill your "company bus" with a highly-talented team—but different talents and passions in every seat of the bus.

In business the allied aim is to drive the bus towards an agreed goal of excellent economic performance.

Collins asks each of us to consider the same simple concepts for our own personal success: "Suppose you were able to construct a work life that meets the following three tests. First, you are doing work for which you have a genetic or God-given talent. And perhaps you could become one of the best in the world at applying that talent. ('I feel that I was just born to be doing this.') Second, you are well paid for what you do. ('I get paid to do this? Am I dreaming?') Third, you are doing work you are passionate about and absolutely love to do, enjoying the actual process for its own sake. ('I look forward to getting up and throwing myself into my daily work, and I really believe in what I am doing.')

How every child develops a unique talent depends on the way nurture builds on nature

For some talents the genetic inheritance can influence the choice of a career

China's basketball star, Yao Ming, is 2.27 meters (7ft. 7in.) tall. His father is 2.08 meters, a former player; and his 1.88-meter-tall mother is a former captain of the national Chinese women's team. In 2007 Yao Ming earned $56 million in sponsorships.

Some schools are now based on similar simple principles: to start with the passions and talents of each student—and then build personal learning plans around those strengths, often flowering inside multi-talented teams, just like work in the real world.

This does not mean encouraging every child into narrow specialization. Nor does it mean skimping on learning the so-called basic skills of literacy, numeracy and science. The opposite: it means learning them in different ways, to suit individual learning styles. But many of those abilities tap into only a limited part of the human brain. And real learning means knowing how to use the rest of the brain—in different ways—by learning many of the "whole-brain" skills like public speaking, creative and critical thinking, research and twenty-first-century communications.

The first step is to get rid of the myths on which so much "education" is based.

Myth 1: *That we all learn best in the same way.*

What we now know: We each have a personal learning style, thinking style and working style. We each have a different way to take in information, store information, retrieve information and turn information into real knowledge.

Even geniuses learn in very different ways, think in different ways and work in different ways:

❏ **George Bernard Shaw** was at the bottom of his class at school, yet became one of the world's greatest playwrights.

❏ **Thomas Edison** was so bored with school he dropped out after only three months, but became the world's greatest inventor.

❏ **Albert Einstein** was a daydreamer. As a youth he failed his college entrance exams. Yet he became the greatest scientist of the last century. Employed as an "inspector third class" in the Swiss Patent Office, he wrote in his spare time three Papers that revolutionized science. The first won the Nobel Prize for physics. The second proved that atoms do indeed exist. "And the third merely changed the world."[4]

Even then, having just solved several of the deepest mysteries of the universe, when Einstein applied for a job as a university lecturer he was rejected. He then applied for one as a high-school teacher, and was rejected there too.

Einstein didn't keep many notes. He worked on intuition. Asked later about his method of thinking, he replied simply that "imagination is more important than knowledge". He worked out the core of his theory of relativity while he was imagining riding on a moonbeam. And, in words that are a challenge to a new generation of creative students and thinkers: "Only daring speculation can lead us further—and not the accumulation of facts."

Myth 2: *That intelligence is largely fixed at birth, and can be accurately determined by IQ or similar standardized tests.*

What we now know: Says Robert J. Sternberg, Professor of Psychology and Education at Yale University: "Skills measured by IQ tests are not the only skills that, in combination, constitute intelligence."[5] He says all children have individual strengths, and "our goal should be to help all children make the most of their strengths and correct their weaknesses. Throw away the crutches and let children use their wings. Help them make the most of the skills they have."

Myth 3: *That there is only one form of intelligence.*

What we now know: There are many forms of intelligence, and certainly many *traits* and *talents*. Harvard Professor Howard Gardner has identified at least eight separate types of intelligence: linguistic, mathematical-logical, musical, visual-spatial, kinesthetic or physical, social or interpersonal, introspective or intrapersonal, and naturalist. There may be many more.

"The single most important contribution education can make to a child's development," he says, "is to help him toward a field where his talents best suit him, where he will be satisfied and competent."[6] America, he argues, has completely lost sight of this. "Instead we subject everyone to an education where, if you succeed, you will be best suited to be a college professor. And we evaluate everyone along the way according to whether they meet that narrow standard of success."

Myth 4: *That all intelligence is inherited.*

What we now know: For decades so-called experts argued which was most important: nature (inherited in your genes) or nurture (developed through environment, expe-

For others, the early family environment can spur future world champions

As an infant, Tiger Woods watched his father practising golf shots, became fascinated with the game, and soon was playing with a cut-down club. He credits the influence of his father and mother as the start of his career to World number one. But he says they never pressured him, and acted as role models in many ways.

For others a national or local culture can spur the launch of a successful career

Spanish tennis champion Rafael Nadal loved the game from an early age, but has been helped greatly by Spain's sporting academies funded by both the Government and Nike.

rience and culture). Now we know that nature and nurture work together. We are each born with certain traits and "propensities" for learning and specific talents—from the physical build of a basketball star to a particular temperament. Our home, schooling, living, working and community environment is then vital to develop those talents and to build new sets of skills and abilities. National, regional and local cultures can also influence many careers. Australia, Spain and more recently China are countries that have poured enormous funds into national sports-development academies. Other cultures have long been strong in many pursuits: from ballet to chess in Russia; literature and dance in Ireland; movie making Hollywood, India and now New Zealand. All tend to attract, enthuse and develop similar talent.

Myth 5: *That intelligence is the same as logical, analytical thinking.*

What we now know: Professor Sternberg says intelligence takes at least three forms: analytical, creative and practical. And intelligence-quotient tests do not measure those latter two. "A high score in an IQ test," he stresses, "is no guarantee of a high level of creative ability, practical or commonsense ability, athletic ability, musical ability or any of a number of other abilities."[7] Again, even geniuses such as Edison, Einstein and many other analytical and creative thinkers have solved problems in different ways.

Myth 6: *That everyone has the ability to succeed at anything.*

What we now know: That is simply not true.

Talent is not an all-embracing ability to be great at everything. Talent is very much based on a built-in series of aptitudes. And different aptitudes help people excel in different ways. The aptitudes that make a great accountant do not necessarily make a great drummer. Attributes that make a fine chess-player do not guarantee success as a creative painter. Great nurses and great surgeons have different talents.

Myth 7: *That school is the main or best place to learn.*

What we now know: From ages five to eighteen, students spend around 20 percent of their waking hours in a school classroom. That time is vital to education. But everything else they learn is with the world as their classroom, and many learn more from that than from school itself.

Take almost any of the great artists, sporting achievers or movie-makers. From Mozart to Beethoven, the great composers learned well away from a school classroom. From Tiger Woods to the Williams sisters, sporting achievers learn by actually playing their sport: on the golf course, the practice range or the tennis court. And Steven Spielberg, George Lucas and Peter Jackson all learned to make movies by making movies.

As the Sante Fe Institute noted in 1995, in a collection of essays entitled *The Mind, The Brain and Complex Adaptive Systems:* "The method people naturally employ to acquire knowledge is largely unsupported by traditional classroom practice. The human mind is better equipped to gather information about the world by operating within it than by reading about, hearing lectures about it, or studying abstract models of it."

Myth 8: That "standards" are the real test of learning, and can easily be measured by standardized written tests.

What we now know: Some standards are important, and *can* be tested. Obviously, students can be tested for their knowledge of arithmetic, chemistry symbols, spelling, geographic data and historical facts. But these are only part of a broad education. And certainly written tests cannot evaluate each students' individual talents, skills and abilities. Many written tests can measure only the ability to memorize.

For nearly every twenty-first-century job—from television and movie making, music and computer skills, to landscaping and cheffing—a digital portfolio showing what you can actually do is much more effective and useful than a written qualification that measures "standardized test" answers.

Such standardized I.Q. testing, as we have covered, grew out of the mechanized, production-line industries of the early twentieth century and the first world war: as easy ways to separate potential officers and managers from the infantry soldiers and simple-skill workers required for repetitive tasks.

In today's high-skill, high-touch and highly creative societies it makes much more sense to rethink education based on our knowledge of the most phenomenal integrated and holistic system of all: the human brain.

Obviously every aspect of all the neurosciences cannot be attempted in a book of

The myth th
will be le
by conce
standardizea

102

The uniqueness of the human race: our total brain structure is inherited by all

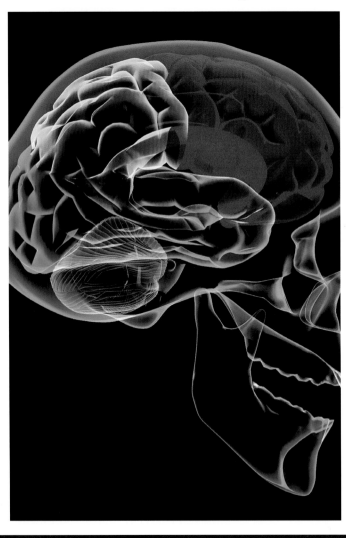

this nature. But at least four can be summarized to show their importance in talent-development:

❏ **The basic brain structure** that makes the human race unique.

❏ **The unique way each individual shapes his or her own brain and future:** how we create our own *mind* by the way we personally build on that basic structure.

❏ **The seven most important systems inside each brain**—and how they can be used to develop individual talent—within the power of the whole brain.

❏ **And the role that parents and teachers** in particular, but also lifelong learners, can play to power-up the ability of the brain, mind and body to work better together.

The basic structure of the brain

For more than a century researchers have been aware of the basic structure of the human brain. But it is less than two decades since the latest fMRI (functional Magnetic Resonance Imaging) machines have enabled neuroscientists and medical specialists to scan, see and record moving images of the brain's innermost workings.

And in healthy humans, the similarity of their brains is obvious:

❏ The brain's two hemispheres—left and right—and the way in which they are joined in the middle by what experts call the *corpus callosum.* Like a highly-efficient international phone exchange, it shuttles thousands of messages between both sides of the brain every second.

❏ The human brain also has a tiered structure: a lower brain-stem adjoining the top of the spinal column; a very large interior part of the brain sometimes called the *limbic* system (for *collar)* because of the way it wraps around the units that make up the brain-stem; a dominant appendage at the lower back of the brain, the *cerebellum,* or "little brain"; and the uniquely-layered cerebral *cortex* (for *bark),* which fits like a thin crumpled sheet over the upper part of the brain

❏ Several obvious parts of the brain—sometimes called *lobes*—which are the main storage and operating zones for many activities: hearing, seeing, talking, writing, moving, touching, feeling, thinking and creating.

❏   Other structures and processes in the brain—including hormones and chemicals—control breathing and heartbeat, process fright, fear and emotions.

All these work together, and are interconnected in many ways around the brain and around the body. But it is the incredible number and strength of special kinds of cells inside the body, and particularly the human cortex, that makes our ability unique.

What makes each individual unique

Around a trillion cell make up the human brain. One tenth of these—100 billion— are *neurons* or active cells: the main phenomenal driving force that separates human brains from every other species.

A fruit fly has 100,000 active neurons. A mouse has 5 million. You've had 100 billion from birth. And each of those 100 billion neurons has the ability to actually grow thousands of tree-like branches, called *dendrites,* that make thousands more connections around the brain and around the body—frequently at least 10,000 each, but in some parts of the brain over 200,000. So the number of connections and *neural pathways* totals trillions.

That uptake soars in spurts during the nine months of pregnancy and then at a phenomenal rate at birth: up to 3 billion "bits" of information in a second from the very first days of life.[8] It flashes that input through those expanding dendritic branches. If it's new information, it grows new branches. If it relates to already-stored information, the brain files "like with like".

And the more you are open to new learning experiences, the more your brainpower soars. In a twenty-eight-week-old human fetus, researchers have found 124 million connections between cells. At birth: 253 million connections; in an eight-month old: 582 million. In the first few years of active life, these connections can explode to about 1,000 trillion.

But those numbers are trimmed back later so that the brain doesn't suffer from "mass overload".

The simplest trim-back example is from spoken language: one of the factors unique

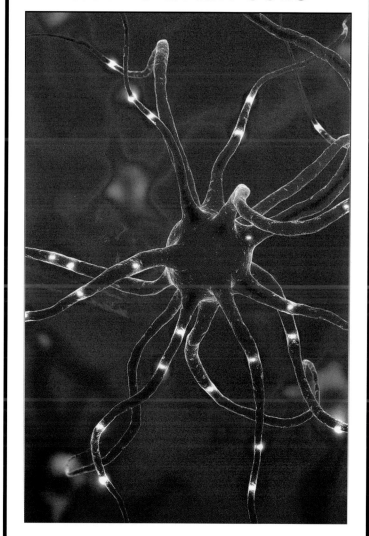

The uniqueness of every individual starts with its 100 billion active brain cells

Every brain cell can grow at least 10,000 unique new learning pathways—fast

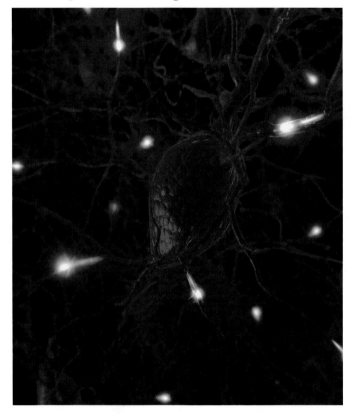

The network expands as you learn from all your senses

to humans. In the first few months of life every healthy child will babble in the sounds that make up the world's languages: about seven hundred in all. That ability is innate: we inherit it with our genes. But we then take in, from our immediate environment, only the sounds that we actually hear. If we hear only English or Spanish in that first year of life, we will start building up a memory-bank, in the brain, of the words, cadence and syntax of English or Spanish speech. If we have an English-speaking mother and Spanish-speaking father, and they converse together, and with the baby, in two languages, the infant will start to absorb both. But if it does not hear hundreds of sounds in other languages, then the infant brain will actually *prune-off* the primitive pathways that process those unheard sounds. That ability will be discarded.

But those pathways which do get used frequently are strengthened—like building individual super wired-highways in the brain.

Says Pulitzer Prize-winning writer Ronald Kotulak in *Inside The Brain*: "The amazing discovery of the brain's plasticity—its ability to physically rewire itself to become smarter—makes mental stimulation, in the long run, more essential to the body than food.* That the brain thrives with good nourishment is a concept that has profound significance for individual achievement and for the way parents raise their children."[9]

And while all the brain's different components can be studied in isolation (as many specialist neuroscientists do), it is much more important, as part of "the learning revolution", to see how they work in unity.

Your brain's main networks

That internal brain system groups its components into at least seven main networks, all of which combine to form the whole brain and link with the body as well:

1. The sensory networks

The structure of our brain, along with our DNA, is a central core of our unique inheritance. From the start of life, the brain starts building on that structure, firstly

---

* *Kotulak is using "journalistic licence" here. As we will discuss: nutrition, both during pregnancy and from early in life, is a major factor in building a fully working brain, mind and body.*

through all its senses: from what we see, feel, touch, taste, smell and actually do.

We also all learn best if we take in information with more than one sense. If a small infant sees an orange, smells an orange, touches an orange, tastes an orange, is told "This is an orange", and sees the word "orange" in at least one written language—each impression will reinforce the total concept of an orange.

Her brain's internal systems will store each of those messages in a different memory bank—and then recall them more easily. The more enjoyable the experience, and the more it is repeated, the better the lesson will be encoded in her different learning banks, for easy recall. The more we link the more we learn.

Maria Montessori, the pioneering Italian educator, was proving this a hundred years ago—by providing classroom experiences where infants could learn through all their senses. All were reading, writing, speaking fluently and doing basic mathematics well before their fifth birthday.

Today, modernized Montessori pre-schools and schools, and their successors, are being used as the basis for effective "experiential" learning.

But it doesn't stop at school. Highly successful business innovators are switching from providing only good products and services to providing great sensory experiences.

Some, like the giant Disney empire, base all their activities on this concept: at Disneyland, Disneyworld, through three-dimensional movies, cruise ships and hotels. That's why Disneyworld is the planet's most popular single tourist attraction, with up to 50 million visitors a year. Other retail centers build on similar "great experiences", from The Mall of Americas in Minnesota—designed around a concept by the creators of the Knott's Berry Farm theme park—to Sweden's IKEA furniture chain.

For schools and college, the lessons, too, are obvious: to act as new experiential centers, not merely one-sense or limited-sense information purveyors.

On a much smaller scale, students now know how to create their own miniature Disneylands as they learn to actually become designers, creative artists, scientists—and expand their other talents.

If a baby sees and tastes an orange, and is told it is an orange, his brain links all those three concepts

As electrical messages flash around the brain they are changed by chemical reactions: the neurotransmitters

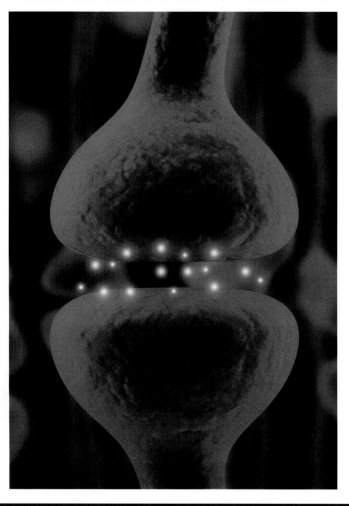

❏ One of Britain's leading high schools has turned itself into the Cramlington Learning Village: a new interactive learning center.

❏ Nanyang Polytechnic in Singapore—one of the finest in the world—has been designed as "a teaching and learning city", where every student, to qualify, has to produce a finished commercial product, from robots to computer animation, in partnership with a commercial corporation.

❏ Carnegie Mellon University in Pittsburgh, Pennsylvania, has built one of America's finest digital campuses. But that does NOT put boring lectures online. "Among CMU's digerati," says *Business Week,* "public enemy No. 1 is the old-fashioned lecture, where a scholar stands before hundreds of snoozing students and drones on for an hour or two. For them the chief role of technology is to help end boredom." And it quotes Professor Raj Reddy, the former longtime dean of CMU's School of Computer Science: "In the future, learning will come from doing. You abolish lectures, and you don't just read about history, you participate in a simulation of it."[10]

2. The transmission network

When those sensory experiences enter your brain, they immediately turn into electrical impulses—to be flashed to the brain's visual, auditory, taste, touch and smell centers. Other major nerve pathways, called *axons,* carry messages around the brain and the body. The transmission network they travel is both complex and brilliantly simple.

While each message starts as an electrical signal, it then quickly reaches the first of a series of switching points or tiny gaps, so narrow they are almost invisible even to many multi-million-dollar brain-scanners. Scientists call these *synapses.* As a message crosses each synaptic gap it is changed by those chemical *neurotransmitters*—and the combined electrical-chemical impulse then carries on.

So far more than fifty neurotransmitters have been identified, and all can have various impacts on health, life and learning.

Some neurotransmitters are triggered by our food and drink. Eat healthy food and drink lots of clear spring-water, and you'll speed messages on their way, and maybe even improve their clarity. But live on a diet of fatty fast foods, washed down with tons of caffeine-rich coffee, toxic sweeteners or strong alcohol, and you'll trigger different chemical neurotransmitters that distort those messages.

Other powerful neurotransmitters come from drugs, such as alcohol and tobacco, which can completely subvert the brain and cause addiction. Others are triggered by exercise, emotions and thoughts.

Perhaps the best known is adrenaline. It is often triggered by fear: fear of public speaking or fear of physical danger. Become frightened, say, by a snake or shark, and fear triggers an "alarm hormone", noradrenaline. This, in turn, "organizes the brain to respond to danger, producing adrenaline and other chemicals that prepare the body to fight or flee. Noradrenaline may play a major role in both hot-blooded and cold-blooded violence."[11]

Noradrenaline is a mood-altering chemical. And so is serotonin: known as "the brain's master impulse modulator" for all emotions and drives. It especially keeps aggression in line. In fact, dangerous impulses often arise from an imbalance between serotonin and noradrenaline.

So neurotransmitters can change moods, create "highs" and "lows". All, of course, can affect learning. We are indeed what we eat, what we drink, what we think, what we exercise and what we do.

The nutrients absorbed in the womb and in the first few years of life are also vital for coating those axon pathways around the brain and the body with insulation known as myelin. Some pathways are insulated before birth, some soon afterwards. The longest axons, from the brain to the feet, are not fully insulated, for example, in the first year of life. That is why infants cannot walk at birth.

Axons that carry the sound of words into the brain's "hearing centers" are myelinated almost from birth, so even a tiny baby can hear those earliest words from her parents. But the axons to the "speech processing" areas of the brain are not insulated till later.

3. The physical network

For years education has been considered a "cognitive" skill: the way we learn by

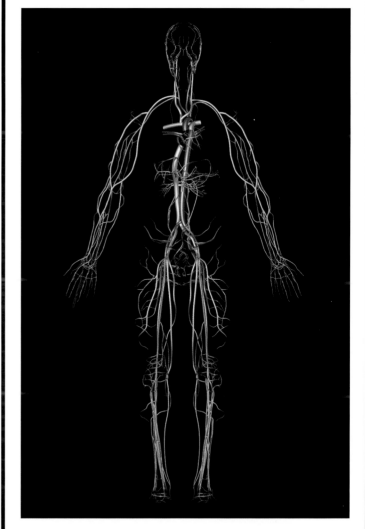

The better the pathway insulation, the faster the messages: and that's how diet helps

What a child does physically often wires up the brain more effectively than study

taking in and processing information into knowledge—by hearing or reading, analyzing, judging, evaluating and comparing: what Yale's Sternberg refers to as "analytical intelligence". This is still at the core of IQ tests and many "standardized tests".

But we also learn physically, *kinesthetically,* through the use of muscles and movement, and tactually through touch.

And now we know how a "physical control network" is coordinated around the brain and the body.

Some parts of that network are centered in the "motor control" parts of the advanced upper cortex. Others are in the lower cerebellum, at the back of the brain. And that cerebellum is linked closely with the balancing area linked to the inner ear. Together that forms the *vestibular system.*

By using all that network, babies learn the vital importance of muscular coordination. Creeping and crawling lead to walking, running, hopping, jumping. Rolling a ball leads to hand-eye coordination, and a sequence of other physical activities—from pouring water to holding a crayon—that eventually lead to hand-writing ability.

As we will see in chapter seven, sequential physical activities in early childhood are more important than "academic" study in laying down many of the most important learning pathways.

And of course the repetition of sporting actions—tennis, golf, table tennis, badminton, pole-vaulting, discuss throwing and all the rest—later "grooves" those into a built-in routine habit.

So physical exercise, along with mental exercise, is vital throughout life. Having children sitting still all day in school is not the way to learn. And hitting the gym, walking, jogging, swimming, tennis, golf and other activities are as vital through all the later adult years as are such mental stimulation as reading, chess and bridge.

4. The emotional, feeling networks

Daniel Goleman sums up the importance of *Emotional Intelligence* in the subtitle of his book of the same name: *Why it matters more than IQ:*

"At best," he writes, "IQ contributes about 20 percent to the factors that determine life success, which leaves 80 percent to other forces. The last decade," he adds, "has seen an unparalleled burst of scientific studies of emotion. Most dramatic are the glimpses of the brain at work. They have made visible, for the first time in human history, what has always been a source of deep mystery: exactly how this intricate mass of cells operates while we think and feel, imagine and dream. The flood of neurobiological data lets us understand more clearly than ever before how the brain's centers for emotion move us to rage or tears, and how more ancient parts of the brain, which stir us to make war as well as love, are channelled for better or worse."

Joseph LeDoux, another American neuroscientist, was one of the first to discover the key role of the *amygdala* in what Goleman calls emotional intelligence. In humans the amygdala (from the Greek word for almond) is an almond-shaped cluster of interconnected structures perched above the brainstem. The brain has two amygdala, one on each side. They're very close to the *hippocampus.* And these are both vital gatekeepers to learning. The hippocampus is often called the gatekeeper to memory—the brain's distribution center to send and sort incoming messages and send new-information messages to specific parts of the brain for long-term storage. The amygdala is the emotional "control center". And, as LeDoux has proven, emotional messages—such as fright, fear, anger, tension and stress—communicate themselves instantly direct to the amygdala and then to other major parts of the brain much quicker than those same messages go to the more "logical thinking" areas of the cortex.[12]

Says Goleman: "In the brain's architecture, the amygdala is poised something like an alarm company where operators stand by to send out emergency calls to the fire department, police and a neighbor whenever a home security system signals trouble."

LeDoux says the amygdala is an emotional sentinel able to hijack the brain. And Goleman summarizes the message even more simply: "Those feelings that take the direct route through the amygdala include our most primitive and potent; this circuit does much to explain the power of emotion to overwhelm rationality."

Emotional intelligence, says Goleman, includes self-control, zeal and persistence,

IQ contributes 20% to life's success but emotional intelligence is more important

How the 'molecules of emotion' turn the whole body on to the learning process

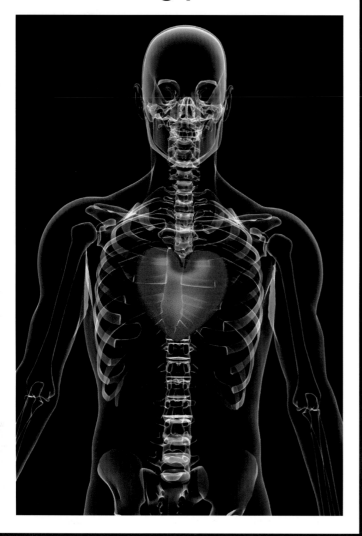

and the ability to motivate oneself. "And these skills can be taught to children, giving them a better chance to use whatever intellectual potential the genetic lottery may have given them." We agree. And as we will see when we look at "the teaching revolution", emotions are the gateway to real learning. Opening that gateway is the first step towards successful teaching.

Other research confirms the way in which brain, mind and body work in unison. No part of the body lives apart from the rest.

Here Dr. Candace Pert's findings are particularly important. Professor Pert first came to prominence in the early 1970s for her discovery of the brain's opiate receptor. Since then she has identified *peptides* as "the molecules of emotion". And those molecules are not confined to the brain. They "run every system in our body". And "peptides are the sheet music containing the notes, phrases and rhythms that allow the orchestra—your body—to play as an integrated entity".[13] Thus memories—so vital for learning—are stored in all parts of the body. And wherever new information enters the body—through sight, sound, taste, touch or smell—memory-traces are stored not only in the brain, but in the body as well. In this way, she says, the body is "the unconscious mind". The mind and body work as one for filtering, storing, learning and remembering: key elements of learning.

In early childhood, at school and college, the role of emotion in learning is vital. Students of all ages learn best when they are emotionally involved with pleasant experiences. They become stressed from fear and fright—from stress itself

5. The social networks

Humans are a social species. Most thrive on interaction in groups.

Socialization of the brain begins in the womb. And babies only a few minutes old seem to recognize their mother from the cadence and rhythm of her voice absorbed during pregnancy.

As each child grows, its first experiences should be social and happy. That interaction between parents and infant is among the most important for learning—language in particular.

During the first three years of life, an average American child hears 1,500 words from his parent for each hour he's with them and awake. But the total varies from 600 words to 2,100 an hour. Over three years that totals between 13 million words to 48 million. Not surprisingly, the infants hearing most words later excel in language.

But the even more important is the type of language, and the personal social involvement of both parents and child. Some infants in "low language families" generally hear only simple statements, like "Finish your food," "Time for bed" or "Let's get in the car". But the dramatic surge in language learning comes from the social interactions that come while babies are being fed, changed, and cuddled—from what researchers Todd Risley and Betty Hart have termed "language dancing": talking to each infant as if she were an adult—even before she can speak—with simple extended sentences such as adding "what ifs", "do you remember when", "wouldn't it be better if", and so on.[14]

The same research shows that babies listening to this type of early speech later become much more creative thinkers—from those early embedded concepts.

Research also confirms what we know from common sense: that young children "mirror" or imitate the actions of those they love—and not just language interaction—especially when they're having fun together. That copying is mirrored in the brain's neurons.

As we demonstrate elsewhere in this book, the new brain-mind-body research proves that loving parents are the world's best first teachers, and family experience in those early years provides the best early "classrooms".

In a crowded country such as China, with its one-child-per-family policy, socialization is a particular challenge for sensible families, spurring the growth of good early-childhood development centers, with the emphasis on happy social interaction as much more important than early "academics".

6. The biological clock network

Sleep is obviously an inherited characteristic of all humans. But we now know that the type of sleep you experience also has an important role to play in the way we

Happy family social interaction shows key to learning language even before speaking

'Relaxed alertness', sleep and the subconscious are big aids to learning and creativity

process information, and particularly in the way we learn.

Important parts of the brain continue to work, almost autonomously, while you're asleep: subconsciously or semiconsciously. Link yourself up to an electronic scanner and you'll soon find out that parts of your brain can send and receive information on different frequencies: on at least four separate wave-lengths. In one sense they're similar to television signals. Tune in your TV set to channel 2, or 22, and you'll be able to receive messages sent out on that wavelength. Scan your brain when you're wide awake and it will also be transmitting or working at a certain number of cycles per second. Scan it when you're dozing and it will be transmitting on a "different frequency". Likewise when you're in the early stages of sleep and dreaming, and later when you're in deep sleep.

Many researchers are now convinced that we can absorb information much more quickly and effectively when our brains are in a state of "relaxed alertness". That's the state we often achieve with certain types of meditation. Or by listening to relaxing music. Or doing yoga or pilates exercises. In the period between full waking and deep sleep, the brain automatically reviews highlights of the day—and seems to "slot" the most important ones into your memory banks. Scientists using brainscans call this REM sleep—for "rapid eye movement"—because it's as if its visual system is flashing pictures of the day's events. "Digital video clips" would be a more apt metaphor.

It's like a subconscious editing, crystallizing process that helps creativity. Think too deeply about a creative problem—writing an article or a chapter of a book, drawing a cartoon or pondering the content of speech that's due—and your waking brain may be too cluttered to find a simple creative solution.

But reflect on the challenge just before going to sleep, play some relaxing music to stimulate "the creative juices", and then, as you drift into sleep, your subconscious automatically shuts out the clutter of the conscious brain. Effectively it takes over the editing-creative process. Those who work on creative problem solving say it's amazing how they wake refreshed after a good night's sleep to find the simple solution to their challenge has been solved overnight—and just "pops out".

A similar process helps at school examination time. Most school written exams test students' ability to remember main points from any course. A good preparation is to start from the end result first: to jot down, say, the twenty main principles learned on any topic. Then play your own version of the television program *Jeopardy* with fellow students: provide those principles as answers, and then think up as many questions that will unearth that answer. Then, before drifting off for a good night's sleep before an exam, think of all the questions that elicited the correct answer—and turn it over to the subconscious. The next day, when you read the questions, the answers are more easily recalled.

Similar relaxation techniques are also highly recommended at the start of each day. The ancient art of Tai Chi, for example, is still highly popular in China. And anyone visiting the Beijing Twenty-First Century School is always impressed by the hundreds of students practising Tai Chi in the playground before school.

7.   *The thinking networks*

Of all the abilities that separate humans from all other species, two inter-related ones are vital:

❏   The ability to think—in many ways: logically, creatively and laterally.

❏   The ability to store thoughts and memories, record their histories and discoveries and pass them on in speech and writing.

Structurally, all human brains are unique "thinking processors" because of the size and power of their prefrontal lobes and frontal lobes—located behind the forehead.

But we also now know that every aspect of the brain's networking structure is involved in thinking and communicating: the information we take in, the way we store it, the way we process it, and the way in which we associate and combine that stored information in our "thinking brain".

For decades scientists came to believe that many of these strengths were controlled solely by the left hemisphere of the brain—and were linked to that hemisphere's ability to speak and write. Some of those beliefs were forged by medical scientists in the mid-nineteenth century after the death of adults with speaking problems.

Chinese 21st-Century Experimental School starts the day with Tai Chi for mental tune-up

The 'split-brain' is obvious, but now we know how the sum of the total is greater than the parts

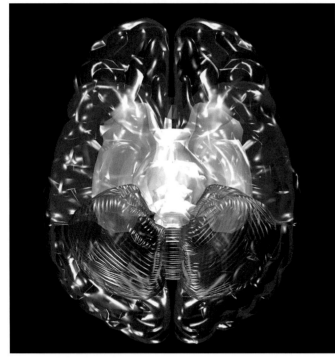

This view from underneath the brain provides a glimpse of both the strong separation of right and left-hemispheres, but also shows the way in which both sides link together to make up the whole. In the foreground is the cerebellum, at the back of the brain, which stores 'muscle memory' and also links with both the brain's intricate inner-ear networks to make up the "vestibular system" which controls the body's balance.

In 1861, French scientist Paul Pierre Broca performed an autopsy on a hospital patient who had been hospitalized with a crippled right side for many years—and with the ability to speak only one word: *Tan.* That autopsy showed that syphilis had severely damaged a cluster of neurons that produce the human ability to speak—located in the left frontal lobe. Ever since, that speech-production center has been known as *Broca's area.*

A few years later German scientist Carl Wernicke discovered that stroke-damage in another area of the left hemisphere impaired the ability to store sounds. It is still known as *Wernicke's area*—behind the left ear.

Later brain-damage research indicated that the major human thinking zone was located in the prefrontal lobes. Because of its proximity to Broca's area, this expanded the left-brain theory. But more recent research using high-powered fMRI brain-scanning equipment has taken this research to new heights—partly by letting neuroscientists actually see each part of the brain working while patients read, talk, write, move and think.

This *does* confirm the dominance of the left hemisphere of the brain in specific tasks, particularly in speech. But it also shows the thinking-creative power of the total prefrontal lobe and areas of the frontal lobe. More importantly, in all aspects of learning—including creativity and speech—this research confirms the most important news of all: the way in which the entire brain works as a unified whole.

The whole-brain system

That takes us back to the example of the subconscious mind: and the way in which the human brain is a unique problem-solving and creative system.

From their first years of speaking, very young children love to ask "Why?" In a simplistic sense, they ask questions through the so-called left brain. But they store their answers and experiences in different parts of the brain's separate but inter-connecting systems.

At many schools, the entire system is based on the ability to recall "the one correct answer" stored in the brain. Almost the entire written examination system is based on that—and on what are mainly left-hemisphere processes. The human brain is much, much more than a simple memory bank. And this presents major potential.

Says Daniel H. Pink in his 2006 book, *A Whole New Mind,* mainly using the United States as an example: "The last few decades have belonged to a certain kind of person with a certain kind of mind—computer programmers who could crank code, lawyers who could craft contracts, MBAs who could crunch numbers. But the keys of the kingdom are changing hands. The future belongs to a very different kind of mind— creators and empathizers, pattern recognizers and meaning makers. These people— artists, inventors, designers, storytellers, caregivers, consolers, big picture thinkers will now reap [each developed country's] richest rewards and share its greatest joys."

Pink says a seismic shift is now underway in most of the "advanced world", where many so-called "left-brain" industries are now being taken over by lesser-developed countries, especially in Asia, where similarly-talented employees work for much less.

"We are moving," he says, "from an [advanced] economy and a society built on the logical, linear capabilities of the Information Age to an economy and a society built on the inventive, empathic, big-picture capabilities. What is rising in its place is the Conceptual Age."

As Pink paraphrases our summary: "The left hemisphere [of the brain] is sequential, logical and analytical. The right hemisphere is nonlinear, intuitive and holistic."

He echoes one of the main themes of this book: the time has finally come to link all those abilities together—and recognize the much greater ability of the whole brain, and the associated systems and networks.

Pink says America's school system has developed as a SAT-ocracy—mesmerized and dominated by scholastic achievement tests—where, unlike real life, most ask for only one "correct" answer. "But this is not just an American phenomenon. From entrance exams in the United Kingdom to cram schools in Japan, most developed nations have devoted considerable time and treasure to producing left-brained knowledge workers."

As developing lands find their place, the affluent world will rely on creative innovation

The unprocessed fresh food that is right for the body is also right for the brain

As we will return to throughout this book, what is now needed is a different kind of school, with different kinds of experiential learning and different kind of assessments. That also means a society where parents as well as teachers open up each child to experience the pleasure of finding meaning, beauty, art, music, culture and confident communication as well as logic, the scientific method and lineal-sequential thinking.

How to unlock the brain's unlimited power

Parents, teachers and students themselves can greatly help brain development. That involves not only total social, happy and emotional support; it also depends on each brain's supply of energy and nutrition. The right food and exercise for the body is also right for the brain.

If a mother is poorly fed during pregnancy, her baby's future is handicapped. Without good food, it will not produce all the nourishing glial cells it needs. And if some foods are missing from the expectant mother's diet, the nerve pathways around the brain and body will not be effectively insulated.

As American researchers Brian and Roberta Morgan put it in their book, *Brain Food:* "The human brain begins growing in the womb, and the majority of this development does not slow down until the age of six. Growth in the brain of the fetus, infant and young child is time-dependent. This means that the brain grows during specific stages at specific times. If it does not have all the nutrients essential for its growth in those times, damage or malformation can result which cannot be corrected at a later date. A developing infant who is fed poorly during its period of brain growth may be left with learning disabilities which will remain for the rest of its life, no matter what is done at a later date to correct the nutritional deficiency."

Scottish Professor Michael Crawford sums up years of research into the impact of nutrition on infant and fetal brain growth: "Wherever we have found low birth-weight babies, small head circumference and intellectual deficits in infants, we have found the mothers concerned had diets before and during pregnancy that were deficient in a large number of nutrients."[15]

One of the major deficiencies is fat. But it's a special kind of fat. "Unfortunately," says Crawford, "we've come to think of fat as lard and dripping. But what the fetus really needs is a highly specialized fat—the essential fats we call them. They are the fats you need to build cells, and not the sort of fats that animals and humans drop on their waistlines."

Many of those fats have traditionally come from marine life. "Now of course it's an old wives' tale that fish is good for the brain. It happens to be that we now have absolute scientific evidence for this. We find that the fats found in fish and seafood are especially relevant to the growth and development of the brain." Those same fats are vital for developing the body's immune system. The core ingredient of fish oil is Omega 3. And if you live in an area where fishing grounds are now affected by mercury poisoning, organic flax seeds and walnuts are good safe sources of Omega 3. A balance of Omega 3 and Omega 6 supplements is also highly recommended.

That continues on for infants and school-age children, too. As Professor Robert Winston records, in *The Human Mind:* "A recent experiment in Durham involved giving fish oil supplements to primary school children over six months. Educational psychologist Madeleine Portwood selected a group of 120 children, aged six to eleven, who all showed evidence of learning difficulties, such as problems with coordination, reading, handwriting and spelling. Some of the results have been dramatic. After only three months of taking the supplements, one child's reading age improved by four years. For others, there has been a two-year leap in learning abilities."*

Both before and after birth, good diet is important to build up that myelin insulation. About 75 percent of myelin comes from those essential fats. Another 25 percent from protein. Breast feeding by a healthy mother is the best source of both. And of zinc, which is also vital to form glial cells. Breast milk also contains specific antibodies which coat the baby's intestines and respiratory tract and fight off infection. It also helps protect the baby from ear infections, eczema and other allergies. And it provides calcium and phosphorous needed for rapidly growing bones. In fact, the only thing

* The British Broadcasting Corporation's television series of the same name, The Human Mind— presented by Robert Winston—is highly recommended. It is available through the BBC online, and snippets are on YouTube. Google: Human Mind + BBC + Robert Winston.

'Whenever we found intellectual deficits in infants we found deficient diets in their pregnant mothers'

The 'real brain basics': natural nutrition

Eat half a banana a day, or a whole one if pregnant, for all your potassium needs

Fresh-fruit smoothies for parent and child

lacking in a healthy mother's breast milk could be Vitamin D. That's why many doctors recommend a vitamin D supplement.

If you're an adult, your brain makes up only about 2 percent of your total weight. But it uses about 20 percent of the energy you develop.

Feed it a low-energy diet, and it won't perform well. Feed it a high-energy diet, and your personal computer will work smoothly, efficiently.

For energy, the brain needs plenty of glucose. That's why fresh fruit and vegetables are so essential. They're rich in glucose.

To send those billions of messages a minute, your brain first has to generate electricity. If you could test it now, you'd probably find it generating about 25 watts. That's the amount needed to run the smallest lightbulb in your home. The source of that brain-electricity: good food combined with oxygen. Obviously you get oxygen through breathing. That's why deep breathing is recommended before and during study: to oxygenate your blood. And that's why exercise is not only good for your body, it's good for your brain. It enriches your blood with oxygen. Cut off the supply of oxygen and you destroy brain cells. Stop it completely and you die.

Your brain also needs the right type of energy to produce the best balance of those neurotransmitters. And that in turn depends on a balanced diet. Scientists have identified around fifty different types of neurotransmitters, including endorphins, the brain's natural painkillers or opiates.

And, as the Morgans point out: "Any deficiencies in nutrients can reduce the levels of certain neurotransmitters and so adversely affect the types of behavior they are responsible for. Conversely, a physical or mental problem can be corrected by boosting the level of the relevant transmitter, and this can be done by making a simple alteration in the composition of your diet."

As an example, they point to the big increase in Alzheimer's disease among elderly people, and add: "Another characteristic of senility is the reduced ability of the brain—by as much as 70 or 80 percent—to produce acetylcholine, the neurotransmitter largely responsible for memory."

Dr. Brian Morgan recommends a diet rich in lecithin to help improve everyone's memory, but especially that of older people. Foods rich in lecithin include wheat germ and soya beans that have not been genetically modified—ideally prepared in the traditional Asian way.

He also recommends lecithin and choline chloride dietary supplements to boost the neurotransmitters that are needed to improve your memory.

Other dietary deficiencies that can impair your mental performance include a lack of polyunsaturated fat called linoleic acid (an Omega 6 fat) which the body cannot manufacture. But fortunately recent research shows the answer: make raw nuts and seeds part of your regular diet. Nuts and seeds, such as walnuts, flax, sunflower and pumpkin, have a vital role in nourishing the brain's billions of glial cells and help to repair the myelin insulation around your brain's and body's "message tracks".

Iron deficiency is a major cause of poor mental performance. It probably affects more people in Western society than any other single deficiency. It decreases attention span, delays the development of understanding and reasoning powers, impairs learning and memory, and generally interferes with a child's performance in school. All minerals, including iron, are available when you eat a variety of raw vegetable sprouts such as mung beans, buckwheat sprouts and alfalfa sprouts.

The brain also needs a constant supply of other nutrients. Among the main ones are sodium and potassium. Each of your 100 billion neurons has up to one million sodium pumps. They're vital for transmitting all your brain's messages. The right combination of sodium and potassium supplies those pumps with energy. Like glucose, potassium is found mainly in fruits and vegetables. Reduce your potassium intake drastically and you risk anorexia, nausea, vomiting, drowsiness and stupor. All could be symptoms of your brain's vital pumps not working. Sodium never occurs as a separate element in nature. It combines with many other elements to form compounds. The sodium-compounds found in sea salt and a fresh vegetable diet are the best for both brain and body. Sodium chloride, or common table salt, is not recommended.

Fortunately, nearly all fruits are rich in potassium, especially bananas, oranges, apri-

Lecithin improves memory: especially from natural soy that's traditionally fermented

Exercise daily to oxygenate the blood and the brain: weights are excellent

cots, avocados, melons, nectarines and peaches. So are potatoes, tomatoes, pumpkins and artichokes.

Thousands of books have been written on good diet and nutrition, including its importance during pregnancy. But if you want your brain to be working efficiently for all forms of learning and work:

1. *Eat a good breakfast every morning, preferably with plenty of fresh fruit.* Include half a banana for its potassium content—a whole one if you're pregnant—with an orange or kiwifruit for vitamin C, and any other fresh fruit in season. If you have children, make sure they do too.

2. *Eat a good lunch,* preferably including a fresh vegetable salad.

3. *Make nuts and raw seeds, such as sunflower and pumpkin seeds, part of your daily diet*—particularly ground flax seeds. *Flax seeds have more than six times as much Omega 3 as the same amount of salmon; and pumpkin seeds have thirty-three times as much Omega 6 as salmon. Eat fish only if you are sure it is not contaminated by heavy metal pollution.*

4. *Exercise regularly to oxygenate the blood.*

5. *Cleanse the toxins out of your body*. One way to do that is to drink plenty of unpolluted water or eat raw plants. Coffee, tea or carbonated "soft drink" dehydrate the body, and fresh water reactivates it. We can't stress strongly enough the importance of a good "brain-food" and toxin-cleansing diet to "make the most of your mind", to improve everyone's learning abilities, develop their different talents and improve what some leading academics call their different "intelligences".

❏   You will recall Harvard's Howard Gardner's list of those intelligences: logical-mathematical, linguistic, musical, visual-spatial, physical or kinesthetic, interpersonal, intrapersonal and naturalistic—which we explore in the next chapter.

Others say even this list is too narrow as it omits common sense and the ability to create new ideas by combining several elements. Gardner agrees that all his "multiple intelligences" could be described as "intelligence traits". But he says the multiple concept is more valid than selecting one sole measure of intelligence.

❏   Yale's Sternberg says all his research[16] indicates that intelligence breaks down into three very distinct sets of abilities:

Analytical intelligence: used in analyzing, judging, evaluating and comparing—very much the heart of IQ tests.

Creative intelligence: used in creating, inventing, imagining.

And practical intelligence: used in putting thoughts and ideas into practice, applying, using and implementing.

Harvard's David Perkins suggests three different types of intelligence:[17]

1.   Neurological intelligence: the intelligence linked to IQ tests.

2.   Experiential intelligence: linked to specialized knowledge and experience over time. And

3.   Reflective intelligence: what some call "metacognition" or thinking about thinking and the ability to reflect.

❐   This academic analysis is well backed by Buckingham and Coffman in their summary of the Gallup business research as a guide for great managers—on how to identify specific talent and turn it into multi-talented teams. Over the last decade, they say, "neuroscience has confirmed what great managers have always believed":

❏   *Everyone is potentially talented, but in different ways.* One of the key tasks of a teacher is to identify and draw out those unique talents.

❏   *Skills, knowledge and talents are distinct elements of a person's performance.* "The distinction between the three is that skills and knowledge can easily be taught, whereas talents cannot."[18] But they can be developed, and differently-talented people can fit into an effective team.

❏   *"Talents are the [major] highways in your mind:* those that carve our your recurring patterns of thought, feeling or behavior."

❏   *Talents can be separated into three categories:* striving talents, thinking talents and relating talents:

"Striving talents explain the *why* of a person. They explain why he gets out of bed

Like professionals in real life, video students learn to link their talents in multi-talented teams

From childhood to senior status, we all learn anything best by actually doing it

every day, why he is motivated to push just that little bit harder."

Striving talents include strong internal drives, stamina, a desire for expertise and mastery, the "missionary" drive to put beliefs into action, and strong achievement values.

"*Thinking talents* explain the *how* of a person. They explain how he thinks, how he weighs up alternatives, how he comes to his decisions."

Thinking talents include focus: the ability to set goals and achieve them; discipline: the ability to impose firm structure on one's actions; gestalt: the need to see order and accuracy; numerical: an affinity for numbers and accounting; and business thinking, including financial talent.

"*Relating talents* explain the *who* of a person: who he trusts, who he builds relationships with, who he confronts, and who he ignores."[19]

Relating talents include empathy: the ability to identify with others; being a team person: the ability to relate to others; interpersonal: good "mixing skills"; relator: the need to build bonds that last; and a stimulator: the ability to create enthusiasm.

❏   Great managers unlock the potential talent of each and every employee. But they also develop skills and abilities. So should schools.

❏   Nearly everyone also learns best by actually doing. We have met no one who learned to walk by attending a school lecture; no one who learned how to use a computer without actually using it; no one who has learned a sport without actually playing it; no one who has learned to draw without drawing .

Nor should the concept of "talent development" restrict anyone to a pre-determined future. Every parent knows that some children are later developers than others. So in early childhood, in particular, and throughout elementary and high school, students should be exposed to as many different opportunities as possible so they can in time find their "right fit". The ideal of working in multi-talented teams at school is also ideal preparation for successful careers later. In fact, as students now work in multimedia production teams, teachers working with them are amazed at how those "natural talents" merge.

Says David Perry, the founder and chairman of Singapore's highly-successful Overseas Family School: "In our pre-kindergarten and kindergarten, we've found it's great to move small children each day into different 'activity teams', so they have the simulation of different activities.

"But throughout primary and high school, we make sure to expose them to a variety of challenges in different ways. We soon find that, by working together in differently-talented teams, the students themselves almost automatically sort themselves according to their strengths. By working together they learn to meld their own talents with those of others; and to appreciate the strengths and talents of others."[20]

Later in life, too, as society changes so people may seek new challenges, and branch off in different directions: often linking core talents with new digital-technology skills. Thus talented chefs might become television presenters and authors, or produce computerized cost-controlling menu software. Or talented journalists may switch to new forms of multimedia production.

But we cannot overstress the way in which nineteenth- and early-twentieth-century learning was based on an industrial-age society—designed to produce standardized products and standardized workers.

As one of America's best corporate trainers, Dave Meier, puts it in *The Accelerated Learning Handbook:* "This approach to learning required a dulling of one's complete self. Its quest: to bring behavior into line with routine production and thinking. The task of education and training was to prepare people for a relatively simple, static and predictable world.

"Today the task of education and training is to prepare people for a world in flux, a world in which everyone needs to exercise one's full powers of mind and heart, and act out of a sense of mindful creativity, not mindless predictability."

Above all, says, Meier, learners should no longer be seen as passive consumers of someone else's information, but as developers of their own talent, and active creators of their own knowledge and skills. This starts not only by identifying one's own talents but one's personal learning, thinking and working style—and how to build on it.

Finding your own talent is the first key to developing it

Everyone has a different learning, thinking and working style to add to a unique talent

How to find your own learning style and build on your unique talent

Winston Churchill did poorly at schoolwork. He talked with a stutter and a lisp. Yet he became one of the greatest leaders and orators of the twentieth century.

Albert Einstein, as we've seen, was a daydreamer. His teachers in Germany told him he would never amount to anything, that his questions destroyed class discipline, that he would be better off out of school. Yet he went on to become one of the greatest scientists in world history.

Thomas Alva Edison was beaten at school with a heavy leather strap because his teacher considered him "addled" for asking so many questions. He was chastized so much that his mother took him out of school after only three months' formal education. He went on to become the most prolific inventor of all time.

Fortunately Edison's mother—a former school teacher herself—was a pioneer in true learning. Says *The World Book Encyclopedia:* "She had the notion, unusual for those times, that learning could be fun. She made a game of teaching him—she called it exploring—the exciting world of knowledge. The boy was surprised at first, and then delighted. Soon he began to learn so fast that his mother could no longer teach him." But he continued to explore, experiment and teach himself.

Einstein, Churchill and Edison had learning styles that were not suited to their schools' teaching styles.

And that same mismatch continues today for millions of others. It is possibly the biggest single cause of school failure.

Obviously everyone has different talents. Every person has a different *lifestyle* and a different *workstyle.* Successful businesses depend on their ability to cater to those different lifestyles. And human-resource consultants spend their lives matching workstyle talents to jobs.

Yet many of our schools operate as if each person is identical. Even worse: most operate with an evaluation or testing system that rewards only a limited number of abilities. And those rewards early in life often separate the allegedly gifted and intelligent from those who are claimed to be less intelligent and underachievers.

Possibly the worst educational innovation of last century was the so-called intelligence test. As we've discussed, some tests may do a good job of testing *certain* abilities. But they don't test *all* abilities. Worse, they gave rise to the concept that intelligence is fixed at birth. It's not.

Better still: we each have access to many different "intelligences" or intelligence traits.

And if the current authors had to choose any one step needed to transform the world's school systems it would be this: find out each student's combination of learning styles and talents—and cater to it; and at the same time encourage the well-rounded development of all potential abilities.

In the new Web 2.0 world of interactive technology, we also see brilliant multimedia experts working with learning-style experts to tailor digital programs to cater to individual styles, as most of our brightest schools already do.

The major fault with so-called I.Q., or intelligent quotient, tests is that they *confuse logic with overall intelligence*—when logic, as we've seen, is only one form of thinking or learning skill. Some IQ tests also confuse linguistic ability and mathematics ability with overall ability.

And, as we have covered from the giant Gallup organization survey, the world's best managers regard talent-selection as their most important task; then make sure that all their teams are filled with the right range of talents.

In recent years Harvard Professor Howard Gardner has been one of many who

Throughout life we all 'walk to a different drummer', except in most schools

From Churchill to Clinton, many political leaders shine as linguistic stars

have made pioneer breakthroughs in shattering the "fixed I.Q." myth.[1] For more than twenty years Gardner has used prolific research to prove that each person has at least seven different "intelligence centers", probably more.

And while it's important that each individual builds on one's own talents, in the new world of multi-talented teams, each needs to learn the core values and working styles of others in the team.

Howard Gardner's multiple-intelligence model

Gardner's different "intelligences" can be defined broadly—with a brief guide to variations within each one:

❏ **Linguistic intelligence, or talent**—*the ability to speak or write well—highly developed in such people as Winston Churchill, John. F. Kennedy, William Shakespeare, Oprah Winfrey and all brilliant writers.*

Overwhelmingly, until the recent multimedia past, this trait has centered around writing and speaking. But even in writing, this talent takes different forms, and is multifaced. Non-fiction authors like journalists write to summarize and convey information. Fiction evokes emotion. So non-fiction writers generally need strong analytical and logical skills. Fiction-writers obviously tap into, and convey, emotions. Non-fiction writers spend hours or days sifting through information to synthesize it succinctly. Non-fiction authors write to convey a word-picture of emotions.

Traditionally, too, most expert public speakers were simply that: they spoke—and brilliantly. Some still do. But in the multimedia world most able keynote and seminar presenters need to be skilled in the use of words, slides, pictures, graphics and video—and how to tap into the expert services of others.

The entire world of television, in itself, has changed much of the concept of linguistic "intelligence". Even now, older television documentary producers write a detailed shooting script first. But most young students, who have grown up in the world of television "jump-cut" stories, often start with music and a theme, then add pictures, and only then start to bring in the words. This is one of the main reasons that twenty-first-century literacy is different to the previous "mainly written" era.

The lesson for schools and teachers follows logically. In a digital, multimedia world, learning in multimedia teams makes sense. And treating even elementary-school students more as multimedia journalists than passive listeners is a great start-point.

❏ **Logical-mathematical intelligence or talent**—the ability to reason, calculate and handle logical thinking: often found in mathematicians, engineers, lawyers, accountants and attorneys.

Overwhelmingly, this is also one of the dominant traits of many academic leaders. They are often systematic, structured, logical, precise, analytical.

Some—but not all—are good problem solvers. Not all are "lateral thinkers".

Some are natural scientists: painstaking in their methods and research. But many, like Einstein, are highly intuitive and creative.

Many are strong on statistics and analysis—high on the need to verify information. Others are "made" to become accountants or detailed figure-people.

Their computer skills will tend to spread-sheets—significantly the biggest business use, to date, of digital technology, with *Viscalc* and *Lotus Notes* showing the way in the 1980s and 1990 and since then Microsoft *Excel* dominating with its *Office* suite: the world's most profitable software combination.

Numeracy and mathematics, and the associated emphasis on scientific research, will continue to play an important part in schooling at various levels.

And it is here new types of digital games will play major roles. In the pre-computer era most families played games, firstly for fun, and then to learn the basics of numbers and logic: card games (from simple snap to cribbage and highly-logical bridge); simple board games such as checkers, *Ludo* and S*nakes and Ladders* or *Snakes and Chutes,* later *Monopoly;* and more advanced board games such as draughts, chess and backgammon.

Already a whole new era of digital games is soaring. And where schools encourage their use, and development in teams, the results can combine to lift logical-mathematical ability with other talents ranging from digital games design to research, art, music, video and artistic design.

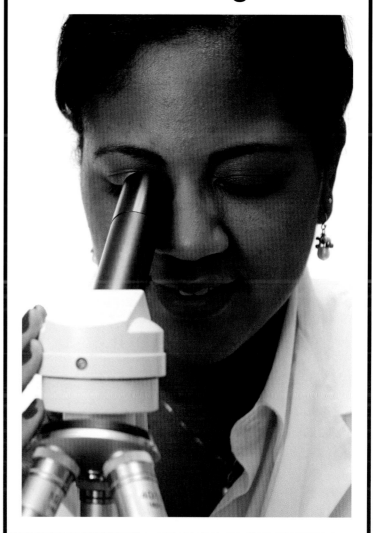

Logical-mathematical flair points to precise, structured, analytical and reasoning mind

In the new digital era, visual-spatial talent provides the choice of many careers

❏   **Visual-spatial intelligence or talent**—*the ability to paint, take great photographs, create sculpture or make Peter-Jackson or George-Lucas movies.*

Howard Gardner couples these together—and, in this sense, we prefer the term "artistic" talent or intelligence. Often, like the great movie directors, they do combine a wide variety of other artistic abilities to their visual-spatial talent. But others may be excellent at visual perception while lacking in spatial ability. All of us know people with great artistic appreciation who are not great followers of street-map or similar "spatial" instructions.

Visual people obviously have a love of pictures, art, drawing, painting—and perhaps building and sculpting. They have a good color sense—an early creative flair. As children they love "dressing up"—organizing even infants to take part in fantasy play-acting.

Throughout school and life, visual people continue to "think in pictures". They create mental pictures, they are good visualizers, prefer to draw diagrams—rather than provide written instructions. They like watching videos or creating their own. Their photos are well composed and shot, with a sense of unity and "visually telegraphing" a message.

As infants they love books like the Dr. Seuss series, with combinations of fantasy artwork and matching rhyme and prose.

As students, they quickly adapt to the Tony Buzan innovation of Mind Mapping: taking visual notes. They doodle, create symbols, highlight with colors.

They love rooms (as most children seem to prefer) with visual stimulation: peripheral posters around the walls. And they love books like this one where the photos are like slide presentations with the words.

They like integrating art with other subjects. And they choose from a variety of careers, depending on their specific talent: professional photographers; advertising agency art directors, visualizers and detailed finished artists; painters or sculptors; movie and television set designers, costume designers and make-up artists. They fit naturally into the new multimedia and other areas of similar creativity.

❏   **Musical intelligence or talent**—*the ability to compose songs, sing and play instruments.*

No need to look far for student role models here: performers, composers, singers, musicians, conductors; others in jobs like recording engineers, makers of musical instruments, piano tuners; and the associated roles as musical audiences.

Many traditional societies maintain their high cultural traditions of music and artistry combined: from the musical-oral communications in many pre-writing societies, the different music and dance traditions of cultures from Central and South America to Asia and Africa. Then the range of classical, romantic and baroque music of Europe to the distinctive African-American contribution of jazz in the United States.

In recent years, musical culture has helped form the entertainment and leisure culture industries of many countries: Abba in Sweden, the *Lord of The Dance* in Ireland, Elvis Presley in America, the Beetles in Britain, and the hit musicals of Broadway and New York.

Musical appreciation generally shows up early in life: a sensitivity to pitch, rhythm, timber—an almost automatic dancing to music; often sensitive to the emotional power of music.

In school years, music plays a major part, whether as a career or for enjoyment. All children can strengthen their learning by learning songs, playing a musical instrument, working out with music—and simply enjoying it.

Teachers who recognize that students have different learning styles find music a great ally. They use it, in particular, for "state changes": to change the mood and help introduce movement, dance and activities to break up the routine of desk-bound sameness. Students can be encouraged to compose raps to remember subjects from mathematics to spelling. Teachers can integrate music with other subjects. It's great, for example, for foreign-language learning; for learning languages to karaoke music.

As we will see, in elementary schools whose year revolves around global themes—with other "subjects" integrated into those topics—music combines with art in all it forms to integrate the study, and involve all types of student talents.

In an iPod, iTunes world, music ability flowers in many from early in life

From swimming to athletics, karate to ballet dancing, kinesthetic ability has many outlets

❑ **Bodily-kinesthetic, physical intelligence or talent**—*the ability to use one's hands or body—epitomized in sports achievers and great actors.*

Again, the range of talents is widely diverse: dancers, actors, athletes and sporting stars, surgeons, karate teachers, racing car drivers, the mechanically gifted who like working with their hands, and many types of outdoor workers.

The well-known achievers range from Tiger Woods to Michael Jordan, Olympic Games medallists to the incredible performers of Cirque du Soleil, the circus without animals: an excellent example of the blending of high physical, musical and artistic talent.

It may seem strange to some to link karate teachers and ballet dancers with lumberjacks. But look at the combined similarities and diversities: exceptional control of one's body, good timing and reflexes, trained responses, often skilled at handcrafts and likes to act, and a love of physical activity, including sports of various kinds.

Traditionally, physical "intelligence" is the most-ignored in classrooms. And that is a pity as virtually everyone loves to learn by actually doing something.

For mathematics, "kinesthetic" students love to learn with manipulatives. They like games such as dominoes, Rubic's Cube, chess and checkers. They are very responsive to, and learn best by, physical movement. They learn well from models, machines, *Tehnic Logo,* robotics and handicraft.

They like physical "state changes", like acting out, dancing, finger snapping and clapping to remember. And, like most children, they love field trips and exchange visits to other areas: with city children visiting and staying with farm families, and country students then coming to town.

Teachers working in "multiple intelligence" schools are amazed at how nearly all students respond so well to physical activity, not just those destined to be great athletes, dancers or choreographers.

And for those working in schools where life revolves around integrated themes, physical activities fit in naturally: great ways to "act out the learning" or main lessons, and regularly using drama, role-playing and real-life activities.

❑   **Interpersonal intelligence or talent**—*what we would prefer to call "social" intelligence—the ability to relate to others.*

This is the kind of talent and strength found in great communicators, political leaders, sales people, counsellors, teachers, religious leaders and "people people".

U.S. talkshow host Oprah Winfrey would typify strong interpersonal and linguistic strengths. So would public relations specialists, flight attendants, guides in the tourist industry.

Overwhelmingly, socially talented people enjoy being with others, they have many friends, enjoy group activities, like to work in teams and groups, relate well and mix well.

Later in life they often seem able to read others' intentions, negotiate well, communicate well, both listen and express themselves confidently, mediate disputes, read "social situations well" and generally like to cooperate.

In school, "interpersonal" people like learning cooperatively, love learning in pairs or groups, they like to help tutor others, and they are naturals at organizing cooperative learning projects around themes.

Given the team-based nature of most creative business today, social skills—including skills in communication and digital technology—are among those that all people need to learn. Not everyone can be an Oprah, a Barrack Obama, Ronald Reagan, Tony Blair or Bill Clinton. But all need to improve interpersonal skills.

The need for this shows up strongly with students in many traditional Asian countries, where hours of study each day and night produce high exam results in memorizing math and science, but often poor skills in social communications and confidence in mixing with people.

In fact nothing shows the difference between seemingly natural *talent* and *learned skills* than confident public speaking and communications. When students work together in multi-talented, "multiple intelligence" teams to research, summarize and report findings, this brings together all their combined strengths, so all start to learn to absorb and apply many of the social skills needed to add to their own specialty.

Some have natural social talent: the future talkshow hosts and 'people people'

Introspective people are deep thinkers, go 'inside themselves', like to study alone

❏ **Intrapersonal intelligence or talent**—*the ability to access inner feelings: what we prefer to call introspective and in some cases intuitive talent.*

The nature of this can vary from wise elders to counsellors, novelists to philosophers, religious leaders and mystics: people who are comfortable by themselves, often working alone "going inside" with their thoughts.

Likely traits include: sensitivity to one's own values, deeply aware of one's feelings, sensitive to one's purpose in life, with a well-developed sense of self, often a very private person, self-motivated but not flamboyant—generally much more likely to be an introvert than an extravert.

Introspective people and learners often prefer to study by themselves, to listen to their intuition, take time for inner reflection.

Good teachers cater to these traits. They encourage time out for reflection and independent study, they encourage students to write about feelings—just like great fiction writers do—as well as writing about things.

Preparing *My Books* or journals can draw on introspective talents while other group-minded minded students gather material for the class or school newspaper.

Schools around the world that now encourage personalized learning plans help intrapersonal students to take control of their own learning as they can then do throughout life.

The traditional one-correct-answer theme of schooling also often inhibits intuition. And yet some of the greatest ideas in history have emerged from private thinking, intuition and imagination.

❏ **Naturalist intelligence**—*the natural flair that many people have to see patterns in nature, and to work as naturalists, ecologists or farmers.*

Howard Gardner has suggested this as an eighth intelligence: strong in people who see patterns in nature, have a keen sense of balance and harmony in nature, are sensitive to environmental and animal abuse.

The late Jacques Cousteau, Britain's David Attenborough, Australia's Steve Irwin and New Zealand explorers Edmund Hillary and Peter Blake fit naturally into that category. And the success of such multimedia organizations as *National Geographic* and *The Discovery Channel* provide excellent study models for schools.

Project work, field trips, using art and nature for study, bringing plants to class and using nature metaphors are natural parts of a rounded education. So are projects that connect nutrition and lifestyle to learning.

The wide range of multimedia available on the Web, and through channels like the public broadcasting networks in Britain, Europe, the United States, Australia, Asia and Latin America provide great online resources. So are the excellent museums of natural history and science.

As we will explore in the last two chapters of this book, a global curriculum like the Primary Years Program of the International Baccalaureate Organization also makes it easy to link natural history and other projects with family visits to museums and civic projects.

❏ **The possibility of existential intelligence or talent**—*what some people call spiritual intelligence.*

Gardner has posed this more recently:[2] the traits found in highly spiritual people, the Mother Teresas of this world: people with a deep self-awareness, often very private people, reflective and with a sense of higher purpose.

Others would say Gardner's first seven "intelligences" indicate different learning styles (as we cover in the title of this chapter), while the first eight might be different talents, and the last one a *spiritual dimension* in life.

We believe his findings have vital importance in planning the future of education. *Every child is a potentially gifted child—but often in many different ways.*

Every person, too, has his or her own preferred learning style, working style and temperament.

Back in 1921, Swiss psychiatrist Carl Jung outlined how people perceived things differently. He classified them as feelers, thinkers, sensors or intuitors. Jung was, as

Some have a great affinity with nature: the future explorers, farmers, naturalists

The confident extroverts are easy to spot, but what combination are you?

far as we know, the first to classify people also as either introverts* or extraverts. It's unfortunate that many of Jung's perspectives were dropped by 1930 and relatively ignored until recently. We all know people who embody many of the concepts he defined, and New Zealand professor of theology Lloyd Geering has summarized them in his book *In The World Today,*[3] which seeks to bridge the gap between religion and science:

The extraverted thinkers, who abound in management, military strategy and some forms of science. People such as automotive pathfinder Lee Iacocca or British wartime military leader Bernard Montgomery.

The introverted thinkers, often interested in ideas for their own sake: philosophers such as Charles Darwin, Rene Descartes and Jung himself.

The extraverted feeling types, interested deeply in other people—the Mother Teresas.

The introverted feeling types, including those who agonize over the world's problems but internalize them and assume them as a burden.

The extraverted sensation types: the sports-loving, thrill-seeking, pleasure-seekers.

The introverted sensation types "who find the outer world uninteresting and unsatisfying and turn inwardly to seek fulfilment"—including some of the great mystics.

The extraverted intuitive people "who enter new relationships with great gusto but do not always prove dependable. They can move quickly from one new interest to another, especially if it is not immediately fruitful. They have visions of new worlds to conquer or to build. They are promoters of new causes. We may name as examples Alexander the Great, Julius Caesar, Napoleon, Hitler, Henry Ford and builders of today's economic empires."

The introverted intuitive people, including the visionaries and dreamers who draw from their own hidden resources.

Geering says "the acknowledgment of psychological types is an essential first step

* Jung himself preferred the "intraverted" spelling of the word; others prefer "introverted".

if we are to appreciate Jung's concept of individuation, the process by which each of us becomes the one unique and whole human person we have the potential to become" Many educators have now built on these concepts. Rudolph Steiner schools, for instance, place great emphasis on identifying and catering to individual temperaments.

Determining your learning style

There are currently about twenty different methods of identifying learning styles. And research by Professors Ken and Rita Dunn, from St. Johns University, New York, provides one of the most comprehensive models.[4] But overall your learning style is a combination of four factors:

❑ *How you perceive information most easily*—whether you are mainly a *visual, auditory, kinesthetic* or *tactile learner;* whether you learn best by seeing, hearing, moving or touching. (The ability to taste and smell can be important in some work-styles, such as wine-tasting and perfume-blending, but these two senses are not major ones in most learning styles.)

❑ *How you organize and process information*—whether predominantly left-brain or right-brain, analytical or "global", using "global" in the sense that you are more "a broadbrush" person than a systematic thinker.

❑ *What conditions are necessary to help you take in and store information*—emotional, social, cultural, physical and environmental.

❑ *How you retrieve information*—which may be entirely different to the way you take it in and store it.

How you take in information

In the Dunns' research, they discovered that:

❑ Only 30 percent of students remember even 75 percent of what they *hear* during a normal class period.

❑ Forty percent retain threequarters of what they *read* or *see.* These visual learners are of two types: some process information in word-form, while others retain best what they see in diagram or picture-form.

Each one of us has an individual learning style as unique as our finger prints

Kinesthetic and tactile learners are the main candidates for failure in traditional classes

❏ Fifteen percent learn best *tactually.* They need to *handle* materials, to write, draw and be involved with concrete experiences.

❏ Another 15 percent are kinesthetic. They learn best by *physically doing*—by participating in real experiences, generally ones that apply to their lives.

According to the Dunns, we each usually have one dominant strength and also a secondary one. And, in a classroom or seminar, if our main perceptual strength is not matched with the teaching method, we may have difficulty learning, unless we can compensate with our secondary perceptual strengths.

This has major implications for solving the high-school dropout problem. *In our experience, kinesthetic and tactile learners are the main candidates for failure in traditional school classrooms.* They need to move, to feel, to touch, to do—and if the teaching method does not allow them to do this they feel left out, uninvolved and bored.

Neuro linguistic programming specialist Michael Grinder says that of a typical class of thirty students, twenty-two will be balanced in their ability to take in information. They will generally be able to cope when the information is presented in either visual, auditory or kinesthetic ways. Two to three of the youngsters will have difficulty learning because of factors outside the classroom. And the remaining youngsters—up to six in a class of thirty, or 20 percent—will be "visual only", "auditory only" or "kinesthetic only" learners. They have great difficulty in absorbing information unless it is presented in the favored style.

Grinder dubs them VO's, AO's and KO's. And he says, "It's not just a coincidence that the initials 'KO' stand for 'knockout.' These kids are 'knocked out' of the educational system. In every study I have seen regarding 'kids at risk,' kinesthetics make up the vast majority of the 26 percent dropout rate."[5]

How you organize and process information

People with strong left-brain traits take information in logically—they can absorb it easily if it is presented in a logical, linear sequence.

People with right-brain dominance generally like to take in the big global picture first; they're much more comfortable with presentations that involve visualization, imagination, music, art and intuition.

And if you can link together the powers of both hemispheres, and tap into those "multiple intelligence centers", you'll obviously be able to absorb and process information more effectively.

The conditions that affect your learning ability

The physical environment obviously affects learning. Sound, light, temperature, seating and body posture are all important.

People also have different *emotional needs.* And emotion plays a vital part in learning. It is in many ways the key to the brain's memory system. And the emotional content of any presentation can play a big part in how readily learners absorb information and ideas. People also have different *social needs.* Some like to learn by themselves. Others prefer to work with a partner. Still others, in teams. Some children want an adult present or like to work with adults only. The Dunns say most underachievers are very peer-motivated.[6]

Physical and biological needs that affect learning

Eating times, time-of-day energy levels and the need for mobility can also affect learning ability. Try learning, for instance, when you are hungry. It's hard for most of us. And some need to constantly nibble.

Some people are morning people. Others are night owls. Again, the Dunns have found that students do better when their class-times match their own "time-clocks." Significantly, they've found that most high school and college students are not morning people. "Only about one-third of more than a million students we have tested prefer learning in the first part of the morning," they report. "The majority prefer late morning or afternoon. In fact, many do not begin to be capable of concentrating on difficult material until after 10 a.m." For daytime learning, the Dunns recommend 10 a.m. to 4 p.m. But who says high schools shouldn't be open evenings for the night-owls?

The Dunns confirm that "the tactile-kinesthetics" face most learning difficulties in traditional schools. They often drop out because they can't focus well sitting down

Be guided by your biological clock:
some learn best in the morning, others late

For a teacher to find out a student's style, often it's as simple as asking and watching

hour after hour. Those that stay on at school often "get into trouble" and get suspended. Others are often unfortunately classified as "learning disabled" and put into "special education" classes—where they do more of the same: lots of sitting still, paying little attention to their true strengths and learning styles.

Every top learning environment we have seen caters to a variety of intelligence-traits and a variety of learning styles. But many high schools in particular still seem geared to "academic" two-dimensional teaching—directed mainly at linguistic and logical learners. Not surprisingly, many high school teachers themselves "shine" in these attributes.

How to determine students' preferred learning styles

One simple way is to ask. A simple request and discussion on learning styles is also often one of the simplest ways to break down barriers between teacher and students. You can also often tell preferred style by listening and watching them talk.

Ask a visual learner for instructions and she'll tend to draw a map. If she is starting to grasp an otherwise difficult subject, she'll say: "I see what you mean." Read her a menu in a restaurant and she'll have to look at it herself. Buy her a present and you can't go too wrong with a book—but check to see whether she's print oriented or prefers pictures. If the latter, she might even prefer a video disc. Most visual learners, but not all, tend to be organized, tidy and well dressed.

An auditory learner generally couldn't care less about reading a book or an instruction manual. He'll have to ask for information. He doesn't buy a car for its looks—he buys it for its stereo system. In a plane he'll immediately strike up a conversation with his new neighbor. And when he grasps new information, he says something like: "I hear what you're saying." If you buy him a present, make it a CD or a DVD player, not a book.

A kinesthetic, tactile learner always wants to be on the move. If she bumps into you accidentally, she'll want to give you a reassuring hug. When she grasps a new principle, "it feels right" to her. And for her birthday present: a laptop computer or a bicycle?

Now: online analysis of learning and working styles

In the early 1990s New Zealand-based Barbara Prashnig, who heads the Creative Learning Company, first introduced the Dunn and Dunn model with great success in New Zealand primary and secondary schools, before spreading it elsewhere.

"People of all ages can learn virtually anything if allowed to do it through their unique styles, through their own personal strengths," she says in *Diversity Is Our Strength: the learning revolution in action.* She has also built on the Dunns' research base to build a practical program for analyzing individual students' learning styles, anyone's individual working style, plus individual teaching styles and training styles. And to do this directly online through the World Wide Web. Cramlington Community High School in Britain is one of several using Prashnig's detailed thinking-style tests for individual students as part of its program of personalizing lesson plans. This is a key part of their official "leading edge" school status, as we will see later.

Four types of thinking styles

Not only do we have preferred learning and working styles, we also have favorite thinking styles. Anthony Gregorc, professor of curriculum and instruction at the University of Connecticut, has divided these into four groups:[7]

- ❏ *Concrete sequential.*
- ❏ *Concrete random.*
- ❏ *Abstract random.*
- ❏ *Abstract sequential.*

We stress, however, that no thinking style is superior; each is simply different. Each style can be effective in its own way. The important thing is that you become more aware of which learning style and thinking style works best for you. Once you know your own style, you can then analyze the others. This will help you understand other people better. It will make you more flexible. To help you we are indebted to SuperCamp co-founder and President Bobbi DePorter[8] for providing this analysis of the various thinking styles:

Even with four college friends, you may find four combinations of thinking styles

We take in and store information in different ways, too: some with MindMaps, others prefer written notes

MindMapping photo courtesy of SuperCamp.

Concrete sequential thinkers are based in reality, according Bobbi DePorter. They process information in an ordered, sequential, linear way. To them, "reality consists of what they can detect through their physical sense of sight, touch, sound, taste and smell. They notice and recall details easily and remember facts, specific information, formulas and rules with ease. 'Hands on' is a good way for these people to learn."[9] If you're concrete sequential—a CS—build on your organizational strengths. Provide yourself with details. Break your projects down into specific steps. Set up quiet work environments.

Concrete random thinkers are experimenters. Says Bobbi DePorter: "Like concrete sequentials, they're based in reality, but are willing to take more of a trial-and-error approach. Because of this, they often make the intuitive leaps necessary for true creative thought. They have a strong need to find alternatives and do things in their own way."

If you're a CR, use your divergent thinking ability. Believe that it's good to see things from more than one viewpoint. Put yourself in a position to solve problems. But give yourself deadlines. Accept your need for change.

Abstract random thinkers organize information through reflection, and thrive in unstructured, people-oriented environments. Says DePorter: "The 'real' world for abstract random learners is the world of feelings and emotions. The AR's mind absorbs ideas, information and impressions and organizes them through reflection. They remember best if information is personalized. They feel constricted when they're subjected to a very structured environment."

If you're an AR, use your natural ability to work with others. Recognize how strongly emotions influence your concentration. Build on your strength of learning by association. Look at the big picture first. Be careful to allow enough time to finish the job. Remind yourself to do things through plenty of visual clues, such as colored stickers pasted up where you'll see them.

Abstract sequential thinkers love the world of theory and abstract thought. They like to think in concepts and analyze information. They make great philosophers and research scientists. DePorter again: "It's easy for them to zoom in on what's important, such as key points and significant details. Their thinking processes are logical, rational and intellectual. A favorite activity for abstract sequentials is reading, and when a project needs to be researched they are very thorough at it. Generally they prefer to work alone rather than in groups." If you're an AS, give yourself exercises in logic. Feed your intellect. Steer yourself toward highly structured situations.

Different ways to store and retrieve information

Not only do we have different learning and thinking styles, we also each have a different way to store information and retrieve it.

And exactly the same principle applies: discuss the entire process with students, and both you and they will soon work it out.

For example, co-author Dryden takes in information, like most print-trained journalists, as a print-oriented linguistic learner. But he stores information in a tactile way: by underlining, highlighting words and touch-typing—the very physical action helps embed it in his memory-banks. And he retrieves information visually: generally, as all TV producers do, by preparing visual presentations. So even if making a presentation without visual aids, he talks from mental pictures.

Co-author Vos is different. She takes information in visually and through tactile notations as she reads. She is print-oriented but enjoys a graphic format of what she reads—charts, for example. She stores information kinesthetically by exercising her body while she is reflecting and jotting her thoughts on paper. She needs time to collect information by reflection and synthesis via the subconscious. And she retrieves information through both the auditory and visual process: often listening to quiet music while preparing, for example, international seminar presentations.

Both are competent logical sequential presenters, but they accomplish it in different styles. One is a logical, sequential television-style presenter, and, especially when videotaping a presentation, is always conscious of the need for sequence, structure and the needs of a later, different TV-viewing audience. The other: a highly intuitive teacher, attuned to where people "are at" and the nuances of individual students' styles

If a lecturer presents information in only one style, many students just won't 'get it'

According to Professor Ken and Rita Dunn's research, only 30 percent of students remember even 75 percent of what they hear during a normal class period. Brilliant bridge players often make poor teachers because they illustrate how to play the game with mathematical symbols on a blackboard—and most learners cannot visualize the playing cards.

Many kindergartens and schools find it best to move each day into different activity centers

and patterns of learning—ever ready to "change the state" with reflection, dialog and often a change of music. Neither style is "right". Both are completely different. And in fact they balance each other when alternating as presenters at seminars.

The implications for home study, schools and teachers

We believe every aspect of this research can greatly improve learning and schooling.

For personal home study, it makes great sense to know your own strengths, know your family's learning styles and build on them. If it's hard for you to sit still for a long time, you're almost certainly a kinesthetic learner. So consider starting to study by previewing your material with a giant Mind Map—on a big sheet of paper. Put it on the floor and use your body while you're working. After previewing the material, play some classical music—and move with its rhythm. Then do something physical. Go for a walk, a swim, or move your body while you mentally visualize what you've just put into your brain.

Especially if you're kinesthetic, feel free to get into your favorite learning atmosphere and position.   If you are an auditory learner, record your notes on to a cassette tape over baroque music. And if you are a visual learner, be sure to draw Mind Maps, doodles, symbols or pictures to represent what you are learning. For a visual learner, a picture represents a thousand words.

For school teachers and seminar leaders, we would hope the lessons are equally obvious: analyze each student's learning style, and cater to it. You won't be able to do this for everyone all the time. But you can make sure that every style is catered for regularly throughout every learning sequence. If you do, you'll be amazed at how easily people can learn—and how much less resistance you will find.

One of the first American schools to be based almost entirely on Howard Gardner's principles is the Key Elementary School in Indianapolis. Walk into the Key School and you'll find youngsters learning in all the different "intelligences". Sure, you'll find all the traditional subject areas, such as reading and math, being covered. But you'll also find everyone involved in music, painting, drawing, physical activity and discussion.

For four periods a week, children meet in multi-aged groups called pods, to explore a whole range of interests such as computers, gardening, cooking, "making money", architecture, theater, multi-cultural games and other real-life skills.

"Once a week," says Gardner, "an outside specialist visits the school and demonstrates an occupation or craft. Often the specialist is a parent, and typically the topic fits into the school theme at the time."[10]

The school is also closely involved with the Center of Exploration at the Indianapolis Museum. "Students can enter into an apprenticeship of several months, in which they can engage in such activities as animation, shipbuilding, journalism or monitoring the weather."

Key School is also alive with projects. Says Gardner: "During any given year the school features three different themes, introduced at approximately ten-week intervals. These themes can be quite broad (such as *Patterns* or *Connections),* or more focused *(The Renaissance—then and now* or *Mexican heritage).* With the curriculum focus on these themes, desired literacies and concepts are, wherever possible, introduced as natural adjuncts to an exploration of the theme."

Both New City School, in St. Louis, Missouri,[11] and the Indianapolis school show precisely what can happen if a country finally uses its great academic research and blends them with well-planned schools, innovative teachers, tremendous community resources and a focus that sees all children as gifted and talented, but in different ways.

We cannot restress strongly enough our own beliefs that everyone, unless severely brain-damaged, has a unique potential to be exceptionally good at something—and we all now know how to identify and build on that talent.

As Britain's Campaign for Learning found when it asked the United Kingdom public to define the aim of learning, the phrase most favored was simply: "To discover the talents within you."

And if you can define those strong talents, and your own preferred learning and thinking style, then it's much easier to apply those to all the simplest ways to learn anything faster, more easily and more effectively.

The most popular definition of learning: to discover the talents within you

Photo courtesy Key School, Indianapolis, one of the first to put Professor Howard Gardner's multiple-intelligence principles into action. It often links students with many different learning styles and talents into multi-talented teams—frequently producing student videotapes to showpiece their work.

To become a master learner, start with the lessons of great sporting achievers

Jack Nicklaus, winner of The Masters golf major six times, the U.S. Open four, the British Open three, and the PGA championship five. Still playing well at 68 years, he says 90 percent of his success comes from being able to visualize precisely where each shot is going to land.

Chapter five: Learning how to learn ■■■■■■■■

How to take your talent and passion and keep adding other skills and abilities

The Gallup organization's survey of one million people is very clear: "Everyone has a talent to be exceptional at something." [1]

But talent alone is not enough. You have to keep adding skills and develop new competencies.

And of course work alone is not the only objective in life. All of us take up new interests, new hobbies or play new games.

In this new era of "personalized learning", the ability to "learn a living" will probably be the most important you'll ever develop, And not just to do that once, in your college and early-apprenticeship years, but to keep on relearning through life. These twenty key steps will help you achieve that:

1. Start with the lessons from sport

Sport probably provides a much better learning model than many schools. You can learn at least eight lessons from it:

❏ ***All sports achievers have a dream.*** They dream the impossible and make it happen. The champion runner wants to break the 3 minute 50 second barrier for the mile. Or take the Olympic gold. Or be in a world series winning team.

All sports achievers, at every level, have dreams. It may be to break 100 at golf, then 90, then 80. Or to become the club tennis champion. Or to run the New York marathon at age sixty-five.

❏ *All have specific goals. And they break those goals down into achievable steps.* So while the dream is always there, they build on their successes. You can't become a world champion overnight; you have to tackle hurdles regularly along the way—and celebrate each success as it is achieved.

❏ *All sports achievers combine mind, body and action.* They know that their goals can be achieved when they link the right mental attitude, fitness, nutrition and physical skills.

❏ *They all have vision; they learn to visualize their goal.* To *see* their achievements in advance—to play through their next football match like a video of the mind. Jack Nicklaus, rated to date as the greatest golfer of all time, says 90 percent of his success comes from his ability to visualize where every shot is going to land.

❏ *They all have passion.* They have an overwhelming desire to succeed.

❏ *Each one has a coach, a mentor, a guide.* In fact, we can probably learn more about real education from the success of the American college coaching system than from most school practice. If you doubt it, how many Olympic athletes, basketball and football stars have emerged from college scholarships, where their coaches were valued role models, guides and friends? Why not the same for all talents in every field, from music to computer studies?

❏ *All sports achievers have a fantastically positive attitude toward mistakes.* They don't even call them mistakes; they call them *practice.* Even Roger Federer, John McEnroe, the Williams sisters and Martina Navratilova belted balls into the net thousands of times on their way to the top in tennis. No teacher marked those shots as failures. They were all essential parts of learning.

❏ *They all achieve by doing.* Sport is a hands-on operation. You don't get fit by reading a book—although that may help with the theory. You don't develop the right muscles staring at a television set. You don't long-jump over 28 feet (8.4 meters) in a classroom. All sports achievements result from *action.*

Former American Olympian pentathlete Marilyn King says all astronauts, Olympic athletes and corporate executives have three things in common:

Sporting greats don't call them mistakes in training; they call them practice

Russian-born, American-based Maria Sharapova was only seventeen when she won the Wimbledon Open in 2004; then the U.S. Open in 2006 and the Australian Open in 2008. She is the world's highest-paid female athlete.

Like a good fitness coach, a great teacher is a guide on the side not a 'sage on the stage'

"They have something that really matters to them; something they really want to do or be. **We call it passion.**

"They can see a goal really clearly, and the 'how to' images begin to appear like magic. While the goal may seem bold, they can imagine doing all these little steps on the road to that goal. **We call** it *vision.*

"Finally, they are willing to do something each day, according to a plan, that will bring them one step closer to their dream. **We call it action.**

❑ **"If you have passion plus vision but no action, *you're daydreaming.***

❑ **"If you have vision plus action but no passion, *you'll be mediocre.***

❑ **"If you have passion plus action but no vision, *you'll get there but find it the wrong goal.***

"Passion + vision + action is our equation for success." [2]

Marilyn King runs courses and seminars teaching *Olympian Thinking* to corporate executives. She has also launched a *Dare To Imagine* project to pass on the same techniques to at-risk young people in her home city of Oakland, California.

So how can you apply the same principles to anything else you want to achieve and learn—and how can you do it faster, better and more easily?

2. Dare to dream—and imagine your future

If, as we believe, nearly all things are now possible: what would you really like to do? What's your real *passion?* The thing you'd like to do more than anything else? Make great wine? Become the district golf champion? Start a new career?

Nearly every major achievement in the world has started with a vision: from Ford to Disneyland, Sony to Apple. So take up Marilyn King's challenge—and *dare to imagine what you'd like to achieve.*

3. Set a specific goal—and set deadlines

Ask yourself first: What specifically do I want to learn? Why do I want to learn it? If it's a new job, a new skill, a new hobby, a trip overseas, a new sport, a musical instrument or a new challenge, what will you need to know?

It's easier to learn anything if you have a set goal. When you've done that, break it down into achievable bite-sized pieces. Then set realistic deadlines for each step, so you can see your success from the start.

4. Get an enthusiastic mentor—fast

Whatever you want to learn, many others have already learned it. When you've set your goals, find an enthusiast you can come to for specific advice. And if you can swap skills, even better.

Let's say you're a printer who wants to learn computer graphics. Obviously you'll be skilled in typography. So find a digital graphics expert. You teach him typography while he teaches you the principles of digital graphic design. If you're new to a firm, do the same thing. Find someone who can help, regularly. Someone nearby or only a phone call away.

If you want to play golf, take professional lessons—certainly. But find a good player whose style you admire, and ask if you can play a game or two together.

The same principles apply if you're learning new technology. No one ever learned to operate a computer solely from a 700-page manual. Each student learned hands-on, with a coach.

5. Start with the big picture first

Learn from the marketers of jigsaw puzzles. If you started to assemble 10,000 pieces of a giant jigsaw puzzle one by one, it might take you years to finish. But if you can see the total picture on the package, you'll know exactly what you're building. Then it's much easier to fit each piece into place.

We're amazed at how often common sense disappears in educational systems. Subjects are taught in isolation. They're often taught in small segments, without students knowing the big picture first.

In real life, that's not the best way. It would take you years to discover New York by walking down every street. So what do you do as a tourist? You go to the top of the Empire State Building. Preferably with a New York guide. And you put yourself

Start with the big-view picture first—then it's easy to see how it all fits together

In the new world of Web 2.0, you are plugged into a giant global library

in the big picture. You can see Central Park, the Staten Island Ferry, Statue of Liberty, Wall Street, the two main rivers, the key bridges, Broadway, Greenwich Village, the United Nations headquarters and the way the city is laid out in numbered avenues and streets. Then when someone tells you an address is ten blocks south of Central Park on Sixth Avenue, or four blocks east of the Lincoln Tunnel, you have a mental picture of where to go. You can build on your overall image Mind Map.

Many traditional schools still introduce subjects through textbook lectures spread over months. You're taught to read each chapter slowly and deliberately—a week at a time—without ever having the "big overview". That's crazy. It's inefficient.

Instead, try this simple experiment. Next time you're planning anything, seek out the simplest overview. If you're visiting a new city, get the color tourist brochures in advance. They'll show you the main highlights.

Now *Wikipedia* is also excellent for the big-picture overview on most topics. Then when you've got the big picture, build up the details. You'll know where they fit. Remember that jigsaw puzzle.

6. Ask—and start with the Web

"Ask!" It's the best three-letter word in the learner's dictionary. Never be afraid to ask. That's what journalists do every day. And for specific information, it's never been easier—with "search engines" on the World Wide Web.

Marc C. Rosenberg, in his book *e-Learning,* says the Web is "nothing short of the world's library". But it is now much, much more than that. It's your passport to museums, art galleries and almost every newspaper in the world.

Start by learning to use Google at *www.google.com*. It's the world's biggest "search engine": an incredible online guide to the world's information. In the "search" line provided, type in whatever information you want. But make it specific: not simply "wine" but perhaps: *Wine + United States gold medal winners 2008.*

For news, *www.news.google.com* gives you instant access to the latest reports summarized from 4,000 different sources, without you having to type in the name of any newspaper, TV or radio station. But don't stop there. Look through all the main features of Google, including their tips on how to search more effectively. Check out the online courses that are available on anything you want to learn—even in your own locality, as we cover at the end of this chapter.

Wikipedia is another great source of information: more than ten million articles, co-created, in the main, by people passionately interested in each subject. It's by far the world's biggest encyclopedia. And it's all available free online. We authors find it best to seek overview information—say on a country's population— simply by typing into the Google "search box" the simplest title for the information you want—in this form: *wikipedia + ireland population*

In less than half a second Google will search billions of websites and rank, in order, the most-searched sites on Ireland's history—starting with *Wikipedia's* entry.

But you access much more. On Wikipedia, you'll find not only a main article but a summary "box". In the article you will find many subjects printed in blue. And in that simple color you've found the simplifying genius of Tim Berners-Lee: the Web-hyperlinks that enable any website to link with others—so you can immediately switch through to other information without reading an entire book or turning a page.

But only a novice researcher would accept any single source of information without verifying it. So, by channelling your inquiry through Google, you'll find a list of all other well-used sites on the same subject. But don't stop there, either. Search through Google for opposing viewpoints. In many fields—particularly in seeking alternative treatments for health problems—a whole array of publicity experts write articles with "key words" promoting clients' products. So if you locate a claimed "cure" for, say, arthritis—after reading it, type the name of that new subject into the Google search box and add simply a plus sign and a request for opposing viewpoints: *+ opponents.*

But do not see the Web as only the world's best factual library. As *Business Week* puts it in an special update issue: "It's a whole New Web. And this time around it will be built by you."[3]

Since we all learn by actually doing, and doing it with all our senses, this new Web offers almost a new sense: a way of participating, sharing, collaborating, socializing

You don't even need to know how it works: simply click on those blue-type Web links

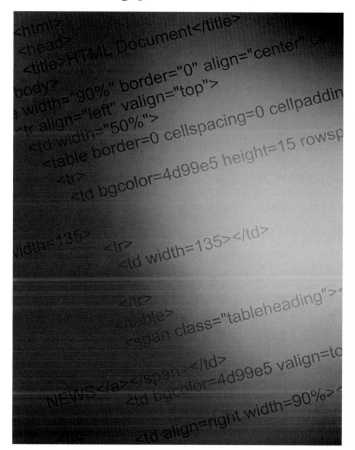

When British scientist Tim Berners-Lee created HyperText Mark-up Language, he invented the World Wide Web. Now anyone can use it to link any webpage to any other. But to use it you don't need to know the software code. Just click on the blue links.

But don't rely only on the Web; public librarians are trained to help you

and actually creating in many different ways. And we have already outlined how social networks, such as *Cyworld, MySpace, Facebook* and *YouTube,* provide other excellent services.

As well as the Web, also learn how to use your local public library. It's not merely a book center. It's a learning resource. Librarians are trained to help you. Call them before you visit; tell them specifically what you want to do; ask them for the best beginner's guide. Use that for your overview; then build on it. But be specific. If you're a business executive planning a visit to another country, ask the librarian for simple guides to the country, its business, its culture, and the industry you're involved in.

If you learn easily by reading, that overview will probably be a book, a booklet or an article. If you learn best visually, seek out a DVD, or at least a book with plenty of colored pictures and graphics. If you learn best by listening, get CDs or audio cassettes, and play them in your car.

But don't use only a library. Find someone from college who's studying the field you're interested in. Ask the name of the best professor—the one who's the best simplifier. And phone him.

Or phone the university library, the nearest research institute, the best firm in the business. And don't be afraid to go to the top. If you want to learn about another country, call its embassy or consulate. Or its trade or tourist office. Or one of its major companies. Make asking a habit. It's probably the simplest thing you can learn from journalism. How do you think all that information gets into newspapers, on to television and radio every day?

7. Seek out the main principles

In nearly every field you'll find one main principle for success. Or perhaps two or three. Find them out first—before you fill in the details.

In photography, the first principle for an amateur: never take a photo more than 1.2 meters (4 feet) from your subject. Second principle: preferably shoot without a flash, with a semiautomatic camera. The third: "frame the photo" so that your finished picture "visually telegraphs" the main action or image you want to convey.

In cost accounting, the main principle: there's no such thing as an accurate cost, unless your business is running twenty-four hours a day, with a guaranteed market for all you produce. Second principle: find the break-even point. Below that you're losing money. Above it you're making a profit.

In talkback radio, the main principle: no matter how big or small the city, if the host asks only for *opinions* he'll get the same thirty uninformed callers every day; if he asks for *specific interesting experiences* he'll get new interesting callers, with stimulating new information.

In education, a main principle: people learn best what they passionately want to learn, and they learn fastest by actually *doing* and enjoying.

In journalistic interviewing, the first principle: ask *what* and *why.*

How do you find main principles? First you ask. Then:

8. Find the best three books by practical achievers

Don't start with academic textbooks. In the area of your interest, find the three best books written by people who've *done it.* If you want to study advertising, call Saatchi & Saatchi or a top agency and ask their creative director what to read. She'll almost certainly recommend *Ogilvy on Advertising* as an overview. And if you want to study copywriting: John Caples' *How To Make Your Advertising Make Money* and *Tested Advertising Methods.*

To practise new skills in thinking, start with the best book we know on the subject, Michael Michalko's *Cracking Creativity.* Then deal cards from Roger von Oech's *Creative Whackpack*—a brilliant ideas-starter. His first book, *A Whack On The Side Of The Head,* is also good. To simplify business, try Don Tapscott's *Wikinomics,* and Buckingham and Coffman's *First, Break All The Rules.*

For three books on effective learning, try one of Tony Buzan's many books; *Accelerated Learning For the 21st Century* by Colin Rose and Malcolm J. Nicholl; and *Teaching and Learning Through Multiple Intelligences,* by Linda Campbell, Bruce Campbell and Dee Dickinson.

From taking photos to learning a new skill, seek out the three main principles

To take good photos, generally shoot close-up to your subject, and without a flash in natural light so that the camera's built-in light meter automatically adjusts to give you pictures that don't look "bleached out". Also: "frame" the picture to "visually telegraph" the action or impact you want to convey. Note the photos in this book that are not attributed to schools. In the main they have been purchased from www.shutterstock.com, with over four million photos. Amateur photographers can learn much from scanning through Shutterstock's website. Professional photographers shoot them and get paid a royalty for each shot sold: typical of the new Web 2.0 marketing principles.

To quickly get its main points, read a non-fiction book like you read a newspaper

If you're a teacher, maybe read *The Everyday Genius* by Peter Kline, *SuperTeaching* by Eric Jensen, and *The Thinking Learning Classroom* by Glenn Capelli and Sean Brealey.

For more about your brain, try *The Amazing Brain* by Robert Ornstein and Richard F. Thompson, *Inside The Brain* by Ronald Kotulak, and *Emotional Intelligence* by Daniel Goleman.

More titles are suggested at the back of this book. But in your own field ask the nearest expert to suggest a beginner's guidebook.

9. Relearn how to read—faster, better, more easily

Amazingly, few people know how to read properly. And we're not talking about super reading techniques at thousands of words a minute.

Let's start with two questions: Do you think you could regularly read four books a day and absorb the main points? Have you read a newspaper this week? If you answered the first question no, and the second yes—think again. If you read a daily newspaper in any major city, you've read the equivalent of at least four books. And the Sunday editions of the *New York Times*, *Los Angeles Times* or any major British paper are equal to dozens of volumes.

And how do you read a newspaper? You read only those things you are interested in. And how do you know? Because newspapers are divided into sections, so you only read the sports pages if you're interested in sports, the business pages for business. But even then you don't read every sports story or every business article. Newspaper headlines highlight the main points, and make it easy for you to select. Even the writing style of newspapers makes it easy to glean the main points. After each headline, you'll generally find them summarized in the first paragraph. So you can either read the summary or devour the whole story.

Over half of a newspaper is advertising. But you don't read every ad. Advertisers flag your attention with headlines and pictures. Classified ads are in alphabetical order. So if you want to buy a house, you don't read all the *Houses for sale* pages. You select those in your preferred suburb, listed alphabetically.

Very simply, you've cracked the newspaper code. You know the formula. You know how to skim-read a newspaper every day. So you already know how to skim-read four books a day or anything else in print.

The secret is to crack each book's code, to find each publication's formula. Court reporters, for example, know the standard format for written judgments. The judge normally reviews the case and the main arguments for many pages, then delivers his or her finding in the last paragraph. So reporters never start reading a court judgment from the front. They start on the last page—generally at the last paragraph—because they are reading the judgment to report the verdict.

And the same principle applies to all non-fiction reading. First ask yourself: ***Why am I reading this? What do I want to get out of it? What new information will I want to learn? Then find the book's formula.***

Nearly every non-fiction book will state its main purpose in an introduction—as this book has done. This will tell you whether the book can provide the answers you want. Then you have to decide whether you need to read every chapter. You've almost certainly come to the subject with some basic knowledge which you're looking to extend. So you don't have to read all the material unless you want to refresh your memory.

Generally, non-fiction authors write books like speeches: in the introduction, the speaker tells you what he's going to tell you; then he tells you; then he summarizes what he's told you. And often each chapter is written in a similar way: the chapter title and first paragraph or paragraphs indicate the theme, the chapter amplifies it, and it may end with a summary. If the book has subheadings, they'll help as well. Many books have other pointers. With color pictures, skim them and their "captions". Tom Peters' *Thriving on Chaos* summarizes each chapter on a separate page at the start of each chapter. In the book you are holding, key points are highlighted in the photo-panel on every page. And we have already suggested skimming the photos first.

In brief, read every non-fiction book like a recipe book. If you want to cook vegetable chow mein tonight, you don't read every page in *The 1,000 Recipe Chinese*

Information books each have a format: learn it and you will have 'cracked its code'

Speed-reading made easy: fast-follow your finger down the center of each page

Cookbook. You read only what you need to know. This tip alone will enable you to read four books in the same time it takes to skim a newspaper.

Another tip: do NOT read "slowly and deliberately". Look out your window right now. Then reflect on your brain's fantastic ability to instantly take in all that information. You've got 130 million light receivers in each of your eyes, with a magic ability to flash that scene to your visual cortex. That's your brain's holistic ability to "photograph" a complete picture. Learn to use it. Even those pages you think you need to read will include much information that can be skimmed.

Remember your purpose, and the key answers you are seeking. For instance, school teachers, young parents, business executives and people approaching "retirement" are probably reading this book for different reasons.

So learn to skim for the points you want. Start by holding this book in one hand far enough from your eyes to see the entire page—generally about eighteen to twenty inches: about 50cm. With your other hand use your index finger or a retracted ball-point pen. Practise running either your finger or the pen quite quickly down the center of each page, with your eyes looking just above the point of your pen or finger, following it down. You'll be amazed at what you can take in, if you know specifically what you are looking for. This is not just speed-reading. It's sensible skim-reading and selective reading.

If you're looking for specific information and quotes to include in a report, article or book, you'll need to stop and note them. If you own the book, use it as a dynamic resource. Mark key information with a highlighter. If the book is not yours, use *Post-It* notes. Return to them and write or type out the key points. The physical act of writing or typing will help embed them in your brain's memory-vaults: your cerebellum— learning through the sense of touch as well as sight. Better still, highlighting will make it easy when you want to retrieve the information later.

10. Reinforce with pictures and sound

Because you've read this far, you may be a print-oriented learner, and a linguistic learner. But you can also learn better if you reinforce the message with pictures and sound. So check out whether simple video or audio discs are available on the subject you're studying.

And if you have family members who are not great readers, encourage them to *start* with their preferred learning style. If one's an auditory learner, make her car into a university with a cassette or CD player.   If one has a visual learning style, then seek out picture books, videos, digital video discs, and interactive computer programs.

11. Learn by doing

We can't stress enough the need to engage all your senses. We give practical suggestions in other chapters.

But for do-it-yourselfers, when you check out introductory courses—or advanced ones—make sure they provide hands-on experience.

You learn to cook by cooking. You learn to play tennis by playing tennis. And even when you take golf lessons, good professionals get you right into action.

Education is generally ineffective when it separates theory from practice. So make an effort to learn through more than one sense. If you're learning a foreign language, try to picture the scene you're learning so you imprint the information through other senses.

Play rhyming games and enjoy other fun ways to remember and embed the new language in your brain's memory banks.

Good teachers and accelerated learning courses use many other techniques, as we'll explore later.   But for do-it-yourselfers, interactive technology can now help greatly. Let's take two of the most complicated non-physical games: bridge and chess. You can learn both by playing— especially with a good coach.

But bridge or chess masters don't really want to spend hours playing with a novice. So, as we have seen, some have now put their knowledge into interactive computer games. So, as well as playing with your friends, you can "play the computer."

At bridge, you can see your cards on the screen and, if you win the bidding, you can see your partner's hand to play it. The computer will play your opponents' hands.

To learn it, do it!
Even young children can learn safety from a safe parent

Visual note-taking like Mind Maps helps embed learning for easy recall

Hand-drawn Mind Maps are excellent to summarize new information. And at many schools students now learn how to use Mind Mapping software so they can display their combined summaries in high-quality color-print. With key statements grouped around a central visual theme, the displays continually reinforce the information. Photo courtesy Thomas Jefferson Institute, Mexico.

And when each hand is over you have a choice of seeing all hands—and checking how the cards should have best been played.

In most computer chess games, you can choose your level of competency, from novice to advanced; the computer will play at the same level.

12. Draw Mind Maps instead of taking linear notes

There's no use taking in important information if you can't recall it when you need it. And here traditional schooling methods are archaic. Tens of thousands of students around the world right now are taking notes. They're writing down words line by line. But the brain doesn't work that way. It does not store information in neat lines or columns. The brain stores information on its treelike dendrites. It stores information by *pattern and association.* So the more you can work in with the brain's own memory-method, the easier and faster you'll learn.

So don't take notes, make Mind Maps. And make them with trees, with pictures, with colors, with symbols, with patterns and associations. Mind Mapping is a method devised by Tony Buzan. Singapore author and Buzan facilitator Dilip Mukerjea has written and illustrated an excellent introduction to the subject, entitled *SuperBrain.*

Swedish publisher Ingemar Svantesson has produced *Mind Mapping and Memory.* And in the United States the finest book on a similar theme is Nancy Margulies' *Mapping InnerSpace.* Margulies has also written a great accelerated-learning book, *Yes, You Can Draw!* and produced a first-class video to go with it. Those books, and some of the Mind Maps in this one, demonstrate the principles. The main points are simple:

1.   Imagine your brain-cells are like trees, with each one storing related information on its branches.

2.   Now try arranging the key points of any topic on a sheet of white paper in the same treelike format.

3.   Start with the central topic—preferably with a symbol—in the center of the page, then draw branches spreading out from it. If you're Mind Mapping New York, use the Statue of Liberty as the centerpoint. If it's Sydney, use the harbor bridge. If it's our chapter on the brain, sketch a two-sided brain.

4.   *Generally record only one word and/or symbol for each point you want to recall—one main theme to each branch.*

5.   *Put related points on the same main branches,* each one shooting off like a new sub-branch.

6.   *Use different colored pencils or markers for related topics.*

7.   *Draw as many pictures and symbols as you can.*

8.   *When you've completed each branch, enclose it in a different colored border.*

9.   *Add to each map regularly.* In this way it's easy to start with the overview and then build up your Mind Map as you learn more about each subject. *On Google: select "Images" and type in "mind maps" for pages of good examples.*

13.   Easy ways to retrieve what you've learned

Since the brain stores information by patterns and associations, and Mind Maps record it in the same way, then it's sensible to use the same methods for easy recall.

Here some more brain-knowledge will come in handy. Your brain has both a short-term and a long-term memory. And that's fortunate. You come to an intersection as the traffic light is turning red, and you stop. The lights turn green and you go. Your long-term memory has learned and remembered the rules about traffic lights. But your short-term memory doesn't have to remember each of the thousands of times you stop for the red light.

So how do you store and retrieve the information you need for long-term use? Partly by patterns and associations.

Mind Mapping is just one method. Another is to use all your intelligence-centers, including those involved with rhyme, rhythm, repetition and music. You don't have to spend hours on boring rote memory. As you've read this book, highlighted key phrases and subheadings and made a Mind Map of the main points, we suggest you do two things immediately you have finished:

1.   Immediately reskim the key points you've highlighted.

As your brain stores information on its tree-like branches, so do Mind Maps

Meditation and relaxation techniques switch on to a 'learning wavelength'

2.   Redo your Mind Map. This will also help you link your main lessons: by pattern and association. Almost certainly, if you're new to Mind Mapping, you'll have found it difficult to list each key point in only one word. But try to do so. It's very important.

Then tonight, not too long before you're thinking of sleeping, play some relaxing music. Take another look at your Mind Map. Reflect on the main lessons you have learned and visualize them.

Think of the associations—because that state of almost reverie, just before sleep, is a vital part of the learning process.

14. Learn the art of relaxed alertness

To make use of the extraordinary powers of your subconscious, *the next real key to effective learning can be summed up in two words: relaxed alertness—your state of mind, especially when you start any learning session.*

We've already mentioned brainwaves. Now let's start to put them to use. Your brain operates, much like a television or radio station, on four main frequencies or waves. We can measure them with an EEG machine (electro-encephalograph).

If you're wide awake and alert at the moment, or if you're talking, making a speech or working out an involved problem in logic, your brain is probably "transmitting" and "receiving" at 13 to 25 cycles per second. Some call this the beta level.

But that's not the best state for stimulating your long-term memory. Most of the main information you learn will be stored in your subconscious mind. Many researchers and teachers believe that the vast bulk of information is also best learned subconsciously. *And the brainwave activity that links best with the subconscious mind is at 8 to 12 cycles per second: alpha.*

Says British accelerated learning innovator Colin Rose: "This is the brainwave that characterizes relaxation and meditation, the state of mind during which you daydream, let your imagination run. It is a state of relaxed alertness that facilitates inspiration, fast assimilation of facts and heightened memory. Alpha lets you reach your subconscious, and since your self-image is primarily in your subconscious it is the only effective way to reach it."[4]

When you start getting sleepier—the twilight zone between being fully awake and fully asleep—your brainwaves change to between 4 and 7 cycles per second: theta.

When you're fully into deep sleep, your brain is operating at between .5 and 3 cycles per second: delta. Your breathing is deep, your heartbeat slows and your blood pressure and body temperature drop.

And the impact of all this on learning and memory? American accelerated learning pioneer Terry Wyler Webb says beta waves—the fast ones—are "useful for getting us through the day, but they inhibit access to the deeper levels of the mind. Deeper levels are reached in the alpha and theta brainwave patterns, which are characterized by subjective feelings of relaxation, concentrated alertness and well-being. *It is in the alpha and theta states that the great feats of supermemory, along with heightened powers of concentration and creativity, are achieved."* [5]

And how do you achieve that state? Thousands of people do it with daily meditation, or relaxing exercises, especially deep breathing. But more and more teachers are convinced that some types of music can achieve the results much quicker and easier. Says Webb: "Certain types of musical rhythm help relax the body, calm the breath, quieten the beta chatter and evoke a gentle state of relaxed awareness which is highly receptive to learning new information."

Of course many types of music can help you remember messages when the music is accompanied by words—as television and radio advertising prove every day. But researchers[6] have now found that some baroque music is ideal for rapidly improving learning, partly because its main 60-to-70 beats-to-the-minute is identical to the alpha brainwaves.

Skilled teachers are now using this music as an essential ingredient of all accelerated-learning teaching. But for learners, the immediate implications are simple: play the right type of music at night when you want to review your material, and you'll dramatically increase your recall. In part that's because of how your brain works most

As songs link rhythm, rhyme and words, music can greatly aid learning

To learn public speaking or anything else: practise, practise, practise

efficiently when you're dropping off to sleep. Some call it R.E.M. sleep. The initials stand for *rapid eye movement*. And EEGs tell you why: it's almost as if your mind—even with your body asleep—is using its visual cortex to take quick frame-by-frame photographs of the day's main events.

Many researchers believe that in this state the brain is sorting out new information and storing it in the appropriate memory banks. And quiet relaxation as you review your Mind Maps, and reflect on the day's main points, opens up the pathways to those subconscious storage files.

That probably also explains why you dream: your subconscious is "dialing up" your old memories to collate the new information. And if you're thinking through a problem, your subconscious sifts through some alternative solutions, as we'll discuss in the next chapter.

The alpha state is also ideal for starting each new specific study period. Quite simply, it makes great sense to clear the mind before you start. Take your office problems on the golf course and you'll never play great golf. Your mind will be elsewhere. The same applies to study. Come straight from a high school French class to a mathematics lecture and it can be hard to "switch gears". It's a poor schooling system.

But take a few moments to do deep breathing exercises, and you'll start to relax. Play some relaxing music, close your eyes and think of the most peaceful scene you can imagine—and soon you'll be in the state of relaxed alertness that makes it easier to "float information" into your long-term memory.

15. Practise, practise, practise

If you're learning to speak French, speak it. If you're learning about computers, use them. If you've taken a course in Asian cooking, cook an Asian feast for your friends. If you're studying shorthand, write it. If you want to be a public speaker, join Toastmasters—and speak publicly. If you want to be a writer, write. If you want to be a bartender, mix drinks. And with the new age of interactive technology, remember: instead of learning *about* science, computers or flying aircraft, you can now simulate *becoming* a scientist, computer programmer or pilot.

16. Review and reflect

When you're learning a physical-mental skill, like typing or cooking, you can practise it with action. But in gaining other types of knowledge, make sure you review regularly. Look again at your Mind Map and review the main points immediately you've finished it. Do it again in the morning. And again a week later. Once more a month later. Then review it, and other associated data, before you have specific need for it: for an examination, an overseas trip, a speech or whatever. Before reading a new book, for instance, many people find it helps to first look at their existing Mind Maps on the subject, or skim-read the highlighted parts of three of four books that they've already read on the subject.

17. Use linking tools as memory pegs

Since the memory works best by association, develop your own "memory pegs". Associate newly acquired knowledge with something you already know.

The association can be physical or tactile: such by actually learning to run a Parisian fashion parade to learn French: to touch the garments as you say their names.

It can be visual: like visualizing scenes to remember names—forging gold in a blacksmith's shop to remember Mr. Goldsmith, a picture of a crocodile under a Mc-Donald's arch to remember founder Ray Krok.

It can be a strong visual story: like picturing a sequence to remember, say, the planets in order from earth—the hot sun shining so strongly it breaks a thermometer, and all the Mercury spills out; this runs outside where a beautiful woman, ***Venus,*** is standing on the ***Earth;*** it keeps running over the earth into the next-door neighbor's red-earth garden—a warlike neighbor, ***Mars,*** appears and starts hurling abuse. But just then a smiling giant appears, ***Jupiter***—the biggest planet—and on his superman-type chest he has the word ***SUN*** emblazoned, for ***Saturn , Uranus*** and ***Neptune,*** and running alongside him is a happy dog, ***Pluto.***

It can be rhyming and visual: like Asians learning English singing to karaoke songs. Or memorizing numbers with rhyming pictorial words, and linking them up with the items to be memorized: so that ***one*** becomes ***sun; two, shoe; three, tree;***

Singing to karoke machines is a favorite Asian fun way to learn English

Always remember: whatever the age, learning is more effective when it's fun

four, door; five, hive; six, sticks; seven, heaven; eight, gate; nine, mine; and *ten, hen.* To remember ten items, such as on a shopping list, link each one *visually* with the numbered sequence—so that if your first three items are butter, cheese and milk, you visualize butter being melted with the sun (one), cheese in a shoe (two), and milk being poured over a tree (three).

But whichever association method you use, *try to make it outlandish, funny and preferably emotional—because the "filter" in the brain that transfers information to your long-term memory is very closely linked with the brain's emotional center. And link your associations with as many senses as you can: sight, sound, smell, touch and taste.*

18. Have fun, play games

Ask a friend what images flash to mind when you mention education or study. Now see how they tally with Tony Buzan's experience. He says: "In my many years of investigating people's associations with the word 'study,' ten major words or concepts have emerged. They are: boring, exams, homework, waste of time, punishment, irrelevant, detention, 'yuck,' hate and fear."[7]   But ask a four-year-old fresh out of a good preschool center and she'll talk about the fun she had. So nearly all progressive educators now stress the need to recapture the fun-filled joy of early learning.

And humor itself is a great way to learn. So include humor with study. Think up games to play to reinforce the key points: games you can play by yourself and games you can play with others.

19. Teach others

"Each one—teach one." That's the recommended theme for the future from California brain-researcher Marian Diamond.

"I want to introduce the concept," she says, "that everyone can learn to be a teacher. One has to be accurate with the facts as a teacher, yet imaginative with creative ideas for new directions in the future. As we learn the facts, we can turn around and share with the next person so that the 'association cortices' can create the new ideas."[8]

Whatever your age, there are few better ways to crystallize what you've learned than to teach the principles to others, to make a speech or to run a seminar.

20. Go digital

Finally, we cannot restress too much that the new era of interactive, instant and co-creative technology is already changing lifelong education more than the mass-produced book did for an earlier era.   To make the most of it, there's now a growing array of other services to let you tailor the Web as you like it, and to help you learn hi-tech skills in new, much easier ways. And you will almost certainly find excellent hands-on training services in your own locality.

❏   **If you're a technology-novice,** we'd suggest you start in the same way as the six-year-olds do at some of the world's best schools: with digital cameras and videos. Then seek out simple community courses to improve your skills.

❏   **If you're into your "third age",** seek out the local SeniorNet, and you'll find others delighted to share their knowledge. Better still, get your grandchildren to teach you, and start sharing photos and family video-clips online. You can start by the simple tips, in this chapter, on taking digital photos.

❏   **If you're a teacher,** either get your students to teach you or sign up for some training. But preferably go to conferences and seminars that link new methods of learning with the new technologies. Here New Zealand has pioneered some great models: two-day, four-day and five-day seminars which alternate sessions between the new learning and teaching methods and hands-on practice to use interactive technology. In two days, teachers can easily learn to master stage-one levels for at least four different digital applications: video editing, digital-photo processing, computer animation, and compiling all these into slide presentations.[9] Better still, the experience sets you up to provide a completely new dimension to the most exciting of all pursuits: creating your own future.

Whatever your age, it's time to join the new world of interactive, instant technology

Idea 1: your personal radio station in your pocket—a new combination of existing elements

A creative thinking course for teachers, students and innovators

For most of the last several hundred years, land, labor and capital have driven the economy. For the first half of the twentieth century, Henry Ford's production lines were the model for creating wealth.

But now brainpower, ideas and innovation are the new drivers. Even more: the new challenge is for creative innovators in different countries to share their talents online—to co-create the future. And, particularly for those in the "developed world", to share their creative abilities with others in emerging countries such as China and India.[1]

But, amazingly, the most important "subject" of all is not taught at most schools: how to do this—to invent a new future. That gives us the opportunity to reinvent education and usher in a golden age of discovery and innovation: to reinvent the way we think, learn, work, live, enjoy ourselves and create. The models already exist. Better still, they work.

Thomas Edison held 1093 patents,[2] and electrified the world. Walt Disney and Apple Computers' Steve Jobs[3] each founded giant commercial empires on the power of a new idea—and a different make-believe mouse. Ray Krok[4] was a middle-aged milk-shake machine seller when he first visited the California hamburger bar of Dick and Maurice McDonald. He was to take their basic concept and turn the result into the world's biggest fast-food chain. And Sergey Brin and Larry Page took a new mathematics formula and turned it into Google.

Bill Gates and his partner, Paul Allen, had a dream to put a computer on every desk and in every home. The result: Microsoft—and two enormous fortunes.

Two of Europe's richest people*, the Rausing brothers,[5] owe their wealth to their father, Richard Rausing. While watching his wife prepare homemade sausages, he became intrigued by how she peeled back the skins to insert the ingredients. That idea, when reversed, turned into the system of pouring milk from cartons. And his heirs still receive royalties every day from millions of *Tetrapak* milk cartons.

All the great ideas in history, all the great inventions, obviously have one thing in common. All have come from the human brain. Just as the brain has fantastic ability to store information, it has an equal ability to reassemble that information in new ways: to create new ideas.

And very simply, ***an idea is a new combination of old elements.*** Write that down, underline it, reinforce it. It could be the most important sentence you ever write. It contains the key to creating new solutions. There are no new elements. ***There are only new combinations.***[6]

Think for a moment of the thousands of different cookbooks around the world. Every recipe in every book is a different mixture of existing ingredients. Think of that example whenever you tackle a problem.   And all the breakthroughs everywhere—radio, television, the internal combustion engine, movies, computers, mobile phones—are new combinations of old bits. A push-button shower combines at least three "old" elements: hot and cold water and a mixing valve. Nylon and other "new" synthetic fibers are new combinations of molecules that have existed for hundreds of centuries. In nylon's case: recombined molecules from coal.

Since an idea is a new mixture of old elements, ***the best ideas-creators are constantly preoccupied with new combinations.***

In most management courses, you learn the overriding need to define correctly the

* Swedish magazine Vecklans Affarer in 2004 put Ingvar Kamprad, the founder of the IKEA furniture empire, as the richest man in Europe and possibly the world, with a personal fortune of $53 billion. Kamprad denies this, stressing that he has placed IKEA control under a charitable trust. Kamprad's brilliant fortune-making idea: to sell simply-designed furniture cheaply by having the end user do his or her own assembly. In 2007 Mexico's Carlos Slim briefly surpassed both Kamprad and Bill Gates.

Idea 2: from problems with filling sausages to inventing the *Tetrapak* carton—and Europe's big fortune

Idea 3: It started with nylon in 1935—now acrylic fashionwear is reborn from molecules of natural gas

problem you want solved. *But now a new revolutionary element has emerged. We can now define the ideal solution in advance—and start creating it.*

This is a revolutionary change. Whereas previously we organized our existing knowledge to solve a problem, within the limits of that knowledge, today we start by defining what we would like to achieve. And then we organize the things we don't know in order to achieve it.

Seventy-five years ago clothing manufacturers were stuck with such basic yarns as wool, cotton and silk. Then Wallace Carothers synthesized nylon in 1935. Today we can define the ideal garment, and then produce the fibers and mixtures to create it. Families became tired of darning socks, so science created a blend of nylon and wool to give us the benefit of both: a new mixture of old elements. Iron-weary mothers wanted shirts that would drip-dry without creases. So science created polyester fibers: a new combination of old elements. Fashion-conscious women liked the easy-care properties of nylon but pined for the fluffiness of wool. So science created acrylics— by recombining the molecules of natural gas.

Peter Drucker, in *The Age of Discontinuity,* has crystallized the new innovative technique in a graphic way. He calls it "a systematic organized leap into the unknown". Unlike the science of yesterday, he says, "it is not based on organizing our knowledge, it is based on organizing our ignorance".

Amazingly these techniques are not taught in most schools, yet in many ways they are the key to the future.

Even worse: school tests are based on the principle that every question has one correct answer. But most questions have multiple answers.

California creative consultant Roger von Oech says, in *A Whack On The Side Of The Head:* "By the time the average person finishes college he or she will have taken over 2,600 tests, quizzes and exams. The 'right answer' approach becomes deeply ingrained in our thinking. This may be fine for some mathematical problems, where there is in fact only one right answer. The difficulty is that most of life isn't that way. Life is ambiguous; there are many right answers—all depending on what you are looking for. But if you think there is only one right answer, then you'll stop looking as soon as you find one."*

So how do you use your own brainpower to make Drucker's systematic organized leap into the unknown? These are the steps we've found most useful:

1. Define your problem

One first step is to define in advance your problem—specifically but not restrictively.

2. Define your ideal solution and visualize it

Step 2 is to define what you would like to achieve—ideally. And then you organize your 100 billion active brain neurons to bridge the gap between where you are and where you want to be. It also helps greatly to visualize the ideal solution, to picture "in your mind's eye" the best possible result.

Let's use a world-famous industry as a typical model: the watch industry. Right up to 1970, the entire industry was dominated by Switzerland.   But its business model had not changed in half a century.   By 1970 it was still making sales of $10 billion a year. But "by the early 1980s most of that value had migrated away from the traditional Swiss business model to new business designs owned by Timex, Citizen, Seiko and Casio. Employment tumbled in parallel with the drop in value. From the mid-1970s to the early 1980s, the number of workers in the Swiss watchmaking industry contracted from 90,000 to 20,000."[7]

So the industry called in consultant Nicolas Hayek. His experience in the industry: nil. But even as a boy "Hayek was always asking his family and teachers, 'Why do we do things the way we do?' He was born with an innate and incurable curiosity about the way things work and where we come from. He consumed every book he could find on physics, astronomy, the Big Bang, and Einstein's theories of mass and speed."[8]

And as an adult he applied that same curiosity to his newest challenge—and ended up reinventing an entire industry. Until he arrived on the scene, most people bought

Actually, the binary code that gave birth to the electronics revolution proves that, even in mathematics, there can be more than one correct answer. Silicon Valley proves it.

Idea 4: how Swatch started the craze for fashion on your wrist and saved the Swiss watch industry

Idea 5: Nike's famous stippled shoe came from Olympic track coach watching his wife make waffles

Nike—the world's biggest sports clothing and shoe marketer— is famous for adopting ideas from many other fields. Like co-founder Bill Bowerman, former U.S. Olympic track coach, dreaming up its famous stipple-soled shoe by pouring liquid urethane into a home waffle iron after Sunday breakfast. Or Nike paying $35 for a logo without any words. And basing its name on the Greek goddess of victory. The Nike logo and name were thought up overnight, and accepted only as interim stopgaps. The company's market value has since climbed to $23 billion.

a watch to last a lifetime. And those flocking to the new Japanese brands were also doing so because of their low cost. But Hayek started with a new series of questions: What did people want from a watch? Fun? Spirit? Style? Variety? Fashion?

Those questions were to lead directly to the invention of the *Swatch* watch—not solely as a timekeeper but as an ever-changing fashion accessory. And with it Hayek launched a marketing program to persuade customers to wear a different-colored watch with every dress or suit. From 1983 to 1992 Swatch sold 100 million watches. By 1996 he had sold his 200 millionth.

Even the name itself emerged as typical of the innovation process. As Adrian J. Slywotzky and David J. Morrison recount in their excellent book, *The Profit Zone:* "Hayek differentiated his watches by giving them a soul. He created a message, an emotional sense that appeals to everyone, conveying a sense of fun, of style, and of lightheartedness. Then he wrapped it around indisputable high quality and low cost.

"All Hayek's new product lacked now was a name. 'We were working with an American advertising company,' Hayek says. 'We had the craziest names in the world and none pleased me. Finally, we went for lunch and this woman wrote on the blackboard *Swiss watch* and *second watch.* Then she wrote *Swatch.* It helped that we were not very strong in English. We didn't know that *swatch* in English meant a cleaning towel. If we had known, we wouldn't have started the company with such a name!'" Problem defined. Vision set. And the two linked by new mixtures of old elements.

3. Gather all the facts

Since a great idea is a new combination of old elements, then the next step is to *gather all the facts* you can. ***Unless you know a big array of facts on any situation or problem, you're unlikely to hit on the perfect new solution.***

Facts can be ***specific:*** those directly concerned with your job, industry or problem. And they can be ***general:*** the facts you gather from a thousand different sources. You will only be a great ideas-producer if you're a voracious seeker of information. A questioner. A reader. And a storer of information.

There is no substitute for personalized, purposeful homework. What comes out must have gone in. The key is to somehow link information filed in, say, "brain-cell number 369,124" on "dendrite 2,614", with another stored on "cell number 9,378,532"—or wherever. Here your brain's patterning ability creates both problems and opportunities. Each one of us uses our brain for every waking minute to take action in a pre-patterned way —from walking to running, from driving a car to stopping at red lights. Your brain tends to store information in narrow channels, on associated "branches" for easy and quick retrieval, so we normally come up with the same answers.

4. Break the pattern

To solve problems creatively, however, you've got to *open up new pathways, find new crossover points, discover new linkages, break the pattern.*

And the easiest way to do that is to *start with questions that redirect your mind.* What would happen to your problem if you doubled it, halved it, froze it, reconstituted it, reversed it, adapted it, rearranged it, combined it?   What if you eliminated it—or part of it? If you substituted one of the parts? If you made it smaller, shorter, lighter? If you recolored it, streamlined it, magnified it? If you repackaged it? Distributed it in a different way? What if you applied all your senses—and added scents or fragrances, added sounds or made it different to see or touch?

5. Go outside your own field

Put your existing preconceptions aside.   The elements you use to solve problems should not be only those that are specific to the industry or process you're involved in. Use only those and you'll come up with the same old solutions.

Ask a teacher to redefine education, and generally he'll start thinking about school, and not about interactive videodiscs or life in 2020. Ask your brain to add 1 plus 1 and it will automatically answer 2. It's programmed that way. Ask bus or train companies to reinvent city transport, and most won't start by abolishing it and redesigning cities with most people working from home.

But your brain has also stored facts about thousands of different interests.   The answers to problems in farming may well come from meanderings in space research. So inventors, innovators and creators develop an insatiable appetite for new knowledge.

Idea 6: how a New Zealand farming engineer reinvented the jet engine to create river tourist industry

New Zealand engineer-farmer Bill Hamilton—the creator of the jet boat for taking tourists around shallow waterways—claimed he never invented it: "Archimedes did—some years ago". Adventure tourism, like jet boating, bungi jumping, skiing, wine trails, farm tours and deep-sea fishing, have together become the country's biggest foreign-exchange earner.

Idea 7: With home video cameras and the Web, anyone can be a TV reporter on YouTube

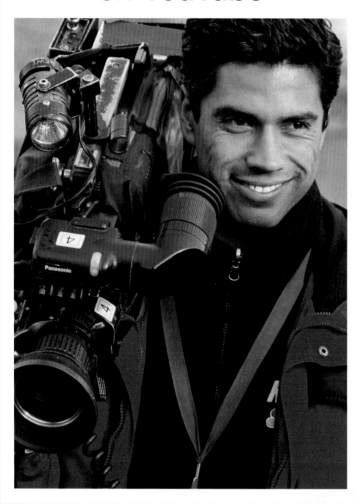

6. Play with various combinations

Next: since an idea is a new combination of old elements, play with various combinations. Jot them down as they come to you. Try different starting points. Choose anything at random—a color, an animal, a country—and try to link it up with your problem and solution. Work at it. Keep your notepad full. But don't concentrate too closely on your specific field or you'll be limited by your own preconceptions.

Read as widely as you can—particularly writings away from your own speciality. Keep asking: *What if?* "What if I combined this with that? What if I started from here instead of there?" And keep asking.

7. Use all your senses

It also helps greatly to consciously try to engage all your senses. If your problem has been defined mathematically, try to visualize some answers. Remember how Albert Einstein's theory of relativity came to him after he'd imagined he was travelling through space on a moonbeam.

Mind Mapping, too, is an excellent for creating—to link information together in new ways, on new branches, in new clusters, so your ideas are not merely listed in one-dimensional lines. Work at it until your head swims. Then . . .

8. Switch off—let it simmer

Like good food after you've eaten it, let your digestive juices take over and do the work—in this case the digestive juices of your own subconscious. Note the relaxation techniques now known as accelerated learning, to put your brain into its most receptive and creative mode.

9. Use music or nature to relax

Many people find it pays to play relaxing classical music, visit an art gallery or go for a walk by a river or the sea. Anything that opens up the mind to new combinations.

Different techniques work for different people. One of the present authors has always found chess a positive creative stimulant—mainly because of the way every move opens up new possibilities. Other people find chess too focused. The other co-author finds music, pilates, swimming and walking more effective.

10. Sleep on it

Just before going to sleep at night, remind yourself of the problem—and the ideal solution. If you have a set deadline, feed that into your "brain-bank" too. And then *your subconscious mind will take over.* It never sleeps. It synthesizes information. But as advertising leader David Ogilvy puts it: "You have to brief your subconscious. Then you have to switch off your thought processes and wait for something, for your subconscious to call you and say, 'Hey, I've got a good idea!' There are ways to do that. A lot of people find that to take a long hot bath produces good ideas. Other people prefer a long walk. I've always found that wine produces good ideas—the better the wine the better the idea."[9]

11. Eureka! It pops out

The next step is the easiest of all: it pops out. You'll be shaving, or taking a shower, or sleeping—and suddenly the answer is there.

In part the process works because it's similar to the way your brain processes information in the first place. Just as you can use your subconscious to file information in patterns, so you can use your subconscious to deliberately break up those patterns and find new combinations. But only if you state your vision and your goal *specifically.* *It also pays to set a deadline, so your subconscious can feed that, too, into its data banks.*

12. Recheck it

When the new answer has popped out, *recheck it.* Does it fully solve your problem? Can you amend it or improve it?

The system we've just highlighted could be called the problem-solving way to creativity. An alternative is a vision or mission approach. That's the same as problem-solving—except you don't start with the problem. You start with a vision of a future where virtually every dream is now possible.

Idea 8: to reinvent 'health', start with good nutrition and exercise

Idea 9: to reinvent a can-opener, they started with a banana and created the teartab top

Australian futurist Dr. Peter Ellyard is one of many who favor this approach. He feels that starting with a problem often limits the solution. "The dangers of a problem-centered approach can be best seen," he says, "in the inappropriately named 'health care' industry. In most first-world countries 'health care' is virtually out of control. The words 'health care' actually mean 'illness cure'. The industry consists of the activities of doctors, hospitals and pharmacies. The size of our health care budget has become an index of the nation's sickness, rather than its health. This forgets that the basic state of humans is to be healthy, not ill. We have adopted a problem-centered approach to health, largely defining health as an absence of illness, and a healthy future as an illness-free one. A *mission-directed* approach to promoting and maintaining health would be very different. It would concentrate on nutrition, exercise, good relationships, stress management and freedom from environmental contamination. This is a totally different agenda. However, the current problem is that we now pour so much money and effort into the problem-centered, technology-driven approach that there are very few resources available for a mission-directed approach."[10]

The current authors certainly wouldn't disagree with this analysis—except to say that the "problem" was not correctly defined. And Ellyard makes a vital point: generally we all try to define a problem too narrowly—and therefore limit the solution.

When consulting engineer William J. J. Gordon was given the task of finding a new way to open cans, he deliberately didn't use the word "can-opener" when briefing his engineers and designers. Instead they toyed with such notions as a banana and its easy-peel abilities. Their eventual solution: the ring-pulls you now see on most teartab cans. A "can-opener" approach would have limited the result.[11]

Whether you use the problem-solving or mission-directed approach, you generally won't come up with a great idea unless you define a specific goal in advance.

There are, of course, many exceptions. Bacteriologist Alexander Fleming stumbled on penicillin when confronted with a strange mould growing at St. Mary's Hospital in London.

And when Massachusetts inventor Percy Spencer was working on a novel radar system in 1945 it struck him that the radiation it emitted could have a culinary use. So he hung a pork chop in front of the magnetron machine he was working on. And, as Peter Evans and Geoff Deehan report, he "produced the first microwave meal in history".[12] In another of history's quirks, it was the Japanese who capitalized on the invention. "When a Japanese firm started to manufacture magnetrons, it was forbidden under the peace treaty to undertake military contracts. Therefore it concentrated on peaceful uses of microwave technology; now Japan leads the world in microwave sales."

Brainstorming checklist for ideas

But most breakthroughs come from a firm vision of the future: a specific goal. Many of those creative techniques can be adapted from other fields. Advertising, for example, has given us "brainstorming"[13]—the original idea of Alex Osborn, one of the founders of Batten, Barton, Durstine and Osborn, the giant advertising agency.

Here are some specific examples of how you can apply the brainstorming, ideas-creation process in practice:

When you're looking for a new idea, can you:

Double it: like London's double-decker buses? *Halve it:* like bikinis or the mini-skirt? *Expand it:* like one-stop shopping centers or the Boeing 747? *Dry it:* like packet soup? *Slice it:* like bread? *Stretch it:* like denims?

What could you substitute?

Ladislo Biro substituted a ball for a nib, and the ballpoint pen was born. *The fax machine* has substituted electronic transmission for posted mail—and the Internet has superseded the fax. *Clarence Birdseye*—after finding frozen fish in Canada's Arctic Circle—substituted freezing for canning to invent the frozen food industry. *Supermarkets* substituted self-service and trolleys for shop assistants. Xerox's Palo Alto Research Center substituted the "point and click" method of running a computer; Apple adapted it commercially, and the world's simplest computing system was born. *Bed-and-breakfast homes* in Ireland have substituted for hotels and become the core of that country's tourist industry.

Idea 10: Shopping carts helped invent supermarkets and self-service replace shop assistants

Idea 11: Combine skate wheels in a different way and you get roller blades

CDs replaced vinyl recordings for music. And now it's the Apple *iPod*.

What new combinations can you make?

Sony combined earphones with a transistor radio to invent the *Walkman*. Pressure-cooked chicken and a special sauce gave us *Kentucky Fried Chicken*. Nylons combined with panties to make *pantyhose*. Walt Disney combined Mickey Mouse with tourism to invent *Disneyland*. Shops and carparks linked together to produce *shopping centers*. General Motors combined hire purchase with a choice of colors and models to build *the world's biggest car company*.

How can you adapt it?

Rollerblades are now a multimillion-dollar seller—realigning skate-wheels into one line. *Rugby football* has been adapted from soccer, *rugby league* from rugby, *softball* from baseball.

What could you magnify or increase?

McDonald's magnified hamburgers to produce the *Big Mac*. *Prince* has made a fortune by enlarging the tennis racket. So has Calloway with its *Big Bertha* golf clubs. *Wal-mart* has become the world's most profitable retail chain, selling through giant discount stores. *JVC* invented *three-hour videotape* and beat off Sony to establish the world standard —because the extra length enabled buyers to record complete sports events.

What could you reduce, reverse or eliminate?

Frank Whittle reversed wind and invented the *jet engine*. *Bill Hamilton* adapted the principle further and gave us the *jet boat*. *The vacuum cleaner* is based on a similar principle. In Australia, *Kerry Packer* of the national Nine television network reduced the time of test matches to invent *one-day cricket,* and a profitable new summer television feature. *Computer spell-checkers* have reduced printing mistakes.

What new forms can you create?

Can you make it: *Hard,* like frozen ice blocks? *Soft,* like easy-spread butter or margarine? *Quiet,* like a Rolls Royce? *Loud,* like rock music? *Thick,* like Doc Mar-ten's famous bootsoles (a profitable fashion industry, based on the initial choice of unfashionable "skinheads")? *Fun*, like *Trivial Pursuit? Vertical*, like rocket takeoffs? *Horizontal*, like reclining chairs?

Can you: *Blend it*, like shampoo and conditioner? *Glue it*, like Glue Stick? *Shake it*, like a milk shake? *Cover it*, like umbrella cocktail decorations? *Uncover it*, like the miniskirt or split skirts? *Color it*, like new lipsticks or cosmetics? *Compress it*, like CD-roms? *Liquefy it*, like shoe-cleaners? *Squeeze it*, in plastic bottles? *Spread it*, like pate? *Raise it*, with self-raising flour?

Can you repack it: *In teartab cans*, like premixed drinks? *In plastic containers*, like cask-wine? *In aerosol cans*, like hairspray? *As roll-ons*, like deodorant? *Sleek*, like Apple *iMac* and Acer *Aspire* computers?

Business innovations like these —and hundreds more —are changing the face of society. *Dell Computers* have gone from a $60,000-a-month business to $50-billion-a-year because of the revolutionary way they have customized individual computers and sold them by direct marketing and then on the Web. *Lego* has developed into a $1.5 billion business, since started by an out-of-work Danish carpenter, Olo Christiansen, as small wooden toy company. Sweden's *IKEA* has become the world's biggest home furniture retailer, with seventy-nine outlets in nineteen countries, through brilliant catalog selling and simple home assembly.

Yet where is the same innovation in the vital field of education and learning?

Come up with a new idea in electronic communication—and it will be carried to a million enthusiasts immediately on the World Wide Web, and within a week or a month by scores of personal computing magazines. Inventors and early-adoptors are making fortunes by cashing in on the new third-wave of economic development. Why not the same verve in education?

We suspect that overwhelmingly it is because of the way schools and curricula are structured. *From the very moment of starting school, most children are taught that all the answers have already been found.* Even more: they are taught that success is learning a limited range of those answers—absorbed from a teacher—and feeding them

Idea 12: Lego was started by a Danish out-of-work carpenter in a depression: now a $1.5 billion industry

Idea 13: Toyota takes lead in world car industry with 1.5 million Kaizen suggestions a year

Kaizen is the Japanese word for continuous improvement. Toyota's 1.5 million staff suggestions every year—95 percent of them adopted—are even surpassed by Matsushita, the National Panasonic electronics manufacturer, with 6.5 million.

back correctly at exam time. Yet that is not the way the real world innovates. The simple questions on the past three pages are typical of the queries posed in businesses every day as they strive to do things "better, faster, cheaper".

Don Koberg and Jim Bagnall, in their book *The Universal Traveller,* have suggested other words to encourage innovation: *multiply, divide, eliminate, subdue, invert, separate, transpose, unify, distort, rotate, flatten, squeeze, complement, submerge, freeze, soften, fluff-up, bypass, add, subtract, lighten, repeat, thicken, stretch, extrude, repel, protect, segregate, integrate, symbolize, abstract* and *dissect.*

Stanford University engineer James Adams[14] suggests thinking up your own favorite "bug list"—the things that irritate you—to start you thinking. And he lists among his own: corks that break off in wine bottles, vending machines that take your money with no return, bumper stickers that cannot be removed, crooked billiard cue sticks, paperless toilets, dripping faucets and "one sock". "If you run out of bugs before ten minutes," says Adams, "you are either suffering from a perceptual or emotional block or have life unusually under control."

Another technique is to focus on 1,000 percent breakthroughs. What can you do ten times faster, better, cheaper? What is the "killer application" in your field: the big "Aha!" that can take your company, your school or your industry to new peaks of excellence? That's what Google has achieved in Web search; what Netscape first did in Internet browsers; what Canon has achieved in color copiers.

Given the tremendous increase in technology, in almost any field 1,000 per cent improvements are possible: in some operations. Learning to typeset magazine advertisements and newspapers, for instance, once took a six-year apprenticeship. To "makeup" pages took five years of training. Today, with desktop computerized publishing, any competent journalist can compress much of that eleven-year training into a week. What would it take to achieve similar breakthroughs in education?

At the other extreme, ***if you learn only one word of Japanese in your life, make it Kaizen. It means continuous improvement. But it also means a philosophy that encourages every person in an industry—every day—to come up with suggestions*** *to improve everything:* themselves, their job, their lunchroom, their office layout, their phone answering habits and their products.

Says Toyota Motor ex-chairman Eiji Toyoda: "One of the features of the Japanese workers is that they use their brains as well as their hands. Our workers provide 1.5 million suggestions a year, and 95 per cent of them are put to practical use."[15] And at Nissan Motors "any suggestion that saves at least 0.6 seconds—the time it takes a worker to stretch out his hand or walk half a step—is seriously considered by management."[16]

Matsushita, the giant Japanese electronics company, receives about 6.5 million ideas every year from its staff.[17] And the big majority are put into operation quickly.

It is beyond the scope of this book to cover all aspects of Japan's Total Quality Management and Kaizen movements. But to test, in part, the effectiveness of their method, try an introductory *Kaizen* on anything you're involved in. One excellent method is to use David Buffin's hexagon *Think Kit.* Staff or students are encouraged to fire in new ideas. The teacher or facilitator writes each on a colored magnetic hexagon and attaches the hexagons to a large magnetic board. The group then arranges the hexagons around various themes or activities, and agrees on the main priorities. These are then left on display as a continual spur to agreed action.

For business we prefer to marry the two methods together: to look for the big *Aha!* idea for strategic planning (what is the really big breakthrough that will change the future of your company or industry?) and *Kaizen* (how can you involve all your staff in continuously striving to upgrade every aspect of that performance?). In oversimplified terms, many would describe *Aha!* as the key to American business success, and *Kaizen* as the Japanese secret weapon. Their "marriage" is *The Third Way.*

In many ways Finland's Nokia company represents this: a traditional forestry company that transformed itself into the global mobile phone powerhouse, with almost 40 percent of the new century's big *Aha!* market—yet is also a global model for fine relations with its 117,000 staff in 120 nations.

Many universities, of course, would say they have always taught thinking as part

Idea 14: Mobile smart phones turn Finland's Nokia into the world's biggest portable brand

So what if we took a Walt Disney approach to 'conceptual blockbusting' in reinventing education?

of logic, psychology and philosophy. But most schools don't teach what Edward de Bono[18] has termed *lateral thinking:* the ability to open-mindedly search for new ideas, look in new directions.

Roger von Oech thinks even the terms logical and lateral thinking are too restrictive. He says we're also capable of *conceptual thinking, analytical thinking, speculative thinking, right-brain thinking, critical thinking, foolish thinking, convergent thinking, weird thinking, reflective thinking, visual thinking, symbolic thinking, propositional thinking, digital thinking, metaphorical thinking, mythical thinking, poetic thinking, nonverbal thinking, elliptical thinking, analogical thinking, lyrical thinking, practical thinking, divergent thinking, ambiguous thinking, constructive thinking, thinking about thinking, surreal thinking, focused thinking, concrete thinking* and *fantasy thinking.*[19]

But most people unwittingly limit their thinking potential. One reason is the brain's ability to file material inside existing patterns. When a new problem is tackled, we're conditioned to go down the track of previous answers. We all have preconceptions, taboos and prejudices, though few of us ever admit to them. They can be emotional, cultural, religious, educational, national, psychological, sexual or culinary.

We are also preconditioned from school to come up with "the right answer"—not the open-minded challenge for a better way. Almost every adult who has succeeded at high school or college will have firm ideas on the best educational system. And it will generally be the system that he succeeded in. Listen to anyone praise a "good school" and you will almost certainly find a school that suits that particular person's learning style.

Now that's not unusual. So perhaps the first step in "conceptual blockbusting"—to use James Adams' term[20]—is to accept that we all have fears, we all have biases. The best way we know to start overcoming them is to combine fun and humor. That often works for students in particular. A fun-filled atmosphere can lead to high creativity.

If you're not used to "far-out" brainstorming sessions, probably a good warm-up exercise is to start with a humorous challenge. Try inventing a new golfball—one that can't get lost. Or planning what you'd do with a holiday on the moon or under water. Or ask some "What if?" questions. Like what would happen if pets became school teachers? Or if computers ran the government? Then use some of de Bono's techniques, such as PMI, CAF, C&S, APC and his "Six Thinking Hats."[21]

PMI standards for Plus, Minus and Interesting. Here the students choose a fairly outlandish statement, and in three columns write down all the points they can think of to be "plus" factors, then all the "minuses," and lastly all the reasons the proposition could be "interesting".

CAF means Consider All Factors. And again write them down, searching for new factors that don't spring immediately to mind.

C & S stands for Consequences and Sequel. Logically, both should be listed under CAF, but de Bono says that most people just do not consider all the consequences unless their attention is specifically drawn to them.

APC stands for Alternatives, Possibilities and Choices. And again the reasons are obvious: a list that encourages you to speculate.

As de Bono summarizes another technique: "The theme of my book, *Six Thinking Hats,* is simple. There is the *white hat* for neutral facts, figures and information. There is the *red hat* to allow a person to put forward feelings, hunches and intuitions—without any need to justify them. The *black hat* is for the logical negative, and the *yellow hat* for the logical positive. For creativity there is the *green hat.* The *blue hat* is the control hat, and looks at the thinking itself rather than at the subject—like an orchestra conductor controlling the orchestra. The purpose is to provide a means for rapidly switching thinkers from one mode to another—without causing offence."[21]

All are excellent techniques. Especially the "six hats"—when you go to the trouble to obtain some bizarre models, in colors and odd shapes, and pass them around so each person can act the part. Many schools have hats in six colors on classroom walls as a constant reminder to switch thinking modes.

But the simple ideas we have suggested earlier in this chapter are the ones we have found to work effectively in virtually any situation: in advertising, business, marketing, selling, exporting, market research and government itself.

What if we used Edward de Bono's Six Thinking Hats to make school 'the best party in town?'

What if we asked the producers of an Olympic opening ceremony to redesign third-world education?

They can also be used to reinvent education, schooling and learning. And here, again, both the problem-solving approach and the opportunity-seeking approach can work in harmony. The problem-solving approach is to start with institutions as they are: early-childhood centers, elementary schools, secondary schools, K-12 schools, colleges and universities. In the last twenty years or so many of these have been dramatically improved. We now call that *The Learning Revolution 1.0:* how to improve the existing system. We recap and add to that in part three of this book.

Then the real challenge is to make the major leap and to reinvent everything about learning, teaching, schooling and education. If you could start with an unlimited mind, and imagine what is now possible: that's *The Learning Revolution 2.0.*

Even in the working examples already summarized in this book, the options are unlimited:

❏ What if we used *Wikipedia* as one model to reinvent education?

❏ What if we used Disneyland and Disneyworld as another?

❏ How can we best tap into the ability of the brightest of the world's 59 million school teachers?

❏ What would emerge if we asked the producers of the Beijing Olympic Games opening and closing ceremonies to redesign China's education system?

❏ Or if we asked India's "Bollywood" movie industry—the world's largest—to reinvent education in a country where almost half the villages don't have schools?

❏ How would the creative geniuses of Google approach the challenge in the 20 percent of their work-time they devote to new ideas?

❏ And what if we asked the most important people of all to come up with creative solutions: the students, who already live in the Web 2.0 world?

❏ *What, in fact, would happen if we reversed current educational spending—and invested as much per student on early-childhood education as we do at university level? After all, that's where the majority of the brain's main learning pathways are laid down.*

Part three
Revolution 1.0

Each of us creates more of our brain's learning pathways in the first four years than in the rest of life

How to enrich your child's learning from birth until age eight

Every country's educational priorities are completely back to front.

Reliable researchers say that we develop around 50 percent of our *learning ability* in the first four years of life[1]—and another 30 percent by age eight.

This does not mean that you absorb most of your *knowledge* or most of your *wisdom* or most of your *intelligence* by your fourth or eighth birthday. It simply means that in those first few years you form *the main learning pathways in your brain.* You also take in a fantastic amount of information in those early years, including much that is absorbed subconsciously. Yet nearly every country spends well under 10 percent of its educational budget on the years where of your ability to learn is formed.

Many compare that growth to laying down an incredible mental highway system. And, in the words of neurology professor Harry Chugani: "Roads with the most traffic get widened. The ones that are rarely used fall into disrepair."[2]

For infants, there are six main pathways into the brain: the five senses of sight, hearing, touch, taste and smell, and the sixth step of what we do physically. Youngsters learn through all the senses. Every day is a learning experience. They love to experiment, to create, to find out how things work. Challenges are there to be accepted. Adults to be imitated.

Most important, a child learns by doing. He learns to crawl by crawling. He learns to walk by walking. To talk by talking. And each time he does so he either lays down new pathways in the brain—if his experience is new—or he builds on, expands, widens and reinforces existing pathways—if he is repeating the experience.

Youngsters are their own best educators, parents their best first teachers. And our homes, beaches, forests, playgrounds, adventure areas and the whole wide world our main educational resources—as long as children are encouraged to explore them safely through all their senses.

Research has also established beyond doubt the importance of every child growing in a positive enriched environment.

We've already quoted research by Berkeley scientists in California who have been experimenting for many years with rats—and comparing their brain growth with humans. "Very simply," says Dr. Marian Diamond, Professor of Neuroanatomy, "we have found with our rats that all the nerve cells in the key outer layers of the brain are present at birth. At birth the interconnecting dendrites start to grow. For the first month the growth is prolific. Then it starts to go down. If we put the rats in enriched environments, we can keep the dendrite growth up. But if we put them in impoverished environments, then dendrite growth goes down fast.

"In enrichment cages, rats live together and have access to toys. They have ladders, wheels and other playthings. They can climb, explore and interact with their toys. Then we compare them with rats in impoverished environments: one rat to a cage, no toys, no interaction. Very simply: we've found that the rat brain cells increase in size in the enriched environment—and the number of dendrites increases dramatically. In the impoverished environment, the opposite." [3]

The rats then take an "intelligence test": they're put in a maze, and left to find food in another part of the maze. The "enriched" rats do so easily. The others don't.

Obviously, scientists can't cut up human brains to test the impact of early stimulation. But they can check with radioactive glucose. "And these checks," says Diamond, "show that the vital glucose uptake is extremely rapid for the first two years of life—provided the child has a good diet and adequate stimulation. It continues rapidly until five years. It continues very slowly from five to ten. By about ten years of age, brain-growth has reached its peak—although the good news is this: the human brain can

We learn with all our senses: what we see, hear, touch, taste, smell, and from what we actually do

Our thanks to the Thomas Jefferson Institute in Mexico for permission to use many of the excellent photos in this chapter. Their early childhood centers in Mexico City, Queretaro and Guadalajara demonstrate why they have twice been voted the best school in the Spanish-speaking world for vision and innovation.

A daily physical routine of fun activities opens up the brain's academic pathways

Part of Professor Lyelle Palmer's daily brain-building program at the New Visions public school in Minneapolis. Minnesota.

keep on growing dendrites till the end of life, so long as it is being stimulated. Very simply, the human brain cell, like the rat's, is designed to receive stimulation—and to grow from it."

That doesn't mean turning an infant's home into a formal school classroom. The reverse, in fact: infants learn by play and exploration. It's the formal classroom that needs redesigning.

"We used to think that play and education were opposite things," say Jean Marzollo and Janice Lloyd in their excellent book *Learning Through Play.* "But now we know better. Educational experts and early childhood specialists have discovered that play *is* learning, and even more, that play is one of the most effective kinds of learning."

The key: turning play into learning experiences—and making sure that most learning is fun.

In fact, activities that good parents take for granted provide some of the best early learning. But we don't mean "academic" studies. *Scientists have proved, for instance, that regularly rocking a baby can help greatly in promoting brain growth.* It stimulates the vestibular system. This is a nerve-system centered in the brainstem and linked very closely with the cerebellum and a baby's inner-ear mechanism, which also plays a vital part in developing balance and coordination.

Dr. Ruth Rice, of Texas, has proven that *even fifteen minutes of rocking, rubbing, rolling and stroking a premature baby four times a day will greatly help its ability to coordinate movements and therefore to learn.*[4]

And Dr. Lyelle Palmer, Professor Emeritus of Education at Winona State University in Minnesota, has completed extensive studies at kindergarten level* to demonstrate the vital importance of such simple stimulation for five-year-olds. Every day youngsters have attended a gymnasium as a key part of early schooling. There they are encouraged to carry out a simple series of routines: spinning, rope jumping, balancing, somersaulting, rolling and walking on balance beams. In the playground, they are encouraged

* *In the United States, kindergarten normally starts at age five. In New Zealand and some other countries, the kindergarten ages start from three and four.*

to swing on low "jungle gyms", climb, skate, perform somersaults and flips. And in classrooms they play with a wide range of games, also designed to stimulate their sense of sight, hearing and touch. All activities are designed to increase in skill-level during the year, and thus help stimulate ever-increasing brain development.

At the end of each year, many of the children undergo the Metropolitan Readiness Test to measure whether they've developed enough to start first-grade schooling. Nearly all have passed the tests in the top 10 percent for the state—and most have been in the top 5 percent. Nearly all of them come from working-class backgrounds. Palmer, a former president of the Society for Accelerative Learning and Teaching, emphasizes that the children are not simply walking, running and skipping—the normal "motor" activities. "The stimulation activities we recommend," he says, "are specifically designed to activate the areas of the brain we know will promote their sense of sight, touch and hearing—as well as their ability to take in knowledge." [5] Most parents, for instance, seem to learn instinctively that infants love to be held firmly by their hands and spun around like a helicopter blade. Palmer's Minneapolis public school research at New Visions School has shown that such activities result in important brain growth. And the greater the intensity of the activity the greater you see the results of the brain-growth in areas that are receptive to further learning.

The overall result is a big gain in competence and self-confidence, increased attention, faster responses and the ability to tackle learning activities of increasing complexity.

Palmer stresses that the activities are not what many schools would regard as "academic." But any classroom visit shows the youngsters "exploding" into true learning. Early reading is taught with word-card games. The youngsters get an early introduction to mathematics by playing with dominoes and big cards with dots instead of numbers. And they play games to develop pre-writing skills.

In another study of at-risk youngsters who were not doing well at school, Palmer's methods produced dramatic gains in reading ability. The children of the experimental group read three to ten times faster than the control group.[6]

Two Swedish vestibular-stimulation experts, Mats and Irene Niklasson, have also

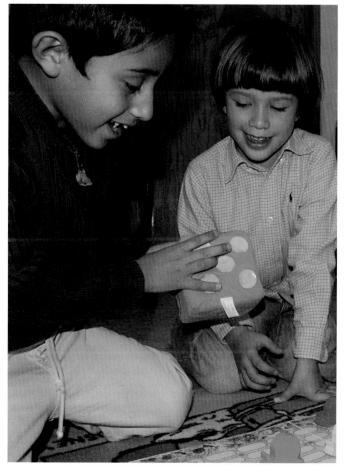

Playing games with giant dice and dots are excellent early steps to building up basic mathematics

Photo courtesy Thomas Jefferson Institute, Mexico.

Crawling, creeping, standing, walking: the right sequence wires up the brain

achieved great results using techniques similar to Palmer. At their Vistibularis organization, they've found that slow spinning and slow movement is ideal for many children, particularly those diagnosed as having severe learning problems. Says Mats Niklasson: "Most learning problems, I found, relate to lack of balance and difficulty with the reflexes." Through spinning and other motor activities, the Niklassons "rewire the brain".[7] They also agree that effective learning starts from the moment of birth—and before. Again, the main points are simple:

1. The vital importance of step-by-step movement

Infants grow in a patterned way. They're born explorers. So encourage them to explore in a safe, but challenging, environment.

In New Zealand two Irish migrants, Jerome and Sophie Hartigan, have combined their talents to introduce a parent-involvement program based very much on children's natural physical development. Jerome is a former Olympic pentathlete, has a masters degree from Ithaca College, New York, and is a scientist and physical training specialist. Sophie is an accomplished music teacher. Their *Jumping Beans* child-development centers, now well-established in New Zealand, involve parents in regular one-hour sessions. They are now being franchised in other countries, starting in Singapore.

Jerome Hartigan says "physical, motor learning" forms the basis for all learning, including reading, writing, arithmetic and music. "Without motor learning," he says," the brain simply will not develop."[8] He says specific movement patterns "wire up" the whole brain, and it's important that physical routines should link in with the way the brain grows.

Janet Doman, director of The Institutes for the Achievement of Human Potential, in Philadelphia, agrees. And those routines should start from day one. "Give children the chance to crawl from as early an age as possible," she says. "Babies can actually crawl from birth, but generally they are restricted by so much clothing that they don't develop this ability till later."[9] So long as children are warm, she says, parents should not limit their movements with too much clothing.

"Very simply, the more they crawl the sooner they're going to creep, and the more they creep the more they'll be able to walk. And each of these stages ensures that the next stage comes at the right moment—and that they have completed the neurological maturation that goes with it. If babies are bundled up for so long that they don't really crawl much at all, but go straight to creeping, then they may well pay a price for that five years later when they get to the point where they need to be able to converge their vision perfectly."

Part of the reason is very simple: to creep and crawl, a baby needs to use all four limbs. And this movement strengthens the 300 million nerve-cell pathways that link both sides of the brain through the corpus callosum. Children who skip creeping or crawling—common in youngsters with severe brain damage from birth—thus find it impossible to fully coordinate both hemispheres.

2. Use your common sense

Almost everything we learn about the world comes in through our five main senses. Very early in life, infants try to touch, smell, taste, hear and look at whatever surrounds them. So encourage them from the outset.

Says Janet Doman: "A baby is born into a world in which, essentially, he is blind, can't hear very well and his sensation is far from perfect. And that's a very uncomfortable place for a baby to be. He's trying to figure out: 'Where am I? What's going on? What's gonna happen next?' Because he can't see, he can't hear and he can't feel very well. So I think the job of a parent is very clear: to give enough visual, auditory and tactile stimulation so that the baby can get out of this dilemma of not being able to see, hear or feel.

"That doesn't have to be complicated. For example, often new parents put children in a pastel environment. For baby this is a disaster. The baby needs to see contrast, needs to see outlined shapes and images, needs to see black-and-white contrasts. If you put him in a room of pale pinks and pale blues, it's like putting him in a world where there's nothing to see—so he can't see it."

Or take taste. Doman says it is one of the most neglected senses. "In the normal course of events, a baby in his first few months of life would probably taste only

From day one in crib or cot, surround babies with bold contrasts, not passive pastels, for visual growth

Infants learn by playing with shapes and colors, and seeing them in the real world

two things: milk and vomit. Now that's not a very interesting taste variety! So we encourage our mothers to introduce some variety: a little taste of lemon or orange or nutmeg."

And sound: "Mothers intuitively speak in a slightly louder, clearer voice to babies, and that's great," says Doman. "And it's even better if you constantly tell baby what's happening: saying, 'Now I'm dressing you,' 'I'm putting your right sock on,' 'Now I'm changing your diaper.'" Playing soothing background music is also recommended, both before and after birth

3. Build on all the senses

As an infant gets older, many parents feel it's even easier to encourage learning through all the senses—because you see the instant feedback.

In *Learning Through Play,* Marzollo and Lloyd stress that children learn from concrete, active experiences. "For a child to understand the abstract concept of 'roundness', he must first have many experiences with real round things. He needs time to feel round shapes, to roll around balls, to think about the similarities between round objects, and to look at pictures of round things. When children are at play, they like to push, pull, poke, hammer and otherwise manipulate objects, be they toy trucks, egg cartons or pebbles. It is this combination of action and concreteness that makes play so effective as an educational process."

4. Use the whole world as your classroom

Turn every outing into a learning experience. On a walk, point out and talk about shapes, such as the circles that form wheels, the sun, clocks and coins; or rectangles such as doors and windows; squares, like paper napkins, handkerchiefs, windows and tabletops; and triangles, like rooftops, mountains, tents, Christmas trees and sails

Every supermarket trip can be a learning journey—and a game: "See who's first to see the cornflakes." Learning to count can be a game, too: "This is one spoon; and these are two spoons." Then make it a natural fun game: "You've got one nose but how many eyes? You've got one mouth but how many ears? And how many fingers?"

Involve him as you set the table for two, three or four people. Let him count the money at the checkout counter.

5. The great art of communication

Language, of course, is a unique human ability. And infants learn by listening, imitation—and practice. So talk to them from the start. Tell them what you are doing. Introduce them to their relatives. Read to them regularly.

Nursery rhymes are great, because rhymes are easy to remember. Every child should be exposed to colorful books from the start—and should be read to regularly. Says New Zealand reading expert and author Dorothy Butler: "Keep the baby's books within reach, and make a practice of showing them to her from the day you first bring her home. The covers will be brightly illustrated, and at first you can encourage her to focus her eyes on these pictures. You can teach your baby a lot about books in the first few months."[10]

Learning to read should be a natural and fun-filled process. Again, the principles are simple. English has about 615,000 words.[11] But 2,000 to 3,000 words make up 90 percent of most speech.[12] And only 400 to 450 words make up 65 percent of most books.[13] Introduce those words to children in a natural way, and reading develops as naturally as speaking. In fact the principle is so simple it's amazing there is any debate. Words, like pictures, are only symbols of reality. A picture of an apple is a symbol of a real fruit. So is the sound "apple". And so is the written word "apple". So if children can hear and see the word *apple,* and can taste it, smell it and touch it, they soon learn to speak and read it.

Glenn Doman has been proving this since before he first wrote *Teach Your Baby To Read* in 1964. He's also had many critics. Yet most of the critics actually recommend many of the same techniques, and often they criticize Doman for things he has never recommended.[14] Says Doman: "It's as easy to learn to read as it is to learn to talk. In fact it's probably easier—because the ability to see is developed before the ability to talk. But don't take my word for it. Ask any producer of television commercials. They use the same simple communication techniques. Look at television any night,

Remember the golden rule: use the whole world as your classroom

Every child should be exposed to colorful books from the start to develop a natural love of language

and you'll hear someone screaming COCA COLA, or McDONALD'S—and at the same time the brand-names appear in large colored words, often tied in with a jingle that's easy to remember. And two-year-olds have broken the code. Now they can read because the message is large enough to be interpreted."[15]*

So Doman-trained parents not only talk new words to their youngsters—loudly and clearly—they show them the words in big type, just like TV commercials or company billboards do.

In many parts of the world parents have found it simple common sense to label as many things as possible, so children can recognize written words as well as those spoken, starting with all the names of important things: from baby's own name to mommy (in America, or 'mummy' in Britain) and daddy, parts of the body and everything around the house. Printed letters, three inches high (about 7 cm.), are recommended. When preschools were combined with parent education centers in the Pacific island of Rarotonga over thirty years ago, they labelled everything in English as well as their native Polynesian language. They found it a great way to encourage youngsters to read and speak in two languages. In Malaysia, the Nury Institute has trained hundreds of parents to teach their three- and four-year-olds to speak and read in both Malay and English—specifically using the Doman technique.[16] English-born teacher and author Felicity Hughes has used similar methods to teach young Tanzanian children to read in both English and Swahili.[17] Many of those children have then helped their parents read.

Felicity Hughes—in *Reading and Writing Before School*—and the current authors agree, but Glenn Doman disagrees, that phonetics have an equal part to play with the "whole language" method of learning. Of the most-used words in English, about half are phonetic—written approximately as they sound: *hat, sat, mat, hit, fit, sit.* The other half are not phonetic, including such difficult spellings as *through, tough, cough, where, tight, weigh* and *bridge.* Learn only "phonetics" and you'll be able to read and

* MIT Professor of Linguistics Noam Chomsky and his followers would disagree with Glenn Doman about reading being possibly easier to learn than speaking. Chomsky has presented convincing evidence that the ability to speak is "wired" into the genetic makeup of humans.

spell *set, bet, get* and *met*.   You'll also quickly learn prefixes and suffixes such as *un, de, dis, re, ing* and *ed*.   But you won't be able to read *Once upon a time* (phonetically: *Wunce upon uh taim*).   And you won't be able to read all the words from one to ten (phonetically pronounced *wun, tu, three, for, faiv, six, seven, ait, nain, ten*). You won't even be able to read the word *phonetically!* The long "e" in English, for instance, can be written twelve different ways: *On the quay* we could see one of these people seize the key to the green machine and give it to the chief officer who threw it in the sea*. So word-cards should include the most-used words, whether spelled phonetically or not. And fortunately 84 percent of English words do have easily-identifiable spellings, such as the "silent e" in words such as *fate* and *kite,* or syllables such as *might, sight* and *fight*.

The first cards should contain "labelling" words—the nouns of the things children first see as their parents are telling them: "That's your bottle. This is your dress. And these are your toes."   Then when they can crawl, roll over and walk, they can start learning the action words, both spoken and written: "Let me see you roll over. Good boy, you can walk." Then come the adverbs: "Roll over slowly." "See how quickly you can walk." And the adjectives, too: "What a big, black dog."

But is too much early learning robbing infants of their childhood? Glenn Doman gives the simple answer: ***"We have a fail-safe law. We teach all mothers this law. When teaching your child, if you aren't having the time of your life, and the child isn't having the time of his life, stop, because you're doing something wrong. That's the fail-safe law."***

 The early years are also the ideal time to pick up more than one language, especially if you live in an area where other languages are spoken regularly. Says Doman: "All children are linguistic geniuses—witness their ability to learn to speak a language in the first three years. If they live in a bilingual house, they learn two. In a trilingual household, they learn to speak three." But Professor Diamond cautions that "love" is the most essential ingredient in early childhood education. "I think that

* In "English English", key, as in waterfront, is spelled "quay".

'Our fail-safe law for parents: if you're not having the time of your life, and the child isn't, then stop'

Regular sight and hearing checks are regular features of Missouri Parents as Teachers Program

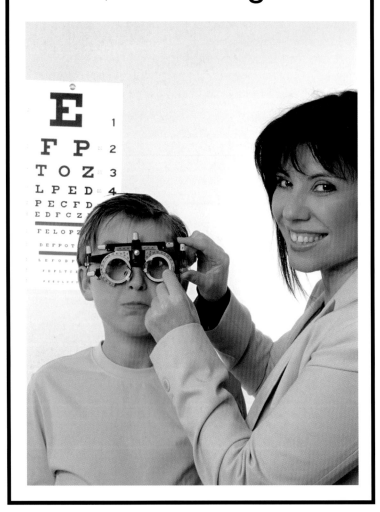

warmth and affection is the prime consideration for healthy brain development. But from then on, expose them to a great variety of experiences. Let the child choose what interests her—and then move out from there."[18]

6. Parents as first teachers

So how can any parent become a better "first teacher"? Or better still, a first coach and mentor? Obviously you can read books on the subject, as you're doing now. But, like any other learning, hands-on experience with a mentor helps. And again the world provides many models.

In America, the Missouri Parents As Teachers program has been an important trailblazer.[19] It started in 1981 as a pilot program—under the Parents as First Teachers title—and its early results were thoroughly researched. When all children in the pilot reached age three, a randomly-selected group was tested against a carefully-matched comparison group. In all significant areas—language, problem-solving, health, intellectual skills, relating to others and confidence—the PAT group scored much better.

PAT later became a state-funded service provided by all 543 public school districts in Missouri. On average in recent years, 60,000 Missouri families, with children from birth to three, have taken part in the program. They've been helped by about 1,500 trained part-time "parent-educators". Every month, each parent is visited by a parent-educator, who offers information about the next phase of each child's development and suggests practical ways parents can encourage sound growth. Parent-educators also offer tips on home safety, effective discipline, constructive play and other topics. At each visit, the parent-educator takes along toys and books suitable for the next likely phase of development, discusses what parents can expect, and leaves behind a one-sheet series of tips on how to stimulate the child's interest through that next stage.

"Families receive three types of service," says parent-educator Joy Rouse.[20] "The primary part is the monthly home visit. We also provide group meetings—a chance for parents to come together with other families who have children in the same age-group. Sometimes it will be for parent-child activities, others to hear a consultant talk about child development or parenting, and sometimes it's just a fun time. The third component is screening, and this is a key component. We screen for language development, general development, hearing and vision. We also have a network where we can refer families with special needs."

From personal observation, we can report a high degree of parent satisfaction. But former Harvard Professor Burton L. White, who played a big part in establishing the PAT, has ended his involvement with it because he says it is "hopelessly underfunded".[21] To do the job properly, he says, would require much higher spending; it should be top priority. *He says not more than one American child in ten gets adequate development in the vital first three years* .

"This state of affairs may be a tragedy," he says, "but it is by no means a twenty-first-century tragedy. In the history of Western education there has never been a society that recognized the educational importance of the earliest years or sponsored any systematic preparation and assistance to families or any other institution in guiding the early development of children."[22] Professor White says the period from when a child starts walking up to two years is most important. "Every one of the four educational foundations—the development of language, curiosity, intelligence and socialness—is at risk during the period from eight months to two years." He says bluntly that "our society does not train people to raise children".

Adds Professor Robert Sylwester: "The best time to master a skill associated with a system is just when a new system is coming on line in your brain. Language is a good example. It's very easy for a two- or three-year-old to learn any language. But if that person waits until eighteen or thirty, learning a new language will be more difficult because the systems governing this have been used for something else. Many skills, like learning to play a musical instrument or developing fine and gross motor skills, are best done as early as possible."[23]

Another home-based parent-education program, which has had excellent success for children from age four to six, is called HIPPY: Home Interaction Program for Preschool Youngsters. It began in Israel in 1969, and has since started in over twenty other countries or states, serving about 20,000 families a year outside Israel. As well

'Many gross motor skills, like learning to play an instrument, are best built as early as possible'

Sweden's best early childhood centers have a neat balance between nature, fun and computers

Children at Sweden's Lemshaga Barnakademi, set up by The Carpe Vitam Foundation as a model school of the future, blending "chickens and computers". It includes a community educational center, teacher training center, multimedia publishing company, all integrated into the community. All Swedish infants grow up naturally learning to be fluent in both Swedish and English.

organizing home visits every month, it also brings parents together for joint meetings in the period between visits.

New Zealand is one country to adopt the system, but with new twist. It was set up initially by the then-named Pacific Foundation, now renamed Great Potentials.[24] Early in the 1990s the foundation designed and built a combined preschool and parent-training center at Kelvin Road School, Papakura, in the heart of an area with many deprived families. The center also links in closely with most other district health and social services. The preschool center also provides a full HIPPY-based development program for infants and their parents. Foundation executive director Lesley Max describes the total project as a "one-stop shopping center for parent and preschool services".[25] Results have been so outstanding that the government has now financed similar centers in other parts of the country.

Again in innovative New Zealand, a parents' cooperative Playcenter movement has been operating since 1941. It was started as a project to provide support for mothers whose husbands were away at the war. The women would take turns looking after a group of children to free the others for shopping or recreation. The movement quickly spread, and one of the early pioneers, Gwen Somerset, organized wider programs to train the young mothers in child development skills. Now there are 600 playcenters throughout the country, catering to 23,000 children. And parent involvement is the key. They take turns in helping a trained, part-time supervisor run each center.

7. Model early childhood centers

Sweden is another country with highly advanced early childhood development programs—but with a tax-rate that most countries might find too high. For every child born in Sweden, one parent can have a year off work on almost full pay to be a fulltime parent.[26] Later, Sweden offers excellent preschool development centers.

For years it also organized one of the world's best refugee-support programs, with migrants from 114 different countries. By law, each preschool center employed adults fluent in both Swedish and the native language of each child. And students spoke at least two languages fluently—and many of them spoke three, including English.

But the prize for pioneering excellence in early childhood education could well go to aspects of a movement that was started over a century ago by Italy's first woman medical doctor, Maria Montessori.[27]

Most Montessori preschools are private, and often have high fees. But at French Camp near Stockton, California—an hour's drive from San Francisco—a New Zealand television crew, videotaping the world's best learning ideas in 1990, found a Montessori center catering to America's poorest working families, Mexican fruit and vegetable pickers.[28] Both parents were working in the fields from 4:30 or 5:00 each morning— for a family income of around $7,000 a year.

Yet their children were benefitting from preschool education that ranks with the top in the world. Their center was one of eighteen set up as a research experiment by the California-based Foundation Center for Phenomenological Research.* In the grounds of the French Camp center, the TV crew videotaped migrant youngsters dancing, singing and playing. Inside, others were engrossed in a wide variety of activities adapted from Montessori's original ideas.

They sat in child-sized chairs, at child-sized tables, used tools and implements specially designed for small hands. They were also learning advanced mathematics the Montessori way, using wooden rods of different lengths and colors to do decimals and numbers up to 2,000.

Among many other innovations, Montessori pioneered cutout sandpaper letters so infants could learn by touch as well as sight. And French Camp children were involved in a full range of similar sensory experiences. Each room had a variety of live animals and fish to help the learning process. Well-trained parents were always on hand to assist, but overall the youngsters were encouraged to be self-learners.

As one of the Foundation's then organizers, Antonia Lopez, told the TV audience: "The major job of the adult is to provide the children with as many opportunities in all of their areas, whether it's cultural, or science, art, music, mathematics or language—to

* Like so many effective pioneering ventures, lack of finance has since forced the Foundation Center to close many of its preschool centers, including the one visited at French Camp.

Maria Montessori's influence lives on, with great results in Latin America

The methods created by the great Italian educator, Maria Montessori, a century ago are used as the basis for many of today's most successful early childhood centers. This photo from the Mexico City early childhood center of the Thomas Jefferson Institute: learning numbers with art and all the senses. At this kindergarten children experience a variety of activity centers every day.

Playing with big-knob puzzles paves the way for writing skills

From playing with big balls when crawling to simple puzzles with big knobs at eighteeen months, all children go through an ideal series of steps to develop "big motor" and then "small motor" skills that lead to hand writing well before their fifth birthday.

provide as many opportunities that are age-appropriate and sequentially developed."[29] Something to eat was being served every two hours, with each meal a lesson in diet and nutrition: low-fat soups, whole-wheat tortillas instead of white-flour tortillas. Children set the tables as they learned to count the spoons and forks and plates. Each meal was a cultural delight. And it didn't stop with nutrition. All family members—male, female, siblings and children—were physically examined each year.

Those who criticize Glenn Doman's early *reading* program would probably gasp with amazement when they hear that French Camp children were *writing* fluently before they reached their fifth birthday.

As Lopez put it: "Montessori tells us that children at about four and a half literally seem to explode into writing. Now that's the official 'I can-write-a-sentence-and-a-word' version of writing. But our children are really being introduced to writing and to reading much earlier. Even as young as two and a half, they're being introduced to pre-writing experiences: they're doing things left to right, top to bottom; learning relationships. And they're obviously exposed to rhymes and story-telling and all kinds of talking—so they're ready to explode into writing well before they are five."

It's perhaps significant that both Montessori's and Doman's initial research began with youngsters who were severely brain-damaged—and they then realized that these children, after multisensory stimulation, were often performing much better than "normal" children.

Montessori set out to fashion materials and experiences from which even "intellectually handicapped" youngsters could easily learn to read, write, paint and count before they went to school. She succeeded brilliantly; her brain-damaged pupils passed standard test after test.[30]

Under the Montessori method, however, a small child is not "taught" writing; she is exposed to specific concrete experiences that enable her to develop the "motor" and other skills that lead to the self-discovery of writing.

Montessori specialist Pauline Pertab, of Auckland, New Zealand, explains: "As early as two-and-a-half years of age, a child will be encouraged to pour water and do polishing, developing hand and eye coordination; to paint and draw, developing pencil control; and later to work with shapes and patterns, tracing the inside and outside of stencils and to work with sandpaper-covered letters about nine centimeters in depth—three to four inches—to get the feel of shapes."[31] The "explosion" occurs when a youngster discovers, by himself, that he can write.

As Maria Montessori was proving in the early 1900s, the key to early childhood deprivation lies overwhelmingly in providing a total supportive environment for all children to develop their own talents.

She demonstrated conclusively that if children can grow up in an environment structured to encourage their natural, sequential development, they will "explode" into learning: they will become self-motivated, self-learners, with the confidence to tackle any problem as it arises in life.

Singapore, too, has some first-rate early-childhood centers: generally one in each of the island state's high-rise housing developments. These have the added benefit of involving grandparents, many of whom live with their grownup "children". Again, one of the best models is Singapore's international Overseas Family School. As covered in later chapters, this is one of the few schools in the world to use the International Baccalaureate "global curriculum" for all grades from age three to senior high school.

From early childhood, children from dozens of nationalities have the chance to learn in a global multicultural environment. They also benefit by the involvement of their multinational parents and grandparents in their education.

The IB's "Primary Years Program" revolves around global and universal themes. These start from age three in pre-kindergarten. Here three-year-olds enjoy dozens of global activities grouped around four themes:

1. Who am I? The central idea: that, as human beings, we have similarities and differences that make us unique.

2. Where do I come from? How are we part of a global family and each family is unique?

3. Once upon a time: how literature is an expression and a reflection of our cultural

Threading large cotton reels or beads (nearing two years) helps develop the grip to hold a pencil

In daily kindergarten activity centers, it's all a matter of balance

heritage—an introduction to classic nursery rhymes, fairy tales and poems.

4. Our best non-human friends: how we share the planet with other species which enhance our lives—and our responsibility towards them.

Youngsters are also encouraged to learn through all their senses, and by spending time each day in different "learning centers": for art, reading (with a choice of books and cassettes), writing (where they develop pre-writing skills at age three and writing at four and five) , math, drama, tactile experiences and a computer center—where they learn both to use the computer as a learning tool and to try out simple software for beginners.

The global themes and learning-center activities continue for four- and five-year-olds:

Four themes in the first-year kindergarten: *Me, my family and friends; All around the world; Stories and rhymes; and What is in my garden?*

Six themes in second-year kindergarten: *The K2 community; Your house, my house; We are the world; Happily ever after (stories about different cultures); Sharing the planet with animals (including how we classify animals into five groups: mammals, fish, amphibians, birds and reptiles); and Sensational senses (how we know ourselves and our world more fully by using and appreciating our senses).*

Three-year-olds at this Singapore school find playing on computers at least as much fun as learning to swim or playing in the school's adventure playground.

Kindergarten principal Rani Suppiah says: "We encourage even very young children to treat computers just like any other learning materials: to be used with all the senses." Wander into the kindergarten computer room and you're liable to find infants from a dozen nationalities learning to become computer literate. There is also at least one computer in each kindergarten classroom. But obviously that is only part of a well-rounded early early-childhood education.

Mexico's private Thomas Jefferson Institute has a very similar early-childhood development program at its three interlinked schools. It offers programs from prekindergarten to senior high school. Each school is bilingual, with half the lessons each day in Spanish and the other half in English. But it is in the schools' early-childhood centers that parents are first brought fully into the learning program—with every child having a thorough psychological examination to identify his or her ideal learning style and talents.

Both parents and teachers are fully briefed by the institute's qualified psychologists, so that together they can tailor programs to cater for each child's unique strengths, while building on overall development. And, like the Singapore international school, students receive the same attention to both individual and group development, as they move through all grades to senior high school. Parents are fully involved in the program throughout, so that home and school reinforce each other.

As today's young students move into primary or elementary schooling, their use of digital technology will also increase: the new discovery, creative and communications tools of the twenty-first century. But it's all balanced in with an overall program of exploration and fun.

A few (but only a few) excellent interactive digital programs also exist for the pre-school years. An excellent one is *BabyWow!* And it can be used with babies as young as twelve months. Simply load the CD-rom on any computer, and your infant can see and play with numbers, colors and shapes on the screen—merely by plonking a tiny hand on the keyboard. Better still, she can learn in a choice of eight languages. And you can learn with her as you play the game and talk about it together. But must obviously be matched by your specific experiences together in real-life learning: spotting and talking about colors, shapes, numbers and animals on your outings.

Kid Pix and *Kid Pix Deluxe* are other fine software programs. But the words of personal-computer pioneer Alan Kay are as valid today as they were when he made them in the 1970s: "Parents ask me what they should do to help their kids with science. I say: on a walk always take a magnifying glass along. Be a miniature exploratorium." xAnd the same exploration-discovery model should be at the heart of all schooling and teaching too—both with and without the use of new digital tools: to turn schools, from the first day to the last, into exciting exploratoriums.

From early childhood to school years, treat every family outing as an 'exploratorium'

Hawaii greets all its tourists with a lei, so why shouldn't school, too, be as welcoming, happy and colorful?

The seven keys to effecive teaching: the proving grounds to reinvent school

This book obviously urges the total transformation of an outdated system of education and schooling. But even without changing the entire system overnight, great teachers, principals and trainers are already showing the wave of the future.

They're doing it by combining lessons from early childhood, brain research, nature, show business, advertising, television, music, dancing, the movies, sports, art and electronic multimedia. Above all they're restoring fun and holistic excitement to the learning process.

Some are doing this brilliantly in "subject classes": using new teaching methods to make it much easier to learn a foreign language or a science unit. And, as we'll show in later chapters, the work of these brilliant teachers can now easily be turned into multimedia "learning tools" that millions of other teachers and students can use. Other trend-setters are doing equally innovative things inside school systems that use a "student-centered" curriculum—and where the teacher's big job is to "turn students back on to learning": to enjoy the fun and stimulation of real education.

Some of the new techniques go by a variety of names. Some carry names that at first may seem strange to most. Like "suggestopedia" and "integrative, accelerated learning".

But the best all combine three things: they're fun, fast and fulfilling. And the best involve relaxation, action, stimulation, emotion and enjoyment.

Says outstanding West Australian teacher and seminar leader Glenn Capelli: "Forget all the jargon. Forget all the big names. What we're really coming to grips with can be summed up in two words: true learning."[1] Says British-born, Liechtenstein-based educational psychologist Tony Stockwell: "We now know that to learn anything fast and effectively you have to see it, hear it, feel it and enjoy it."[2] From our own research around the world, and practice in schools, colleges and business, all good training and educational programs involve seven key principles. As a lifelong learner of any age, you'll learn quicker, faster and easier in any classroom if all seven are organized brilliantly by a teacher who is an *involver*—not a *lecturer*—who, acting as a *facilitator*, orchestrates these factors:

1. **The best learning "state":** including the whole welcoming atmosphere of the classroom;

2. **A stimulating format** of inquiry and discovery that involves all your senses and is relaxing, fun-filled, varied, fast-paced and stimulating;

3. **A process that builds thinking skills,** including creative, reflective and critical thinking;

4: **"Activations"** to access the material, with games, skits and plays, and plenty of opportunity to practise;

5: **Real-life experiences** so students can put it all into practice to "show they know";

6: **Regular review and evaluation sessions;** and with them opportunities to celebrate learning;

7: **A flexible, holographic approach**: the almost intuitive flexibility that all great teachers have—to "seize the moment" and look for the "magic hooks" that "turn students on", rather than rigid, unchangable "steps".

1. The best learning "state"

Not surprisingly, each of those principles works well for an adult in almost the same way it works early in life, when learning develops quickly and easily through exploration and fun.

'To learn anything fast and effectively you have to see it, hear it, feel it and enjoy it'

Why should all the fun and activity disappear after the absorbing years of early childhood?

Orchestrating the environment

Can you imagine a two-year-old youngster learning by sitting still on a classroom seat all day? Of course not. She learns through doing, testing, touching, smelling, swinging, talking, asking and experimenting. And she learns at a phenomenal pace. She is highly suggestible, and absorbs information from everything that goes on around her total environment. But once she gets past kindergarten, too often education starts to become boring. The fun disappears. In many classrooms youngsters are told to sit still, in straight rows, listening to the teacher and not exploring, discussing, questioning or participating.

Good teachers know that's not the best way to learn. So they plan a classroom setting that facilitates easy learning. They use fresh flowers for scent and color. They cover the walls with colorful posters, highlighting all the main points of the course to be covered, in words and pictures—because much learning is subconscious. Students absorb the lesson-content even without consciously thinking about it.

More and more teachers have music playing to establish the mood as students enter the classroom. Many use balloons and swinging mobiles to create an almost-party atmosphere.

"The total atmosphere must be non-threatening and positively welcoming,"[3] says Mary Jane Gill, of Maryland, U.S.A., formerly in charge of staff training for Bell Atlantic. Her techniques on one accelerated learning course cut training time by 42 percent, on another 57 percent. And the first thing they did was change the atmosphere.

Top Swedish teacher, the late Christer Gudmundsson, would agree: "The atmosphere from the time your students enter the classroom must be thoroughly welcoming."[4] And the late Charles Schmid, of San Francisco, California—a world pioneer in new teaching methods—found mood-setting music one of the major keys to achieving learning rates at least five times better than before. "And that applies everywhere, from preschool to a business seminar teaching computer technology."[5]

Liechtenstein's Stockwell—one of Europe's leading new-style trainers in both schooling and business—says the importance of well-designed colorful posters cannot be overstressed when teachers or trainers are planning a "subject" lesson: "Posters should be up around the walls before any learning session begins. They're peripheral stimuli. Their constant presence engraves the content into your memory, even when you're not consciously aware of them." He also says color psychology is important. "Red is a warning color; blue is cool; yellow is seen as the color of intelligence; green and brown have a pacifying effect and are warm and friendly. Never forget that effective posters make a strong impression on the long-term memory. They create memory pictures which can be called on when required although they were never consciously learned."[6]

It's also the kind of lesson that all educational institutions can learn from the best businesses:

❏ The Seattle-based Nordstrom chain of clothing stores is used in dozens of management seminars as a model in profitable service—and it always has freshly-cut flowers in its customer changing rooms.

❏ Every international airline welcomes passengers on board with soothing, calming music—before presenting safety demonstrations.

❏ Visit Hawaii, the tourist capital of the mid-Pacific, on a package tour and you'll soon slip into a welcoming vacation mood as you're greeted with a lei of island flowers.

❏ Visit Disneyland or Disneyworld and you're immediately struck by the cleanliness and total welcoming atmosphere.

Think of that the next time you visit a school or company seminar-room that persists with uncomfortable straight-backed wooden chairs and an atmosphere that is cold, lifeless and often colorless.

Setting the right mood and getting students' attention

Canadian teachers Anne Forester and Margaret Reinhard, in their excellent book, *The Learners' Way,* talk of "creating a climate of delight" in every school classroom. They say variety, surprise, imagination and challenge are essential in creating that climate.

From the coffee shop of this Mexican school you can take in a musical preview

The coffee shop at the Thomas Jefferson Institute's Mexico City campus adjoins the K-12 school's performing arts center and its videotape presentation suite. There visitors can sit in on student rehearsals of Broadway musicals like Wicked (in photo).

Juggling, Jazzercize and left-right activities are great to get both sides of the brain into gear for learning

"Surprise guests, mystery tours, field trips, spontaneous projects (old-fashioned days, pet displays, research initiated by the children) add richness to reading, writing and discussion. The production of plays and puppet shows is stimulated by the children's reading and is masterminded more and more fully by the children themselves. "Your classroom will rarely be totally silent. Sharing and interaction are the vital components of a climate of delight. Discoveries, new learning, the sheer joy of accomplishment demand expression."

Creating that "climate of delight" is the first critical key in setting the right mood for more effective learning.

Early activity is vital

The next key is activity: precisely what students or trainees are encouraged to *do*. The colorful setting, posters and mobiles will already have started to stimulate those who are mainly *visual learners*. The music will have "touched base" with the mainly *auditory learners*. And early activity makes the *kinesthetic learners* feel instantly comfortable. Interspersing these three learning styles also makes sure that all levels and networks of the brain are activated. But there are other good reasons for instant activity:

Jazzercise-type exercises to music encourage an increased flow of oxygen to the brain—and the brain runs largely on oxygen and glucose.

Other exercises to music—such as simple juggling and left-foot/right hand, right foot/left-hand movements—can stimulate instant communication between the "right brain" and the "left-brain" .

Others can loosen students up—mentally and physically: to help them relax. Canadian psychologist and astronomer Tom Wujec covers many in *Pumping Ions—Games and Exercises to Flex Your Mind.*

Other activities can break the ice and help participants get to know each other—and the talents that are available to be tapped, inside and outside the specific setting.

The authors of this book frequently start international seminar sessions with a game of *People Search*. Participants have two minutes to meet as many people as possible—often to the tune of *Getting To Know You*. In two minutes they learn about the tremendous array of skills in the room. They also identify those who may be able to share specialist knowledge.

At England's Cramlington Community High School, which we will meet in chapter 12, all "subject" lessons start with high-participation activities for students to have fun recapping the main points of a previous lesson. All Cramlington teachers have been trained to use digital, interactive whiteboards. So if students in a previous class learned the Spanish names of body parts, at the start of this follow-up class they might play an electronic version of "pin the tail on the donkey". They'll digitally place body-part names on a projector-outline of a human body. It's fun, interactive, ice-breaking, and it quickly rehearses knowledge already learned—to quickly connect with the new lesson. The teachers have even written their own handbook of similar ideas.[7]

Other activities can put you in a positive mood. Australia's Capelli often gets his adult seminar-learners to:

❏ Sit in pairs—with someone they've never met before—and spend forty-five seconds recounting the most interesting aspect of their background; so that each person starts the session by focusing on projects that have been personally successful—reinforcing their ability to learn.

❏ Or massage each other's neck and shoulder muscles to encourage relaxation.

Obviously the techniques will depend on whether you are teaching a regular school class, running a specific-topic seminar, or introducing an international symposium. Eric Jensen, author of *SuperTeaching* and co-founder of SuperCamp, believes two core elements affect learning: they are *state* and *strategy*. The third is obviously *content*. "State" creates the right mood for learning. "Strategy" denotes the style or method of involvement. "Content" is the subject. In every good lesson you have all three.

But many traditional school systems ignore "state". Yet it is the most critical of the three. The "door" must be open to learning before true learning can happen. And that "door" is an emotional one—the "gatekeeper to learning", part of being in a fully resourceful state.

In this Singapore school the 'big picture' for the year is laid out like a corridor TV storyboard

A typical corridor scene that greets visitors to the elementary campus at Singapore's Overseas Family School, displayed like a giant movie or television storyboard.

Music like Vivaldi's *Four Seasons* can establish the right brain wavelength for 'relaxed awareness'

The right brain wavelength

One of the main steps to achieve this is to get everyone working on the "right wavelength". **And here probably the most ironic contradiction occurs: to learn faster you slow down the brain.** One of your brain's "wavelengths" is obviously most efficient for deep-sleep. Another is more efficient for inspiration. And another, the one you're most conscious of: the wideawake alertness of daily living. But many studies now reveal that a fourth brainwave is the most efficient "frequency" for easy, effective learning: what some call the alpha state.[8]

Bring on the music

Dozens of research projects have found that music is a very efficient dial to tune into that alpha frequency. "The use of music for learning is certainly not new," Californian accelerated-learning innovator Charles Schmid told us not long before his death. "Most English-speakers learn our alphabet to music, *The Alphabet song:* ABCD—EFG—HIJK—LMNOP.

"But in the last twenty-five years we've gretly expanded our music knowledge. We've found out that in a special kind of relaxation, which music can induce, our brain is most open and receptive to incoming information. That type of relaxation is *not* getting ready to fall asleep. It's a state of *relaxed alertness*—what we sometimes call *relaxed awareness.*" [9]

Much recent knowledge in this field has been built on the pioneering research started in the1950s by Bulgarian psychiatrist and educator Georgi Lozanov. Lozanov set out to determine why some people have super-memories.

After years of research, he concluded that we each have an "optimum learning state". This occurs, he says, "where heartbeat, breath-rate and brainwaves are smoothly synchronized and the body is relaxed but the mind concentrated and ready to receive new information." [10]

In putting that research into practice, Lozanov achieved some amazing results, particularly in foreign-language learning. By the early 1960s, Berlitz—then the world's largest language-training school—promised students could learn 200 words after several days' training—a total of thirty hours. But Lozanov's research reported Bulgarian students learning 1,200 words *a day* and remembering a remarkable 96.1 percent of them.[11]

Many others have built on his research. According to Schmid: "We now know that most people can achieve that ideal learning state fairly easily—and quickly. Deep breathing is one of the first keys. Music is the second—specific music with a certain beat that helps slow you down: anywhere from fifty to seventy beats a minute."

The most common music to achieve that state comes from the baroque school of composers, in the seventeenth and early eighteenth centuries: the Italian Arcangelo Corelli, the Venetian Antonio Vivaldi, France's Francois Coupertin and the Germans, Johann Sebastian Bach and George Frideric Handel.

Lozanov found baroque music harmonizes the body and brain. In particular, it unlocks the emotional key to a super memory: the brain's limbic system. This system not only processes emotions, it is the link between the conscious and subconscious brain.

As Terry Wyler Webb and Dougles Webb put it brilliantly in *Accelerated Learning With Music: A Trainer's Manual:* "Music is the inter-state highway to the memory system."[12]

Vivaldi's *Four Seasons* is one of the best-known pieces of baroque music used to start the journey along that highway. It makes it easy to shut out other thoughts and visualize the seasons.

In a model New Zealand school, Tahatai Coast, six-year-old children in one class not only created their own computer-animated short story of two children finding a kiwi flightless-bird trapped in a forest trap, they used *Four Seasons* as the background music. And then they computer-animated an orchestra playing it. Finally they added in a brief visual story of Vivaldi's life.

Handel's *Water Music* is also deeply soothing. And for teachers trained in new learning techniques, Johann Pachelbel's *Canon in D* is a favorite to relieve tension. Many teachers also use specially-prepared tapes, CDs and DVDs to start each learning

Handel's *Water Music* is perfect to relax and achieve an ideal state for foreign language-learning

All great sporting coaches start with individual goals: and so should schools

session—with soothing word-pictures to match the music and encourage relaxation. Tapes can be either self-made or bought as CD or online *iPod* tracks. Their key first use in education is to put students into a relaxed, receptive state so they can focus on learning.

Break down the learning barriers

Lozanov says there are three main barriers to learning: the *critical-logical* barrier ("School isn't easy, so how can learning be fun and easy?"); the *intuitive-emotional* barrier ("I'm dumb, so I won't be able to do that"); and the *critical-moral* barrier ("Studying is hard work—so I'd better keep my head down"). Understand where a student is "coming from" and you gain better rapport. Especially in systems where students are bored with old teaching methods: step into their world and you overcome any resistance quickly, smoothly.

Encourage personal goal-setting and learning outcomes

Encourage students to set their own goals—and to plan their own future. If they know where they are going, then their path is focused. *Most people will over-achieve personal targets that they set themselves*—possibly the soundest principle in management goal-setting.

In classroom settings, we both encourage the "Station WiiFM" game—to focus on "What's In It For Me?" Not in a selfish sense, but to get participants, perhaps in pairs, to tell each other and teachers what they specifically hope to get from the session, the day or the year.

The way this is introduced is vital, especially in school. Many at-risk students get very angry with the traditional "You-will-learn-this-today" introduction. Instead, good teachers invite students to set their own goals, right from the outset, and the outcomes they would like from the session.

In the International Baccalaureate elementary-school program, every grade spends six weeks collectively researching one global project. It might be "endangered species", "great inventions" or "the solar system". And their research projects always start off by the students themselves listing their own questions first. And then they set out to find the answers—and record their findings in interesting multimedia ways.

But often students in less interesting environments come with "hidden agendas"—and they don't always "buy in" to the a subject agenda. The key is to make learning a partnership, where the teacher prepares a smorgasbord of possible "curriculum pieces" and the students get a big say in what they want out of it.

Try visualizing your goal

Visualizing is a powerful learning tool. An ineffective teacher might well say: "Don't forget to study or you might do poorly in the upcoming test"—a negative reinforcer.

Eric Jensen suggests two better ways. One is to encourage students to visualize precisely how they would use their new-found knowledge in the future. The other is to plant a positive thought that will encourage students to browse through their study-book looking for specific answers that might be used in the future. We cannot stress this point too strongly: many teachers do not realize how damaging negative suggestions can be.

Trigger the emotions

Nor can we overstress that the emotional part of the brain is the gateway to long-term memory, so all good teaching encourages warm emotions. This fuses what you have been learning into deep memory.

2. The presentation: through exploration and inquiry

Positivity and linking are the first principles

All good presentations must be learner-centered and linked to students' own goals and existing knowledge. The flower is the perfect metaphor: "What does it take to make your flower grow?"

Another technique to guarantee involvement from the start is for the learners and the instructor to toss a squashy, brightly colored Koosh ball to volunteers to tell one main point they already know about a topic, and to draw Mind Maps covering the same points—from a pre-prepared map that lists the main "learning branches". The sequence encourages the learners to start by identifying what they want to know, and

Juggling balls and Koosh balls are ideal as a game to bring out what students already know on the subject

Field trips and video clips can help to show the big picture first before students fill in the details

The ancient pyramids of Teotihuacan, a favorite site for school field trips from nearby Mexico City.

then proceeding from what they already know—generally an amazing amount.

The entire presentation must also be positive. The facilitator should never suggest in any way that the session is anything but fun—no "now the break's over, let's get back to the hard work" talk.

Lozanov called his fast-learning process "suggestopedia," from "suggestology"—but that is a difficult word to translate. Says Stockwell: "The name is rather unusual, but if you see 'to suggest' in the sense of 'to propose' or 'to recommend' then it is easier to understand the relationship."[13]

The power of suggestion is paramount in learning: we all do best when we think we can do it; we fail if we expect to fail. Every adult has seen how infants' learning abilities soar in a favorable, positive atmosphere. All good Lozanov-style facilitators try to recreate the same kind of positive fun-filled atmosphere in the classroom. And like all good advertising copywriters, they go out of their way to stress how easy the project is.

Lozanov stresses the important links between conscious and subconscious presentation. He believes each of us has an enormous reserve of brain power waiting to be tapped. He believes that by far the most important part of all learning is subconscious; and that good teachers remove the barriers to learning by making their presentations logical, ethical, enjoyable and stress-free. Hence the importance of posters and "peripherals" as part of the total presentation: whether those posters are made in advance by a seminar presenter or, in inquiry-based school classrooms, are made by the students themselves.

Getting the big picture first

A major presentation technique is to present "the big picture" first—to provide an overview, like the total jigsaw puzzle picture, so that all the later pieces can then fall into place. Again, posters or other classroom peripherals may well present the big picture—so it's always there as a focusing point.

Telling a story is also a great preview technique.

And field trips are highly recommended at the start of any study—to see the big picture in action. At the "Vivaldi trapped-kiwi story" project we've already mentioned, all classes study four schoolwide projects a year, and all other "subjects" are integrated into them. And if that schoolwide project is, for example, conservation, regular field trips will be held to explore all aspects of the subject. One of their nearby middle schools holds yearly adventure camps, videos all their confidence-building activities, and then uses the finished video to teach other teachers how to edit videos.

Drawing Mind Maps at the start of study, including all the main "limbs", allows students to draw in the smaller branches later.

Involve all the senses

All good presentations also appeal to all individual learning styles.

The most neglected learning style in nearly every school system is kinesthetic—or movement.

Every good learning experience has plenty of verbal stimulation, plenty of music, plenty of visuals—but the really great teachers make sure to have plenty of action, plenty of participation, plenty of movement. Even though students will have different combinations of learning styles, everyone *embeds* new information by *doing: by actually using what they have been taught.*

Step out of the lecturing role

This is probably the major personal change required in teaching styles. All the best "teachers" are activators, facilitators, coaches, motivators, orchestrators.

Always orchestrate "non-conscious" processing

Since Lozanov practitioners say most learning is "subconscious", the room setting, posters, body language, tone of speech and positive attitude all are vital parts of the learning process.

Plenty of role playing and "identities"

Lozanov teachers also encourage students to "act the part". There are few faster ways to learn science than to act out the roles of famous scientists; or to learn history by putting yourself in the historical setting.

After the big-picture, then class study from student-made models to Mayan videos

Elementary school class on pyramids, Mexico City Campus, Thomas Jefferson Institute. They also study the pyramids' history on the Discovery Channel's online network.

All 'subjects' now integrated into global topics in International Baccalaureate programs

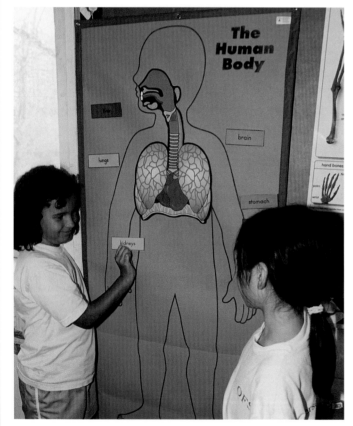

Young elementary students in an interactive art lesson as part of a six-week integrated course on the human body. See also the associated computer-studies photograph opposite.

Organize plenty of "state changes"

In subject-based classes, the best teachers organize plenty of "state changes" so that students switch from singing, to action, to talking, to viewing, to rhyme, to Mind Mapping, to group discussions. This has a two-fold purpose:

1. It reinforces the information in all learning styles; and

2. It breaks up the lesson into memory chunks for easy learning.

Both have a major bearing on how well the information is absorbed. and remembered. For example, it is now well proven that, in any presentation, students can generally remember easiest the information at the start, the end and any "outstanding" examples that gripped their imagination. Regular "state changes" provide the opportunity for many more "firsts", "lasts" and emotion to aid memory.

But in project-based study, students working in teams, and sharing their own strengths with others, generally get too caught up in the action to get bored. And the very act of learning-by-doing, while you learn the talents and skills of other team-members in the process, is stimulating enough.

In the International Baccalaureate global curriculum, which we analyze in detail in the final chapter, its Primary Years Program divides each year into six-week or seven-week global themes. Thus, when students are studying the human body or some other topic for six weeks or seven weeks, every other "subject"—from art to computer studies, math and language—is integrated into that theme. Each part reinforces the rest.

Make learning-how-to-learn a key part of every course

This is probably the main overall desired result from all learning. So the techniques should be blended into all activities.

The Lozanov "concerts"

Possibly Lozanov's greatest contribution to education has again been in the sphere of music: not only to relax your mind and put it into a highly receptive state—but to use music to float new information into your memory system. This is particularly useful when learning detailed information on a new subject—like a foreign language.

Lozanov recommends two *concerts*. And again, Charles Schmid has summarized the theory and practice neatly: "If, say, a class is learning a foreign language, as the first step the teacher sets out the new vocabulary in the form of a play, and with an overview of it in pictures. The student sits there taking a 'mental movie' of it.

"Immediately following this comes the first concert—what Lozanov called the *active concert*. With the student looking at the text, the teacher turns on some selected music, and he reads the foreign language in time to the music. He deliberately acts out the words dramatically in time to the music.

"Now there's no magic to this; it's precisely why it is easier to learn the lyrics of a song, rather than remember all the words on a page of notes. The music is somehow a carrier and the teacher surfs along with the music—almost like catching a wave."[14] Lozanov's second learning phase is called a *passive concert*. Charles Schmid again: "The second concert follows immediately after the first. And here we use very specific slow baroque music—around sixty beats to the minute—very precise. And while the first reading of the language was very dramatic, the second is in a more natural intonation. Now the students are invited to close their eyes if they want—although they don't have to. They put the text aside, and imagine, say, that they are in a theater in the country they're studying, and somebody is acting a story in the background. Generally this will be the last part of a particular language session—and the students will then go home—and probably skim through their foreign-language 'play' just before they go to sleep." Overnight the subconscious goes to work—and the seemingly automatic start of the transfer to long-term memory storage. Lozanov fans claim the use of music in this way can accomplish 60 percent of learning in 5 percent of the time.[15]

We hasten to add that even great Lozanov enthusiasts do not recommend using his full "concert" technique in every session. Even in something as clearly defined as learning a foreign language, perhaps only three "concert" sessions might be held in a week. But all the other key principles of learning would be used in other sessions.

At one of our favorite international primary schools—The Overseas Family School in Singapore—[16] for example, all students spend one hour a day learning a foreign

Computer software on the human body links with art, math, science and foreign language on same subject

Interactive computer software now makes it easy to explore the inner workings of the human body, and many other aspects of biology at Singapore's Overseas Family School.

New technology also helping children with developmental delays in early language learning

A child with early-learning speech difficulties can often be helped by listening to the spoken language recorded on special CDs. In this way, language spoken more slowly and distincly is easier for many children to understand and copy. This method is used extentively at the New Visions School in Minneapolis and at 250 schools around America under the SMART program.

language—with a choice of six: English, Mandarin, French, Spanish, German and Japanese. In three typical classes in one week eight-year-olds might be:

❑ Learning French by presenting a Parisian fashion parade, with their own French-language commentary—and then teaching French to their audience of parents.

❑ Learning the Chinese written language and spoken Mandarin by showing their parents a multimedia presentation, in Chinese, on the best nutrition for learning.

❑ And learning German by staging a German version of *Snow White*.

No need for Lozanov "concerts" here. The students add in their own French, Chinese and German music to their own shows. And now videos of each are on the school's website for others to share.

With the growth of global technology, and extensive music downloading on the Web and though mobile phones, online foreign-language learning is a major growth industry. Colin Rose's United Kingdom company Accelerated Learning Systems, is one that has specialized for many years in producing learn-it-yourself digital language-learning programs based in part on the Lozanov method.

Recorded music and differently-paced language cassettes are also now being used, along with brain-stimulation exercises, to help children with developmental speech problems, at Minnesota's New Visions School and 250 other centers around the United States. Children who find their brains "jumble sounds together" are helped greatly by playing cassettes with slower and more distinct language—under the SMART program (Stimulating Maturity through Accelerated Readiness Training).[17]

3. Thinking about it, and deep memory storage

Education is, of course, not only about absorbing new information. It involves thinking about it and storing it into deep memory as well.

Learning how to think is a major part of every educational program, and good facilitators use "thinking games" and "mind games" to synthesize information—and provide "state changes". In business seminars we've found it best to introduce this by fun projects such as "What if?" game on subjects outside that business.

For deep memory storage, Lozanov's active and passive concerts are tops—specially for storing detailed new information. They are designed to access the long-term memory system in order to link new information subconsciously with data already stored.

4. Activate to draw out the learning

Storing information is also only one part of the learning process. The information also has to be accessed. So the next step is "activation".

And here games, skits, discussions and plays can all be used to "activate" the memory-banks—and reinforce the learning pathways. Again, this needn't make more work for the teacher. The opposite, in fact. Students love to organize their own plays, presentations, debates and games. Give them the chance to present their new information to the rest of the class or group—any way they prefer.

Schmid explains a typical fun-based activation session, after French-language students have slept on a concert-session: "The next morning, or within forty-eight hours, the students come in; they haven't said a word of French yet—or at least not in the new vocabulary. Now comes three or four hours of what we call activation.

"Now we play games with the vocabulary. We're feeding their brains in different ways. We've already done it consciously in showing them the words and pictures of their French play. Then we've fed it into their subconscious, with the aid of music. And now they're activating their brains in different ways to make sure it's stored. And I tell you: now I wouldn't teach in any other way."

Schmid, who died not long after our interview, had degrees in music, psychology and foreign language instruction. He taught at the University of Texas and New York University for years with traditional methods before "getting hooked" on the new techniques. "I started to teach French and German with these new methods; I wanted to see if the system worked, if it really was all it was cracked up to be. And I was amazed. I would teach students in a three and a half hour class. I'd give them 400 words of French, say, the first day. And by the end of the third day they were able to repeat them in forms of conversation. And that had never happened before.

"Recently at a New England telephone company students were using these methods

All types of games, skits, dicussions and plays can help reinforce learning

Examinations?
The real test is whether you can do it and apply it

to study optic fibers and some technical telecommunications work. The trainees were sitting on the floor, playing with wooden blocks, fitting them together and understanding what goes on in an optic fiber. The trainer said: 'OK, it's time for a break.' And the trainees said: 'You take a break; we're having fun; we're learning; and we're getting this finally.' That's what I mean. It works and it's fun."

5. Apply it

In our view, the real test of learning is not a written examination through multiple-choice questions. The key is to use the learning and apply it to purposeful situations, preferably real-life. The real test of a French course is how well you can speak French. The test of a sales course is how well you can sell.

You learn to play a piano by playing a piano, you learn to type by typing, to ride a bike by riding a bike, to speak in public by speaking in public.

So the best teachers and business seminar organizers plan plenty of action sessions to back up the theory so students can purposefully use and apply the learning.

Turn your students into teachers

As in the activation phase, it makes sound sense to have students work in pairs or teams, with a free hand to prepare their own presentations of main points. Groups in a teacher-training class, for example, may each be asked to crystallize a specific aspect of educational psychology. And more and more schools are using the "buddy" system, where an older or more qualified student helps another, and both benefit.

Encourage Mind Mapping

We've already covered the principles of this and suggested you use it to preview the learning, but it is also a remarkable way to review and make notes. *It really is what it says: a map that records main points in the same way the brain stores information— like branches on a tree.* It's also a major tool in the next process.

6. Review, evaluate and celebrate

Even highly efficient learners will not always be conscious of whether they "know what they know". One way to bring the learner to that awareness is through a quick

Koosh-ball throw at the end of a lesson. This will jog students' memories of all the important learnings of the day. Another way is a "passive concert" review, which also covers all the points handled.

And then comes one of the most crucial steps: the self-evaluation. This is where a student truly "digs within" to uncover those precious gems of the day. Self-evaluation is a tool for higher thinking: reflecting, analyzing, synthesizing, then judging. Peer-evaluation and instructor-evaluation are also important parts in culminating a lesson, but the most important is self-evaluation. Another way to review is to skim over your Mind Maps or "highlighted" notes, or both:

❏   Before you go to sleep on the day you've been studying;

❏   For five minutes each morning for the next week.

❏   For five minutes once a week in the following month.

❏   For five minutes once a month for six months.

❏   And just before you need to use it—or before an exam.

If you're on a one-week course with an examination at the end, spend at least fifteen minutes a night on that day's Mind Map and highlights, and at least five minutes on each of the previous days. Or if you're writing an article or even a book, it's amazing how much you can recall by skimming your Mind Maps and underlined books.

And always remember to celebrate every victory—just as any sporting achiever would celebrate. Praise the entire class effort, and whenever possible turn that praise into a recap of the main points learned.

7. Holographic and holistic teaching

We stress, however, that none of these keys to teaching are intended as dogmatic, automatic steps—always in the same sequence. Virtually every teacher in America knows the name of Madelaine Hunter. For years she influenced U.S. schooling by laying down a dogmatic formula for organizing every classroom lesson in exactly the same sequence. But there is no "one best way" of teaching and learning. Different students and teachers learn and teach in different ways. Great teachers use checklists

Not only sporting winners deserve trophies: learning success should also be celebrated

Visually, St. Louis Missouri means its famous arch, but not when its students use all their 'intelligences'

only as guides. And great teaching is holistic and holographic, intuitively changing the sequence and style to tune in to students and switch-on the learning-process.

Transforming an entire school

But how does all this theory work in practice? The answer is "great"—as we summarize in the final two chapters of this book, with models from around the world. But if a school board decided to start with only one of the new theories of learning to dramatically improve its performance, what would it be? The answer could well come from the best working examples of Howard's Gardner's theories.

Here one of the outstanding models is New City School in St. Louis, Missouri. It serves 360 students from three years up to sixth grade. New City is an independent school, in an area that cannot be described as wealthy. Around 33 percent of its students are minorities, mostly African-Americans. Almost 27 percent receive need-based financial aid. Other students come from all parts of the city, with parents choosing the school because of its mission and philosophy.

And that philosophy is very strong. New City is a "multiple intelligences" school. A few years after Harvard Professor Gardner proposed that theory in the 1983 book, *Frames of Mind,* New City principal Thomas R. Hoerr, read it. And, in his own words: "Life has never been the same for any of us."

In that first book, as we've seen, Harvard's Gardner identified at least seven different types of "multiple intelligence": mathematical-logical, linguistic, visual-spatial, musical, physical-kinesthetic, interpersonal and intrapersonal: since increased by naturalist and possibly existential. New City School has been implementing that MI theory since 1988, the second school to do so in America—following the Key School in Indianapolis

Says Hoerr: "MI theory teaches us that all kids are smart, but they are smart in different ways." So Hoerr and his faculty started their quest to bring out that individual talent in all its students, and to expose them all the other flowering talents and learning styles in the school. To the school's principal, "MI seemed to offer another way to recognize the uniqueness of each individual".[18] And not just in students, but in faculty, too. The early enthusiasts formed themselves into a Talent Committee, and gave themselves the task of using all their own "multiple intelligences" in studying each chapter of Gardner's book. Soon the enthusiasm spread, not just to other faculty members but to the students' parents as well.

The school started by using a yearlong, schoolwide theme. And because of the role the Mississippi River plays in their district, they chose *Life Along The River* as the first. Says Hoerr: "The theme was enjoyed by everyone. The synergy of siblings in different grades, talking at dinner or on the way to school about what they had learned about the Mississippi River in their respective classes, was great. And so was the dialog among teachers from different grades as they were trading ideas and talking about how they were bringing the river into their classroom."[19]

But the next year they all opted to concentrate, instead, on one theme for each grade level. For three- and four-year-olds, the theme was *All About Me:* "Who I am and how do I fit within my family and class?" For kindergarten: *Busy bodies*—"How do different systems in my body function?" Second grade concentrated on *All kinds of homes:* "Why and how do people make homes different in their communities." And fourth graders studied *Making a difference:* "What are the characteristics of someone who makes a difference?"

And all faculty, staff and parents soon discovered they *were* making a difference. As faculty delved more into the depths of "multiple intelligences", the more they realized the individual strengths in both students and teachers. And, like other great schools around the world—including those we'll meet in other chapters—that combined faculty-study led to some unusual results.

For a start, the faculty not only shared their own talents and investigations, they set out to share them with the world. In 1994 the whole school produced its first book, *Celebrating Multiple Intelligences: Teaching for Successs.* And in 2000 they followed up with *Succeeding with Multiple Intelligences: Teaching through the personal intelligences.*

In the first, the faculty took the entire Missouri state curriculum and showed how

When St. Louis students researched their history, they found other, much older, arches

America's model for multiple-intellligence schools found every child had a different way to learn

"Kinesthetic students" at the New City School in St. Louis, Missouri. When their teachers wrote two guidebooks on different intelligences, they discovered ways all students can learn through their own individual strengths.

to teach that by concentrating on and sharing the great strengths and talents of each student. And by building on these strengths, all children were able to then learn from the talents of others. That first book set the agenda to achieve that, at every grade level:

❑ How musically-talented students could learn third-grade math or social studies to music—and share that music with others.

❑ How second-graders with visual-spatial "intelligence" could use those talents to learn geography or history—and to share their resulting artwork, sculpture or demonstration-models with others.

❑ How those with great mathematical or logical strengths could use those to learn language-arts.

❑ How those with physical or kinesthetic skills could use those to learn anything—by physically doing something.

But these were not just theoretical experiments. In that first book, the faculty, students and staff pooled an enormous amount of knowledge. Every section of it includes:

❑ *A complete resource guide for teachers.* Not just a great range of books to use, but musical resources, video resources, art examples—and "tools" to develop each of the MI talents.

❑ *Student resources:* a great array of things to do, in class, at home and in the community, to build and share different talents.

❑ *And resources for parents, too:* books they might read, movies they might see together with their children, galleries and museums to visit, music to play, activities to enjoy.

Soon the entire school was buzzing with "multiple-intelligence" activities. Instead of pen-and-paper multiple-choice questions, all students were collaborating to actually demonstrate their multiple talents.

Even now, Tom Hoerr is amazed at how long one-dimensional "IQ" tests have dominated schooling. "Despite the fact that the misuse of tests and test-scores flies in the face of common sense, many people continue to embrace the IQ model, assuming that there is one measure that can assess an individual's intelligence. Of course, we know this is nonsense."

And not just "know": New City School students actually prove it by *showing that they know*. Regularly they demonstrate this by projects, exhibitions and presentations: what the school calls PEP.

But the innovation doesn't stop there.

❏ The faculty have together devised their own "Multiple-Intelligence Progress Report" for each child, on each curriculum subject, but related to how each student specifically demonstrates an ever-widening range of "multiple strengths".

❏ And the exercise extends well beyond school class hours. The school's day officially runs from 8.30 to 3.30. But New City offers a range of services from 7 a.m. to 6.30 p.m.

The before-school program is free, and is staffed primarily by teacher-aids. As many as 150 of the 360 students stay after school for a fee-based Extended Day Program. This is mainly recreational, although a study hall is offered for upper-grade students. And the school offers Talents Classes, all framed around MI, and often taken by parents, teachers and outsiders with specialist talents. The school also offers a ten-week summer holiday program, including a live-in camp.

With 45,000 copies sold of the two faculty-produced books, New City has made its multi-talented learning model available to others. Now, of course, new technology makes it possible to turn such co-creative contributions into online success stories to share with the world, as we will explore in chapters 12 and 13.

New City School is a prekindergarten-to-sixth-grade school. And around the world elementary-school reform has often been easier to achieve than at high school—where, if anything, the need is even greater, and fortunately new models are already emerging.

America's first multiple-intelligence school also shows how diverse talents can combine in teams

When elementary students at the Key School in Indianapolis decided to explore space with their own "mission to Mars", they used each child's own talents as part of the team. And when their "Animators' Pod" reflected on their own journey (above) with one of their teachers, the conclusion: Mission accomplished. Students in the Animators' Pod first made their own space rocket (photo at start of chapter 1) and then planned their space journey. They talked with space scientists at NASA and saw the Disney Imax film, Roving Mars. They wrote their own application for a grant that funded all their computer, video and animation equipment. And they even made clay models of their simulated Mars landing.

> # 'Most American high schools are obsolete, and the system needs to be completely redesigned'

New recipe for secondary school reform: to learn it, do it—in real-life partnerships

Of all schools ripe for reinvention, high schools would lead most lists.

Microsoft Chairman Bill Gates considers America's high schools were designed fifty years ago to meet the needs of another age. He says most are obsolete, and the secondary school system needs to be completely redesigned.[1]

Harvard Professor of Innovation, Dr. Clayton M. Christensen, says the one-size-fits-all textbook-based school is completely outdated. By 2014, he forecasts, 25 percent of high school courses will be delivered mainly online—and by 2019, 50 percent.[2] He says all courses for learning new skills will be available to all age groups in module-units, anywhere, anytime—and all will be personalized to individual learning styles.

But even inside existing structures, much can be done by rethinking the way high schools can work. At its simplest, the alternative can be summarized in one sentence: *If you want to learn it, do it.*

Equally simple: *Start by tapping into students' own inherent interests.* Encourage them to develop their own talents, seek out their own goals, develop their own real-life projects, so that they then find real-life solutions. In this way, most students find it much easier to develop higher-level skills in math, science and other "subjects"— because they relate directly to specific integrated tasks.

Just as simple: *Instead of relying only or mainly on standardized written memory-tests to gain a credential, make sure students "show they know" by completing real-world projects.*

This is not the complete answer, of course. But it crystallizes the core of almost every successful learning experience we can think of. Yet many high-school systems around the world ignore that simple truth. So do many tertiary institutions, with the notable exception of good polytechnics and specialist and research universities.

Fortunately, an increasing number are now putting the "doing" back into learning. Thus they're solving the dropout dilemma at middle and high schools—again, simply because they're connecting learning to real life.

❏   A survey of West Coast high schools in America identifies the key practices that set top-achieving high schools apart from others. Nearly all involve high-quality, rigorous work, most with hands-on practical experience to "show you know".

❏   In Alaska, students from some of America's most deprived "academic" backgrounds have succeeded at high school by setting up and running four successful pilot companies. All have been run by "native Alaskan" students in a state where most of others of their background lag well behind.

❏   In California, more than 200 "school-within-a-school" Partnership Academies have been set up to provide hands-on job experience for students otherwise at risk of dropping out of high school.

❏   In Washington state several school districts have pioneered "project-based", "performance-based" or "applied learning" programs at high school.

❏   And in New Zealand some schools have achieved highly by "using the whole world as a classroom" and working out in "the real world" to put their learning into practice.

The only "surprise" is that the success of this approach should surprise anyone. Says Professor Roger C. Schank, an American authority on learning: "There is really only one way to learn how to do something and that is to do it. If you want to learn to throw a football, drive a car, build a mousetrap, design a building, cook a stir-fry, or be a management consultant, you must have a go at doing it."[3]

There's no secret in this, he says. Parents usually teach children in precisely this way. They don't give a series of lectures to their children to prepare them to walk, talk,

'There is really only one way to learn how to do something, and that is to do it'

For a student whose passion is electronics, working with a circuit board turns him on more than a lecture

climb, run, play a game, or learn how to behave. They just let their children do these things.

"When it comes to school, however, instead of allowing students to learn by doing, we create courses of instruction that tell students about the theory of the task without concentrating on the doing of the task." Throughout history, says Schank, youths have been apprenticed to masters to learn trades. But educators have not found it easy to apply the apprenticeship system to education. "So in its place," he says, "we lecture."

Not only lecture, but, particularly in America, base the entire high school system around "standardized" units of study and memory-based "standardized test scores".

That system is a disastrous failure—and it starts much earlier than high school. As Jack O'Connell, California State Superintendent of Public Instruction, put it in 2004: "Fewer than 10 per cent of Californian high schools have reached optimum levels on state achievement tests. Fewer than half the students who enter the California State University system are proficient in reading and math." [4]

How the best schools succeed

Schools that are already achieving success are generally doing it by changing the archaic present system, not perpetuating it.

In 2004 *The Oregonian,* in Portland, Oregon, completed a survey of high-school achievement. Its conclusion: "Creating a high school that ensures success for nearly every teenager is rare. But it can be done, as shown by the results of a handful of West Coast high schools. These schools get extraordinary results, and they do it without spending more tax money than the schools around them." [5] The newspaper found "plenty of determined principals who have turned their struggling *elementary* school into a star in a couple of years". But overwhelmingly they found high schools failing their students.

Their criteria for success? "The hallmarks of such a school would include a low dropout rate, high student achievement, a high proportion of graduates going to college and evidence that they're succeeding in college. The school would need to enroll enough minority, low-income and special education students to show it was succeeding with them too. And, on campus, students work with a sense of purpose that shows they see a connection between school and their future. Held to that standard, about 99 percent of high schools fall short, according to state achievement statistics and education experts."

Of the key factors the newspaper found in the best schools, two stand out.

1. Captivate students with real-world lessons.

At David Douglas High, in east Portland, Oregon, students can now find classes that match their diverse interests: electronics, Japanese and even golf-course maintenance.

"After David Douglas High paired senior Chris Czupryk with a pathologist, the teen watched him autopsy a man who had died of a massive brain infection. It involved cutting open the skull and examining the swollen brain. Now he can't wait to study microbiology and cytology, and wants to become a pathologist himself."[6]

At the Center for Advanced Learning, a charter school in Gresham, Oregon, students build Web sites, weld furniture, and use defibrillators on mannequins to study information technology, engineering and health sciences. "Students say they shift into overdrive," says the newspaper, "to fulfil the demands of a program that aligns with what they want to do in life."

2. Assign academic work worthy of being showcased.

"At San Diego's High Tech High, students learn by doing ambitious projects: documentaries of World War 1, a public debate on evolution, a working submarine." Every student at High Tech High is involved in producing finished "products" as he or she "learns a living". And in a typical year every graduate of High Tech High went on to college, even though fewer than half have college-educated parents.

Says *The Oregonian:* "Teachers there cover many of the same basics as other schools. But they say students understand and retain the basics better when they're tied to meaningful projects, not dictated in a lecture." Similarly, at high-achieving David Douglas High, "all juniors gather their best essays, research reports, shop projects and other work into a portfolio that showcases their advanced skills. Then they must top

If your passion is nursing, you'll learn more as a hospital understudy than from a lecture

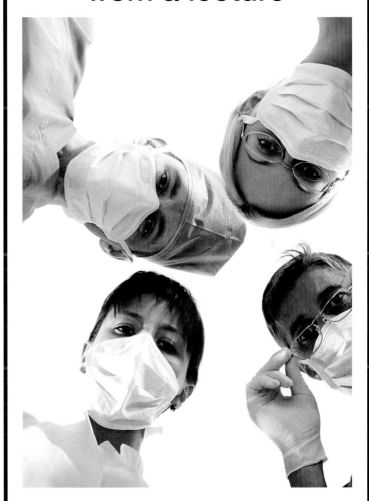

In business-school partnerships, even young students learn with mentors from local industries

it up with a senior portfolio with more elaborate samples. Those get displayed at a 'portfolio' fair for students and parents.

Business-school partnership academies

Other schools are building very specific partnerships with business: some through Partnership Academies. This model originated in Philadelphia in the late 1960s. Now 290 Partnership Academies operate in California. These are linked with more than 500 California employers, in over twenty industries, including health, marketing, international trade, agriculture, electronics, construction, tourism, printing and high-tech manufacturing.

Each is a school-within-a-school. And each is designed to help students who are otherwise headed for failure and probable unemployment or lowly-paid jobs.

In San Jose, Silicon Valley, for instance, the East Side Electronics Academy has been successfully operating since 1985. Based on three schools in the East Side Union High School District, it sets up at-risk students with hands-on experience in the electronics, computer, semiconductor and telecommunications industries. Students work throughout the year with mentors from industry. And they take paid summer jobs for nine or ten weeks in partnership companies. *In a typical year, 96 percent of seniors graduate not only with diplomas but with strong hi-tech work experience.*[7]

Also in San Jose a Biotech Academy has been set up to link Andrew P. Hill High School with some of Silicon Valley's best-known corporations. These companies provide guest speakers, job-shadowing opportunities and field trips. Some offer working internships. Many corporate mentors volunteer each month to work with high school students. Erica Diaz and Miguel Villafana are typical of students who have benefitted. When Erica began high school she did not expect to graduate. "As a freshman, I just thought I was going to be a single mother and at my age—at sixteen!" she recalls.[8] But she flowered in the academy, has since graduated and hopes to become a doctor. Miguel thought he would graduate from high school, but college was not in his plans. Now he's attending San Diego State University and mentoring high school students. Both say their lives were turned around by the hands-on learning methods.

In Minnesota, employers have actually helped design "an MBA for high school students": the Minnesota Business Academy, one of the state's most unusual public charter schools. "Opened in 2000 in the renovated former Science Museum of Minnesota in downtown St. Paul, the ninth-through-twelfth-grade school known as MBA boasts a technology-oriented, project-based curriculum that incorporates a business element in everything from art to English," says a report prepared for the George Lucas Educational Foundation.[9]

"Every school should make the curriculum more practical," says Bob Kaitz, chief executive officer of BestPrep, the privately-funded charitable group that helped MBA become a reality. "A lot of kids don't do well in school because they don't see a connection between what they're studying and what they're going to do."[10] BestPrep conceived the idea of the 480-student MBA and mobilized 150 volunteers from the business and education community to create the school. It helped design the school building and curriculum, and raised money towards the $12 million building and operations startup costs.

Singapore shows the way

In other middle-school and high school systems around the world, students flower when producing real-world results.

Middle school students at Singapore's Overseas Family School each have to complete a specific science project every year and "show they know" in demonstrations to fellow students and parents. Those demonstrations range from making blueprints for rocket models to tracing the history of human exploration.

All 3,500 students at OFS assemble digital portfolios demonstrating all their major abilities; and they also have the opportunity to sit certificate and rigorous diploma examinations to qualify for college entry.

As at all International Baccalaureate high schools, to qualify for a senior IB Diploma, and thus entry to top universities, all senior students have to undertake a major inter-disciplinary project, and report on it. Where needed, they also have to make a working model to accompany their thesis.

At this international Singapore high school, art students balance practical proof with academic study

High school art at Overseas Family School, Singapore.

Washington students build Battle Robots as part of project-based learning movement

Robot Battle is free programming game where players design and code adaptable robots. Players can download several prototypes, then create and program their own: a sound introduction to software programming. Google 'Robot Battle' for background or: wikipedia + robot battle.

Project-based learning takes off

Similar project-based learning is also growing in popularity elsewhere. America's Washington state is one that has recently adopted both "project-based" and "performance-based" learning as the cores of its high school policy.

Some schools there have built these methods into their curriculum for years. Lake Washington is one of the school districts that already has what they call "a culminating requirement" in operation. As with the IB international Diploma, all students to graduate have to produce practical project proof to show what they have learned.

"Because students choose their own projects," says researcher-reporter Diane Curtis, "the nature of their study is as varied as the teenagers themselves. Projects can range from working with real scientists on the Human Genome Project and sharing their experience through video or written reports to writing and producing a play, or building a 'Battle Bot' robot and explaining how it was built and how it works."[11]

One Lake Washington student who suffers from dyslexia conducted research on the disease and then used this information to work with younger boys troubled by dyslexia. Another student created a steam engine out of plexiglass. Another used computer-aided design (CAD) software to design a sailboat.

"Technology should be a natural component of everything students do," says Heather Sinclair, district director of secondary curriculum and staff development for Lake Washington. "It should be a natural tool they use on a day-to-day basis. It shouldn't be something that is scary or contrived. It should be authentic and realistic."[12]

But producing a "culminating project" is not done in isolation. The Washington State Legislature has laid down very rigorous educational goals for high school students: mastery of reading, writing and communications; knowing and applying the core concepts of math, the social, physical and life sciences, civics and history, geography, the arts, health and fitness; thinking analytically and creatively and integrating experience and knowledge to form reasoned judgments and to solve problems; and understanding the importance of work.

But the "culminating project" enables all students to prove how they have integrated all these learning concepts into real-world results.

Start with the hands-on experience

Too many other schools, however, start with "the academics" and wrongly concentrate first on theory and abstract principles.

Seymour Papert, distinguished professor at the Massachusetts Institute of Technology, is one who has long tried to reverse this process. He strongly believes that it's much more effective for students to move from hands-on work to abstract thinking by solving real-world problems. "At the moment, we generally teach numbers, then algebra, then calculus, then physics. That's wrong. Start with engineering, and then from that abstract out physics, and from that abstract out ideas of calculus."[13]

That is exactly what's now being done at San Diego's High Tech High, set up in 1999 in the city's former Naval Training Center. Since then it's built up an excellent record through courses in telecommunications, biotech, computer software, biomedical and electronics manufacturing. Again, all students study math, science, Spanish and integrated humanities while completing hi-tech projects inside and outside the school. The school also serves as a national model for educational entrepreneurship.

High Tech High started as a single charter high school launched by a coalition of San Diego business leaders and educators. It has evolved into a school development organization that is even accredited to train its own teachers in new ways of learning and teaching. And by 2006-7 the movement had grown nationally into seven schools: four high schools, two middle schools and one elementary school.

While the first one started out to "bridge the digital divide", particularly between "minority" students in San Diego, it has done much more than that. All its final-year students have been accepted to college. Around 80 percent have enrolled at four-year universities, including Stanford, Harvard, MIT, University of Southern California and University of California at Berkeley. And the school has proven so popular that each year it gets over 3,000 applications for around 300 slots open in first-year classes.

The school has also reversed a long history of separating technical and academic subjects. And learning-by-doing is the byword here and all the other High Tech High

Software programming and graphic design are part of hands-on High Tech High appeal

The High Tech High model: if students are building a hovercraft, school makes sure it gets off the ground

This hovercraft manufactured in Britain, not San Diego.

Schools following the same model. And they are doing it with similar success.

While all use twenty-first technology as the core catalyst for change, principal and CEO Larry Rosenstock says the main aim is to "stimulate kids to assume responsibility for their own learning" in real-world condition. Says Harvard's Chester Christensen: "The atmosphere is one in which teachers are more like coaches. They rarely lecture. They do always help, guide and evaluate."[14]

And their aim is to ensure that all students leave school with the confidence and competence to keep on learning and with an ethic and drive to produce valuable products and services in the real world. As Rosenstock puts it: the school makes sure if students are building a hovercraft it gets off the ground.

Significantly this also forms the basic guideline for the Singapore's Nanyang Polytechnic, one of the world's most successful. To graduate qualified in any discipline—from robotics to computer-aided product design—students have to produce a working finished product under contract to a major company. And you cannot achieve that unless you have mastered many academic disciplines, including math, science and specific skills.

Setting up school-based companies

Another pioneer in hands-on learning is Mt. Edgecumbe High in Sitka, Alaska.[15]

Its success is all the more remarkable because of Alaska's traditional high school record. In area it's the biggest of the 50 United States—twice the size of Texas. But it has the second lowest population: about half a million people, and only one metropolitan area, Anchorage, with a population as high as 200,000. Its native population is diverse: Caucasian, Eskimo, Eleuts and several Native American Indian tribes. Many are centered around small community towns of only 150 to 200 people, living on extremely low incomes, in a climate where the temperature in winter can reach -17 degrees Fahrenheit or -20 degrees Centigrade.

Hardly a recipe for soaring educational success. And it shows. In Alaska's 2001 high school exit examinations, 78 percent of white students passed in reading, compared with 37 percent of "native Alaskans". In writing: 56 percent of white students;

23 percent of "native Alaskans". In mathematics: 53 percent white to 22.[16]

In a damning 2002 report on Alaskan under-achievement, academics Ken Jones and Paul Ongtooguk are highly critical of the entire U.S. system that relies on testing and test results to determine educational success. Even worse, as Alaskan Natives are passing tests at half the rate of white students, "the students leave their schools for college and are assigned to remedial classes. Faced with paying college tuition to obtain what amounts to a high school education, many of these youngsters soon drop out."[17]

The notable exception, say Jones and Ongtooguk, is Mt. Edgecumbe High School in Sitka. For years it has been the leader in showing how great ideas can stem from other fields—in this case from Japan's quality revolution inspired originally by the American W. Edwards Deming.

TQM (Total Quality Management) and CIP (the Continuous Improvement Process or Kaizen) have been among the main processes used to transform Japan from a devastated, shattered and beaten society into a world economic leader.

Now Mt. Edgecumbe High School has pioneered similar methods for education. It is a "alternative" public boarding school with 210 students and thirteen teachers. Eighty-five percent of its students come from small villages. Most are Native Americans. Forty percent of its students had struggled at other schools. But in recent years the school has achieved one of America's best records for students moving on to higher education and interesting jobs.

In many ways it was transformed by the vision of two people: former Superintendent Larrae Rocheleau and former teacher David Langford. Mt. Edgecumbe was originally opened in 1947 as a school for Native Americans. But in 1984 it was converted into an alternative experimental school, with Rocheleau in charge. One of his first objectives was "to turn these students into entrepreneurs who would go back to their villages and make a difference". Although Rocheleau is now dead and Langford has left for wider fields, their achievements live on as models for high school reform. Among the highlights of the period when they were in charge:

How an Alaska high school copied its revolution from total quality management in Japan

See page 176 for fuller description of Japanese Kaizen.

The high school that sold $500,000 of packed salmon to Japan while learning export marketing

❏ *Teachers and students became co-managers. They set their own targets and goals, individually and collectively. And they evaluated themselves regularly against agreed standards of excellence.*

❏ The first computer course began by teaching speed typing. All students do their homework on a computer, using word processors, spreadsheets and graphic programs to produce 100 percent perfect results—just as their future businesses will demand excellence in typing, spelling, accounting, financial and sales reports.

❏ Students and staff started by drawing up their own "mission statement". Among many other points, it stressed that: "The school places high expectations upon students, administrators and staff. Program and curriculum are based upon a conviction that students have a great and often unrealized potential. The school prepares students to make the transition to adulthood, helping them to determine what they want to do and develop the skills and the self-confidence to accomplish their goals. Students are required to pursue rigorous academic programs that encourage them to work at their highest levels."

❏ *Students decided it was inefficient to have seven short study periods a day, so the school switched to four 90-minute classes. This schedule allows time for lab work, hands-on projects, field trips, thorough discussions, varied teaching styles and in-depth study. The reorganized schedule also allows for an extra three hours of staff development and preparation time each week.*

❏ Because students are viewed as customers, the school tries to provide what they want. Students repeatedly requested more technology, so the school added dozens of computers, and opened the computer lab, library and science facilities at night.

❏ *CIP has prompted teachers to rethink their teaching styles. One teacher says he has changed from being an 80 percent lecturer to a 95 percent facilitator.*

❏ *Because one of the school's goals is to develop "Pacific rim entrepreneurs",* the students set up four pilot "companies": Sitka Sound Seafoods, Alaska Premier Bait Company, Alaska's Smokehouse and Fish Co. and the Alaska Pulp Corporation—all under the umbrella of Edgecumbe Enterprises. The "parent company" started its first salmon-processing plant in 1985, run by students themselves. The goal was to give students the skills and experience needed to run an import-export business aimed at Asian markets. By the 1988-89 year, the company was already making four annual shipments of smoked salmon to Japan, with sales of $500,000.

Each subsidiary company linked hands-on experience with the academic curriculum. So mathematics students calculated the dollar-yen exchange rate. Pacific Rim geography became part of social studies. Art students designed promotional brochures and package labels for products. And business and computer students learned how to develop spreadsheets to analyze costs and project prices.

❏ *All students can learn either Chinese or Japanese, and their curriculum is strong in the history, culture and languages of the Pacific rim, English, social studies, mathematics, science, marine science, computers, business, and physical education.*

And the success ratio? Mt. Edgecumbe's simple goal: to produce quality individuals. Almost 50 percent of all graduates have entered college and are still there or have graduated—much higher than the national average. There have been few dropouts—in a state where dropouts are the norm among native Alaskans.

Integrated studies use the world as a classroom

If Alaska is an unlikely place to start a revolution, the lush, green, heavily-afforested national parks and soaring mountains of New Zealand seem even further removed from the traditional schoolroom. But has now proved an excellent setting for a project introduced at New Zealand's Freyberg High School in the city of Palmerston North.

The Freyberg integrated studies program started in 1986 as a joint venture with IBM (providing computers), Massey University (which supervised the research) and Freyberg. The aim was to use the entire world as a classroom: studying real-life problems in the real-works, linking other "subjects" in with these—and presenting results in computerized reports. Typical projects: one class camping out for a week on a major river, to study its history, geography, and the impact of farming and tourism on the ecology; and replanning the entire city's traffic flow as a project. The initial results, with senior

Tourist river research can be great project for high school study of ecology and environmental impact

From America's Cup luxury yachting to teaching students to create new industries based on 3D design

New Zealand is basing a series of new three-dimensional software industries on its world success in high-cost America's Cup racing: twice winner and twice runner-up in the global competition. Its early success led to the development of 3-D graphic software to televise such events, then to creating a major export industry building luxury yachts at up to $70 million each. One of the major New Zealand 3-D design companies, Right Hemisphere, then built a multi-million-dollar business largely on a unique 3-D system now used in by the world's leading aircraft and aerospace industries. Now Right Hemisphere and the New Zealand Government have formed a joint-venture partnership company, NextSpace, to involve educational institutions and companies in building new export industries with a $1-billion-year sales goal.

high school students, were outstanding. When sitting straight subject-examinations in their senior year, students scored 10 to 15 percent above the national average.

High school business courses

In another highly successful New Zealand innovation, Onehunga High School in Auckland has become the country's first to set up its own business school. Students have flocked to enroll and learn real-life business skills: one of the most popular innovations in an innovative country.

Like the Freyberg project, Onehunga's business school started as a three-way partnership between the school itself, the University of Auckland Business School and New Zealand entrepreneur Tony Falkenstein, a former student of the high school. Falkenstein's Just Water company kicked in $200,000 for financial underwriting. And, when the company floated publicly, it donated the equivalent of $US750,000 ($NZ1 million) in stock to the high school, and the same amount each to the university and Auckland's Business School and the Unitec Institute of Technology. Since then the value of the stock has doubled. And Auckland University provides scholarships for the top-scoring students to study business.

Another Auckland project questions whether moving straight from high school to college is the best route for all interested in hi-tech jobs. The Media Design School takes all its new students at age 20 or over—after they have had at least two years' job experience. Then those who may have worked as juniors in the TV, movie or advertising industries come back to school with a specific vocational goal: graphic designer or artist, computer animator, digital games developer or in the movie industry. And because they know specifically what they want to do, they qualify in about third of the normal time. Over 95 percent have jobs lined up before they graduate, and the rest soon after. This compares with a 35 percent university dropout rate in New Zealand at the end of year one 50 percent by the end of the second year.

But how can the entire system be transformed?

So is there a need for a complete rethink of high schooling? Bill Gates is in no doubt. "America's high schools are obsolete," he told an American National Educational Summit on High Schools. "By obsolete, I don't just mean that our high schools are broken, flawed and under funded—though a case could be made for every one of those points. By obsolete, I mean that our high schools—even when they're working exactly as designed—cannot teach our kids what they need to know today. Training the workforce of tomorrow with the high schools of today is like trying to teach today's computers on a fifty-year-old mainframe. It's the wrong tool for the times.

"Our high schools were designed fifty years ago to meet the needs of another age." And, echoing one of the major themes of this book, Bill Gates added: "Until we design them to meet the needs of the twenty-first century we will keep limiting—even ruining—the lives of millions of Americans every year."[18]

In Bill Gates' view, this is not by accident or a flaw in the system: it is the system itself that needs to be changed.

And Harvard Business School Professor Clayton M. Christensen says most countries are tackling the change in completely the wrong way. In his new book *Disrupting Class*—subtitled *How disruptive innovation will change the way the world learns*—he says school leaders are being asked to do the impossible. He likens this to expecting the captain and crew of a modern giant jet passengers to fly it across the Pacific or Atlantic while rebuilding the aircraft in full flight.

Christensen has a world reputation for analyzing the disruptive technologies that transform entire industries. And he argues that no industry has been able to reinvent itself inside its existing structure. The big breakthroughs that are transforming the rest of the world are coming either from:

❏　Completely new innovative companies, like Nokia, Vodafone, Google, Apple, DoCoMo and many others—not locked into total existing structures and systems;

❏　Or from completely separate divisions set up in existing companies: like Toyota with its new hybrid car division, or IBM when it introduced its personal computer.

So how might the new Web 2.0 disruptive innovations help reinvent education? What makes the twenty-first century so different, and how should high schools reflect this? Can that change take place in isolation? Or is it really possible—as this book

'Public schools have been required to do the equivalent of rebuilding an airplane in mid-flight'

When a kindergarten student can program robots with help from MIT's MediaLab, what else is possible?

At Mexico's world-leading Thomas Jefferson Institute, a kindergarten student learns to program Scribbler robot software, one of the great new learning-tools developed by the Massachusetts Institute of Technology's MediaLab. At elementary school, he will be working with methods learned at one of both Microsoft's and Apple's model schools of the new century. And at high school he will take the Harvard Business School's business program. **Read the full details in the final part of this book.**

argues—that "a new renaissance" is about to trnsform "education" globally?

Are we correct in arguing that the new world of *Google, Facebook, YouTube,* the *iPod* and Nokia is already creating a new planet-changing paradigm that will transform schooling more than the invention of the mass-produced book—and demand for universal literacy—did over three hundred years ago?

The challenge, we believe, will be resolved only by recognizing another main theme of this book—the vital difference and interconnection between:

❏ **Individual talent.**

❏ **Information and knowledge.**

❏ **Skills**—and the ability to learn new ones continually throughout life.

❏ **Interactive technology** and its ability to both globalize and personalize.

❏ **Instant communications**—everywhere, including the developing world.

❏ **Co-creativity**—and the new-found ability to share the world's best learning methods with the planets' two billion poor people.

❏ **Individual learning styles** — as unique as our fingerprints.

❏ And the ways these can combine to redesign systems that put each one of us in charge of our continuous learning process.

Those systems will include great early-learning centers, schools, colleges and universities—but they will also take full advantage of the new renaissance tools.

So are specific new *disruptive innovation models* emerging? The answer: a resounding *Yes.* They come, in part, from newly-created schools as diverse as California's High Tech High, Mexico's Thomas Jefferson Institute, Singapore's Overseas Family School, several of its fellow International Baccalaureate schools around the world, Canada's Master's Academy, many new-type schools in countries as diverse as New Zealand, Britain, China and Sweden, and some of the world's top research universities.

We highlight their success stories in the final part of this book. Then tackle the far bigger challenge: the way the new Web 2.0 revolution provides both the instant and interactive digital tools to share their success with all.

Part four
Revolution 2.0

To cater for demand, the world would need to complete one new university every week for next ten years

How to the new Open Web will anchor the emerging cyberspace learning era

From Google to *iPod* and *iTunes*—mobile TV-phones to the supersonic speed of fiber optics—the future is racing nearer. Revolutionary new technologies are emerging as catalysts to reinvent education. The challenges are enormous. But the world's leading research universities and many of their brightest graduates are tackling them with the same imagination and drive that has already changed everything else.

❑   Eighty million students now attend the world's 8,000 universities.

❑   Another 30 million are qualified to enter but can't gain places.

❑   On present trends, university student numbers will increase by at least 80 million over the next decade.

❑   *To cater to that number, the world would need to complete one new university every week for the next ten years.*[1]

❑   At least 125 million children never get to school at all. Hundreds of millions more get next to no schooling—in a world where 1 billion people live on under $1 a day and another billion on under $2 a day. And half the world's population is under 25 years of age—mainly in poor nations.

"In most of the world, higher education is mired in a crisis of access, cost and flexibility," says the former head of Britain's Open University, Sir John Daniels. "The dominant forms of higher education in developed nations—campus-based, high cost, limited use of technology—seem ill-suited to address global needs of the billions of young people who will require it in the decades ahead."[2]

Even in the world's most affluent country, *Time* magazine highlights another major problem: "American schools aren't exactly frozen in time, but considering the pace of change in other areas of life, our public schools tend to feel like throwbacks. Kids spend much of the day as their great-grandparents once did: sitting in rows, listening to teachers lecture, scribbling notes by hand, reading from textbooks that are out of date by the time they are printed. A yawning chasm (with an emphasis on yawning) separates the world inside the schoolhouse from the world outside."[3]

Time headlines this cover-story: *How to bring our schools out of the 20th century.* It's actually worse: most schooling remains the only "industry" based on a system designed before the last century, even before the industrial revolution—a system based around classrooms, teachers, chalkboards, textbooks and desks.

But even a glimpse at two large nations highlights the way in which the current education debate is about very limited alternatives:

❏ **The United States of America: over 300 million people.** Its research universities are overwhelmingly the best in the world: leaders in creativity, Nobel Prizes, and the ability to turn student innovation into new world-changing products and ideas. But with a poorly-performing public school system. Yet the political debate is generally about "standardized test scores"—with success measured only by the ability to memorize textbook facts.

❏ **India, with a population of 1.1 billion.** Now with 300 million of those in an affluent middle class. Their millions of children also cram textbook facts seven nights a week—with the final 180,000 test-ranked "survivors" then competing in exams for only 3,500 places available each year in India's seven high-quality Institutes of Technology. At the other extreme, 70 percent of India's poor families remain locked into the "informal" no-wage economy, most wracked by poverty. Forty million Indian children never get any schooling, and 65 million are so undernourished their future learning ability is severely impaired.[4] Almost half its villages don't have a school.

Yet India's achievers have made it possible for that country to take advantage of

Imagine a country with one billion people where almost half the villages don't even have a school

We can now carry on a few fiber-optic strands a thousand times more messages than all wired technologies

the best new technology breakthroughs to bring its new hi-tech cities, like Bangalore, into world leadership.

So let's reframe the debate by seeing how those new breakthroughs could help provide a new infrastructure-platform to educate everyone:

❏ **The new world of fiber optics:** the ability to carry—on a few strands of glass fiber one-tenth the thickness of a human hair—a thousand times more information on one path than all the world's traditional wireless technologies put together.[5] For the first time in history, we now know both how to store all the world's information, in almost any form, and transmit it on demand to almost anyone—free, or next to free.

Says digital technology expert George Gilder: "When anyone can transmit any amount of information, any picture, any experience, any opportunity, to anyone or everyone, anywhere, at any time, instantaneously, without barriers of inconvenience or costs, the transformation becomes a transfiguration."[6]

❏ **The new era of wireless:** where Albert Einstein's brilliant explorations into photons,* the speed of light and quantum physics are at last merging into new photonic and multi-channel wireless technologies.

Thomas Friedman, in The Earth is Flat, calls the emerging wireless and associated breakthroughs "the communications revolution on steroids"—ready to take off spectacularly.

❏ **Today's other new era of low-orbit earth satellites:** hundreds of them sweeping across the skies at 27,000 kilometers an hour between 500 and 1,400 kilometers above the earth, and transmitting information at low cost.

China has already installed satellite dishes and computers at 70,000 schools in remote regions, with distance learning programs to cater to tens of thousands of children—and to retrain teachers in new methods of learning.[7]

---

* A quantum is the smallest unit of energy—and a photon is a quantum of light: at least 10 million times smaller than the smallest atom. Photonics is the science best known for the way in which it can take the same light emitted by a flashlight and, by organizing it into coherent quantum vibrations, boost its laser power enough to slice through steel or send millions of messages a second across oceans—or through the atmosphere.

❏   **The almost unlimited bandwidth of these converging technologies:** fiber optics, wireless and LOE satellites.

Gilder's book, Telecosm, is subtitled: "How infinite bandwidth will revolutionize our world." He dubs the convergence as "new technologies of sand, glass and air" that will soon have a total carrying power at least a million times larger than the total global networks of 2000.

❏   **The new computer era—the mobile "teleputer":** the computer-phone in your pocket—based on the mobile phone and video-screen, but now surpassing both them and the PC in power and multimedia scope.

Already 3.3 billion mobile phones are in use: more than twice the 1.4 billion personal computers. By late 2009: at least 4 billion— each with the computing power that cost millions of dollars only a few years ago.

Instant wireless technology also makes it easy to link hundreds of millions of teleputers to television consoles and village-based screens—and to link even the world's poorest villages into a global learning Web.

Visionary educators are already well down the road to bring that dream to life: to create a Global Cyberspace Interactive Learning Web—which everyone can access, anywhere, any time. Not only to access it—but contribute to it.[8]

And if you think that is utopian daydreaming, think again. Many of the steps to achieve that goal are outlined in an eighty-page report released in early 2007 by the Hewlett Foundation—based on a five-year, $68-million research project funded from the estate of one of Silicon Valley's co-founders, Bill Hewlett of Hewlett-Packard.

The report is available free at *http://www.oerderves.org* for instant down-loading. It bears the modest title: *A Review of the Open Educational Resources (OER) Movement: Achievements, Challenges and New Opportunities.*[9] But it is much more than that.

It outlines the infrastructure needed to build that Global Cyberspace Learning Web and make it work. The final four chapters of this book spell out how this could evolve—and how the concept has the power to change education more than the original invention of schools and textbooks.

The other face of Asia: in a world that now has 3.3 billion mobile phones, China has over half a billion

A decade ago we had never heard of Google; now it answers almost any question in half a second

Some keys to create this reinvention are already obvious. One can be summarized in a word: *Google.* Yet that term didn't exist as recently as 1996. It was invented a year later by two young university students: one born in Russia, one America.* Today the company Sergey Brin and Larry Page co-founded in 1998 is valued at an incredible $150 billion.

Now Google provides by far the world's most-used Internet search engine. Well over 300 million people visit it every day to ask for information: more than 200,000 inquiries every minute. And it takes less than another half second to scan billions of pages of information and images to find and rank answers.

But the Google key has barely nudged the door open, even though it is already much more than an information-and-image "search engine":

❏ **Google Language Tools** instantly translate anything into a choice of 115 languages.

❏ **Google Scholar** makes millions of university research papers and their abstracts available for study.

❏ **The Google Library Project** is digitizing millions of books stored in some of the world's biggest university libraries.

❏ **Google Maps** let you zero in on virtually any site in the world and in some countries already provide instant driving maps on demand.

❏ **Google News** continually scans 4,000 news sources and provides summaries—personalized on request: From *the news* to *my news.*

❏ **Google's YouTube**—a Web 2.0 concept that didn't exist even two years ago—is now at the heart of the online video revolution, with millions of amateur producers sharing their talents.

❏ **Froogle**—Google's online e-commerce directory.

* In 1997, Stanford University students Brin and Page decided their prototype Backrub search engine needed a new name. After days of brainstorming, Page suggested Googolplex, after "googol"—a math term that means the number 1 followed by a hundred zeros. Fellow student Sean Anderson suggested shortening it. Page typed "google.com"—with incorrect spelling—into a primitive search engine and immediately registered it.

❏ **Google Gmail** provides a free personal email service with storage space 500 times greater than Microsoft's Hotmail.

❏ **Google Video** is an e-commerce site for video sales.

❏ **Google** is also a dictionary, thesaurus, phonebook, weather forecaster and instant menu-maker on demand. All that from a company under ten years old.

Even Google CEO Eric Schmidt admits "we don't know what is coming". But when asked to guess, he says: "I personally believe the right model is to think of all the world's information in the equivalent of an Apple iPod. What happens when you are carrying all that information with you and there is a real-time update? What does it do to teaching when every student can do the answer quicker than any professor can get it out of her mouth?"[10] Now his own company, with its Android software, is about to offer all Google's services free to any cellphone manufacturer.

So we're talking about a new world where *information* is available virtually on demand—in virtually any form, and free. So the teachers' role as mainly a purveyor of up-to-date information is changed forever.

But *information* is only part of the new equation. *Communication* is much more important to our humanity than computing or other tools. Says George Gilder: "Communication is the way we weave together a personality, a family, a business, a nation and a world. The *telecosm*—the world enabled and defined by new communications technology—will make human communications universal, instantaneous, unlimited in capacity, and at the margins free."[11]

Experts say the Google breakthroughs to date represent no more than 5 percent of what will come in online "search" in the next decade.[12] The other 95 percent—co-created by millions—will transform the world, and education, more than anything else in history: spurred by what some are calling the second coming of the Internet: Web 2.0. Google itself says it has tapped no more tan 2 percent of the search-future.

And if two young university students can achieve Google's current results in under ten years, what can the combined talents of 59 million K-12 schoolteachers, 2 billion students, 3.5 million university faculty and 80 to 180 million university students achieve

'The telecosm will make human communications universal, instant, unlimited and free'

Yesterday students learned <u>about</u> science; now they can actually <u>become</u> a scientist, in lab and online

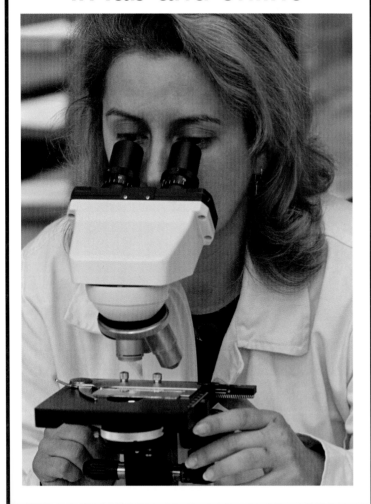

if working together as producers, co-creators and learners? The revolution, as we've suggested, has seven keys to open the lock:

1. It's GLOBAL

No one suggests abolishing the world's existing schools and universities. We're sure they'll continue. But not as expensive buildings occupied only five or six hours a day, five or six days a week, for under forty weeks a year. And not with systems designed over 250 years ago, when the new "blackboard" was "state of the art" and pencils were unknown.

Almost certainly, they'll become open-any-time hands-on community centers for lifelong learning—in partnership with cyberspace learning programs and specialist local coaches, mentors and skilled teachers. But, according to the Hewlett Foundation, the big over-riding global opportunity can be summed up simply:

❏ *To merge the combined abilities of the world's most passionate and talented innovators into a new Global Cyber Learning Center, co-created by all, available to all, of any age, at any time, and regularly updated and expanded by all—in all languages.*

Instead of same-place, same-time learning in a school or university, this proposed Global Cyber Learning Web could provide anywhere-any time learning tools for everyone, everywhere.

That recommendation is the most important to emerge from the worldwide research program funded by the William and Flora Hewlett Foundation. Its initial Education Project started in 2002 with a simple but challenging aim: "How to catalyze universal access to—and the use of—high-quality academic content on a global scale".   But it soon became clear that the task must involve much more than "academic content". In a world of constant change, one challenge is to lift "education" away from simply memorizing old "content".

New technologies also make it possible, for the first time, for millions of people to learn not merely <u>about</u> science, biology, music, drama, history, chemistry or computer animation. But to actually <u>become</u> a scientist, biologist, musician, playwright, any *character in history, a research chemist or an expert in computer animations.*

And to share those results with others around the world so millions can be involved in the co-creation process: to create a platform that is, at the same time, personal, interactive, global, instant, free or nearly free, easily shared and co-creative. The additional challenge: to achieve that in ways that finally solve the appalling divide where at least half the world's population is locked out of quality education.

To evaluate its research, the Hewlett Foundation then engaged three of America's best creative minds and highly respected scientists, each personally involved in major aspects of the Web 2.0 challenge:

❏ **Daniel E. Atkins,** Director of the Office of Cyberinfrastructure, U.S. National Science Foundation, and a Professor of Information, Computer Science and Electrical Engineering at the University of Michigan, which is also prototyping new alternative learning centers.

❏ **John Seely Brown,** former Director of the Xerox Palo Alto Research Center (PARC) in Silicon Valley, which in the 1970s invented nearly every aspect that became the personal-computer revolution.

❏ **Allen Hammond,** Vice President, Special Projects and Innovation at the World Resources Institute, which has recently completed a major report on *The Next Four Billion:* on practical programs to lift the poorer two-thirds of the world out of poverty by new skills and productivity.

Their report provides scores of practical examples to create the proposed *Global Open Cyber Learning Web*. It is recommended reading for every government and education system planning the future. And its excellent and extensive research-links provide detailed examples of how everyone everywhere could benefit, especially in developing nations.

2. It's PERSONAL

Among the linked sources, John Seely Brown provides an excellent summary of *New Learning Environments for the 21st Century.*[13] First, he stresses the importance of

Why shouldn't the 'next four billion' have the same educational chance as the rest?

In the lifetime of many people alive today, our concept of literacy was framed by the power of the typewriter

switching the focus from "education" to lifelong learning and the continual upgrading of personal skills.

"Today's students," he says, "want to create and learn at the same time." They want to take truly interactive templates and use them immediately. They are collaborative learners.

The Hewlett Report wants a world where learners anywhere —at any age—engage in "experimenting, exploring, building, tinkering and reflecting in a way that makes learning by doing and productive inquiry into a seamless process".

As the Gallup Organization's research shows, everyone has a talent to be good—and perhaps great—at something. And the new era of interlocking global networks now make it much easier to share one's talents with others—both freely and as the basis for new careers.

"Technology by itself is seldom if ever the solution," says Brown. The former Xerox Corporation Chief Scientist says Web 2.0 also provides the first medium that can honor the notion of multiple intelligences. "The last century's concept of literacy," he says, " grew out of our intense belief in text, a focus enhanced by the power of one particular technology, the typewriter. It became a real tool for writers, but a terrible one for other creative activities such as sketching, painting, notating music, or even mathematics. The typewriter prized one particular kind of intelligence, but with the Web we suddenly have a medium that honors multiple forms of intelligence: abstract, textual, visual, musical, social and kinesthetic. As educators, we now have a chance to construct a medium that enables all young people to become engaged in their ideal way of learning. The Web affords the match we need between a medium and how a particular person learns." [14]

But this is only part of the educational debate that is needed. As *Time's* cover story puts it: the real debate is "the one that will ultimately determine not merely whether some fraction of our children get 'left behind' but also whether an entire generation of kids will fail to make the grade in a global economy because they can't think their way through abstract problems, work in teams, distinguish good information from bad or speak a language other than English."[15] Most of the existing debate, of course, is conducted by adults. But motivated young students themselves are now among those most fitted to reinvent the world of the new co-creative age. This is simply because—in a society where schooling takes up no more than 20 percent of waking time—they live most of their day in the new world of *iPods, PlayStations, YouTube,* mobile phones, and multi-player digital games.

3. It's INTERACTIVE

Brown stresses the need for all learning to be interactive. He says most older adults don't appreciate the brilliance of what he calls "serious games" that enable today's "digital natives" to actually simulate real-life and creative experiences.

One of Brown's predecessors as a Director of PARC, Robert Taylor, grasped the importance of the same concept early in his postgraduate life in the 1960s, when he worked selling flight simulators to the military. "What caught his attention here was the tremendous power of information delivered interactively. You could teach pilots from books and theory until your voice gave out, but find a way to place their hands on a joystick and their eyes on a simulated landscape, and it was as if they were learning everything for the first time." [16]

Significantly, Taylor headed up PARC throughout most of the seventies when his hand-picked team of computer-scientists together conceived the personal computer. All its components were based on the simple interactive concept: if you can both see it and do it, you'll learn much faster. The new click-move-change-create-and-play era was born.

Most senior adults think of games as old-type hobbies and pastimes: card games, board games, dice games. But, in the new age of digital learning games, millions of online players can now design and co-create new cities—in *SimCity;* or invent ideal new societies—in *Civilization.* Now some of American's top science universities are designing game formats and templates to teach any subject by active participation.

The Hewlett Report mentions several. But *Immune Attack* is an ideal example: a game that models the human immune system. Funded by the Federation of American

Now your keyboard can access email, encyclopedias and the ability to make music and edit video

With trains so packed, the Japanese banned talking on cellphones, so their students invented texting

Scientists and produced by Brown University and the University of Southern California, the game lets students actually control immune cells, battle disease and solve infection problems—as if inside the cells.

"Another example of 'getting a feel for' a subject-domain involves new deeply immersive 3-D visualization of protein-folding that allows students to walk inside a protein and to touch and explore proteins." [17] Not long ago, says the Hewlett Report, this required millions of dollars of computing. But now, by using cluster computing and a set of Nvidia game boards, these visualizations can be rendered cheaply in real time.

But you don't have to be a university science team to produce such new learning tools. In New Zealand, children as young as five, in three-day school holiday programs, learn to produce 3D computer animations, design templates and create their own digital games. [18]

4. It's INSTANT

Every one of the world's 1.4 billion computer-users already connected to the Internet knows how easy it is to gain instant access to information through Google, Yahoo and other search engines. Billions more will soon have the same access through mobile teleputers: the combined PC-phone-and-video network in your pocket.

"From a small base, the number of mobile phone subscribers in developing countries grew more than fivefold between 2000 and 2005, to reach nearly 1.4 billion. The fastest growth was in sub-Sahara Africa, to a total of nearly 77 million. Nigeria's subscriber base grew from 370,000 to 16.8 million during those five years, while the Philippines grew sixfold to 40 million." [19] But now the global number has soared to more than 3.3 billion in 2008, soon to be four billion.

But the most spectacular lesson of how new wireless, mobile phones can change the world—and education with it—comes from Japan. It can be summed up in one word: DoCoMo.* Here is a mobile phone company that has gone from virtually zero

** DoCoMo: an abbreviation of **Do Co**mmunications **O**ver the **Mo**bile Network, but the Japanese word dokomo also means "everywhere".*

in revenues in the late 1990s to $45 billion a year, profits of $7 billion —and a stock-market value over $400 billion: more than double Google's.

But it's done it like no other cellphone company: by capturing the passion of millions, linking them direct from mobile phone to the Internet—and into online social communities. With patented *iMode* technology, years ahead of the rest of the world, DoCoMo went from scratch to 30 million users in two years. Now more than 50 million Japanese use it for Internet access, banking, shopping, digital photography and a big range of directory services—from restaurant bookings to movies. It's done it by tapping into the same kind of philosophy that we believe applies to great teaching methods: with passion, emotion, fun and interaction. Every foreigner who has spent time in Japan is fascinated at the contrast between formal and social behavior. In business hours, Japan seems one of the most formal of all societies. Away from the office at night: the world's biggest entertainment-expense budgets.

Japan is also home to the world's biggest digital-games creators, with names like Nintendo, Sony *PlayStation* and *Hello Kitty*. And entertainment and games like *Karaoke, Pokemon* and *Sudoku*. With 127 million people packed into an island country the same size as New Zealand, housing space is small, commuter-trains crowded. So much so that speaking on mobile phones is banned on most train trips. Somehow DoCoMo has linked all these factors—with fun, games and texting the national travel pastimes. And, as in China, learning English by mobile phone is highly popular—specially when it's karaoke-type fun.

5. It's FREE—or nearly free

The overwhelming weight of the Hewlett Report, however, is thrown behind the concept known as *open source,* or *open standards*. This is the grassroots movement where thousands of students and learners actually combine in cyberspace to produce complex new digital programs. The results are available free—for further development by volunteers. And this output provides open standards that are easy to share.

The core examples read like a manual for Web 2.0—open-source computer programs so good they have already transformed the world:

Karaoke is Japan's gift to entertainment, but also now one of the great ways to learn a language to music

How China slashed laptop prices by 90% through the benefits of open-source sharing: downloading OS* free

* Computer operating system, such as Windows or Mac OS.

❑ **The World Wide Web**—free and used by everyone with access.

❑ **Linux** open-source computer operating systems —used by Google as the base for the world's biggest installation of 175,000 computers.

❑ **Apache** software, now used in 70 percent of the world's computer Web-servers, including IBM, Amazon and Google.

❑ **Java** —a common software language that enables all computers of whatever type or brand to communicate without expensive software.

❑ **Firefox** free Web browser—also created collaboratively.

❑ **Open Office** (the alternative to Microsoft Office's top-selling three programs)— downloadable free by anyone.

But "free" as in *free speech* and *free standards,* not as *free cookies.* "Open source" means sharing and co-creating *open standards:* like the alphabet, dictionary, grammar and syntax form the open standards for languages. This doesn't stop anyone improving or adding to their language, or creating and selling their book or dictionary. This, of course, is what research universities and scientists have always done until recently: share freely the results of each others research, build on it, and add improvements to the common pool.

Google is a classic example. Even its original logo was designed using *GIMP,* the open-source alternative to *Photoshop* basics. Not only is Google's computer system based on co-created, open-source components, it gives away most of its searchable information completely free. But, like Yahoo, it earns millions of dollars a day providing low-cost linked access to related products and services.*

6. It's EASILY SHARED

The new open-source movement also typifies the learning benefits of sharing one's talent in new social communities.

For it does more than invent computer systems and software. It also enables young computer-science students to actually *become* computer and software designers: in new

* Google's "business model" is dubbed by John Battelle, in his book The Search, as "a mechanism to make a billion dollars one click at a time".

real-life learning communities. What better way to become a computer or Web software designer than to actually design software, in partnership with worldwide teams? The total concept is also one incredible step forward in making the best computer and Web software available to the developing world. Instead of 1 billion PC operating systems and 1 billion sets of *Office*-type programs being bought for 1 billion computers, alternatives can be "stored" on the Web—and downloaded free or at low cost on demand. This is how China, in 2003, was able to reduce laptop prices by 90 percent.

Wikipedia provides another excellent example: the world's biggest encyclopedia, written and added to daily by people who are passionately knowledgable about their subject. And available free to anyone on demand, so far in seventy-five languages, and growing.

The Hewlett Foundation, with support from many major world institutions and universities, wants to extend that concept into the entire field of curriculum design and lesson-plan sharing.

Probably the biggest single university contribution has come from the Massachusetts Institute of Technology, with its Open CourseWare (OCW) Project, launched in 1999 under the leadership of MIT President Emeritus Charles M. Vest, with Dr. Anne Margulies as Director.

Dr. Vest's 2006 summary of the MIT initiative is called Open Content and the Emerging Global Meta-University*—and is one of dozens linked to the Hewlett Foundation open-source report.

In it, he addresses four questions to university leaders in pondering the challenges posed earlier in this chapter:

❏ What is the appropriate use of "educational technology" in teaching, learning and scholarship?

❏ What will be the nature of globalization in higher education?

❏ Will the Internet fundamentally reshape higher education?

❏ Are residential colleges and universities dinosaurs or the wave of the future?

* http://www.educause.edu.apps/er/erm06/erm0630.asp?bhcp=1

With MIT lecture notes free online, now all can start to benefit from first phase of global meta-university

India's industrous engineering students can benefit, too, from pondering MIT's free 'problem sets'

Note: MIT (Massachusetts Institute of Engineering) stresses that this is only phase-one of the global meta-university program. See iLab proposals, from opposite page.

When he first pondered these questions himself, he had "a recurring nightmare in which students all over the world are sitting in front of a box, all viewing the same videod lecture". But when MIT's then Provost Robert Brown set up a university faculty-student-administration committee to find alternative answers, the result surprised many: it recommended giving away all MIT's course materials by putting them on the Web—free for everyone, anywhere. Vest agreed almost immediately—largely because of a great precedent set by a joint American-British Government partnership with MIT during World War II. This ran a world-leading Radiation Laboratory, with radar research as a major project.

"When the war ended," Vest recalls, "the U.S Government did something that seems unimaginable today. It closed down this successful RadLab, whose wartime mission was then complete. But before the government turned off the lights and locked the doors, it funded key staff members for six months to record the technical essence of their work. The twenty-eight volumes that resulted did document the work, but they also had a greater significance. These volumes formed the basis for a new science-based approach to the practice of electrical engineering and, indeed, engineering more broadly." [20]

This approach moved engineering away from being mainly an experience-based "handbook" profession to being one more centrally based on scientific first principles. "This stimulated an educational revolution," recalls Vest.

"Subjects were developed on a base of science, and new teaching materials were generated throughout MIT: lecture notes, problem sets and experiments." Much was later used in textbooks. "But what really propagated the 'engineering science revolution' was that many of the rapidly increasing numbers of engineering PhD's educated at MIT joined faculties of universities and colleges across the country, bringing with them their lecture notes, draft textbooks, problem sets and laboratory experiments."

Fifty years later, it now seems obvious to MIT's visionary leader to use the same sharing model globally—especially with poor countries: the start of the proposed Global Meta-University.

MIT's Open CourseWare program is a first step to this: to provide easy and free access to all the almost 2,000 subjects taught at MIT. MIT materials for 1,800 courses from thirty-three academic disciplines are now readily available online for free access. Currently these are provided mainly as pdf and HTML* documents. The Hewlett Report envisages such material being available soon on the Web as interactive learning plans and modules, easily used by anyone. Vest says the next stage of open content is an online laboratory.

"The principle is simple," he says. "Most experiments are controlled by computers. Therefore experiments can be controlled from any distance through the Internet." One of the first prototype projects is iLab, a joint initiative of Microsoft Research and MIT. It was designed to enable MIT students to operate experimental equipment from their dorm rooms or from other study venues—"when they wanted and where they wanted". iLab started with microelectronics experiments. But it has now expanded to teaching experiments involving chemical reactors, mechanical structures, heat exchanges, polymer crystallization and a photovoltaic weather station.

The MIT group also makes available *iLab Shared Architecture,* a toolkit of reusable modules—like "electronic Lego blocks"—and a set of standardized protocols for developing and managing online laboratories.

Vest sees this as only the beginning of the MIT vision of "Open iLabs that someday may provide free and open access to online laboratories throughout the world".

Visitors to the MIT site *(http://ocw.mit.edu)* are located on every continent, except Antarctica, and average over one million visits a month. Educators make up 15 percent of the traffic, students 31 percent and self-learners 48 percent.

More than 120 institutions are linked into the consortium. CORE (China Open Resources for Education) is translating MIT OCW courses into Chinese and making them available across China. And CORE is beginning to make Chinese courses available and to translate them into English. Another partner, Universia, a consortium of

** pdf: portable document format—free, downloadable software that converts any document into a file that can be viewed on any computer screen and printed. **HTML:** Hypertext MarkUp Language—the Web language that makes it easy to link any document with any other document.*

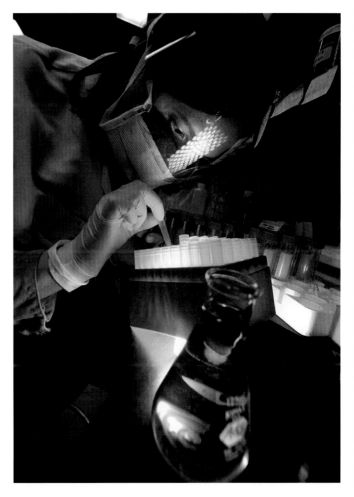

New modular **toolkits now bas** **MIT online iLab: lik** **scientific Lego blocks** **for students' reuse**

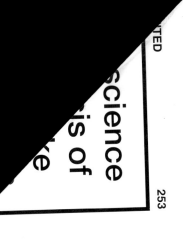

s best
s and
-creating
a of 1.8
species

253

840 institutions in the Spanish-speaking world, has translated MIT OCW subjects into Spanish for free access by anyone. At least fifty OCW initiatives are already operating internationally, with thirty more planned.

And Vest sees the total concept—when matched with cheap, widely available high-speed broadband access—being exactly the right type of globalization for institutions of higher learning: to bridge the digital divide between rich and poor regions.

7. It's CO-CREATIVE

But it's in the entire new concept of cyberspace-based *co-creativity* that the new Web 2.0 architecture provides the innovation to transform education.

To anyone working in another industry it seems absurd for the world's 59 million teachers to work largely in isolation: either "reinventing the wheel" each day or recycling yesterday's teaching plan to students itching to get back out into the real world.

Fortunately, Web 2.0 now makes it possible to change that. The drive for change is coming from many of the brightest leaders in education, government and philanthropic foundations:

❏   In 2007, some of the world's greatest universities and museums announced plans to compile the *Encyclopedia of Life* [21]—to tell the story, in words, pictures, video, sounds and graphics of everything they know about all of the Earth's 1.8 million known species. Seed funding has already come from some of America's biggest not-for-profit foundations: the MacArthur Foundation and the Alfred P. Sloane Foundation.

❏   The British Broadcasting Corporation is digitizing the entire contents of its seventy-year archival collection of cultural and historical television masterpieces—to make them available for resharing, and recombining, in what BBC Director-General Mark Thompson calls "the new on-demand, pan-media universe we are hurtling towards." [22]

❏   The U.S. National Science Foundation's Office of Cyberspace Infrastructure is spending $700 million a year to promote new ways to share great interactive science learning programs globally.

❏　　And the Hewlett Report lists dozens of other projects similar to MIT's, including Stanford, Carnegie Mellon, UC Berkeley, Harvard, Johns Hopkins, Tufts, UC Irvine, Yale, Utah and Washington universities in U.S., leading Chinese and Japanese universities, Britain's Open University, the Netherlands Open University and the African Virtual University.

But the Hewlett Report stresses that projects like these will fulfill their potential only if they actively involve the talents of millions around the world to co-create the future: a grassroots revolution.

Here we believe millions of young students will themselves create some of the most useful interactive-technology tools to transform education. Here, too, a challenge from Marc Prensky, a leading world designer of interactive digital games, mirrors the vision of MIT. Prensky's vision* is breathtakingly simple:

❏　　*That the educational software we all use—"all of it, games, non-games and anything else, at all levels, preschool to adult"—should be created by a "world mind" of students, teachers and passionate learners.*

❏　　*It should not belong to any of us, and should be available free to anybody, anywhere, who wants to use it.*

❏　　*Universities, colleges, teachers colleges and other schools around the world each pick a subject and a level.*

❏　　*The school that picks each particular topic becomes the "home" for all educational software developed in that field—by everyone in the world working together. And that pool to be easily indexed, available to anyone off the Web—for recombining and adding to, then reshared.*

Prensky says the "absolute requirement" would be that everything every school does be open in at least three ways:

1.　　They will be required to constantly comb the world for good things that are

* His articles listed at www.marcprensky.com include the one that summarizes this vision: "Proposal for Educational Software Development Sites", subtitled: "An open source tool to create the learning software we need".

Not only can s
play compute
now they're ...
to design them
for easy learning

256

Anyone who believes there won't be a massive input to the challenge is living in a pre-Internet world'

out there and add them to their system, organizing them in useful ways for learning and teaching.

2.   Their software and organization will all be *Wiki* (as in *Wikipedia* or some variation) so that anybody can easily add to it. All teachers and students around the world in the subject would be encouraged to do so.

3.   Anything good and useful —idea, tool, content or anything else— developed by any of these sites anywhere in the world would (because the system would require it) be quickly adopted by all the others, so that the software at all the sites would remain state of the art.[23] What would that give us?

❏   *First, says Prensky, an educational technology system that is worldwide and where everything works together.*

❏   *Second, an educational technology system that everyone in the entire world interested in education—student, teacher, expert—contributes to.*

❏   *Third, an end for schools having to decide which proprietary system to "go with", only to forfeit the benefits of the ones they don't pick. "Our free, open system will have all the best of the components of all of them."*

❏   *Fourth, a way for classroom teachers, home scholars and all students and learners around the world to have access to the best and latest ideas and technologies—free.*

"Sound fantastical? Pie-in-the-sky? It's NOT. This is what the Internet brings—or should bring us. MIT has all of its content online already. This just takes things a bit further." [24] Prensky says anyone who believes there won't be massive worldwide input into such a challenge program "is living in a pre-Internet world—the problem will be *too much* input".

He accepts that a lot of help will be needed to organize and control the project. "And this is where the colleges come in. This is work that is both important to world education and appropriate for college students, and students should certainly get credits for doing it. And who better to write the software than the world's best engineering students?"

One prominent industry leader who has already taken that concept further is Scott McNealy. A Stanford graduate, McNealy is co-founder and chairman of Silicon Valley's SUN Microsystems, the corporation that developed and donated to the world the free *Java* computer language that lets different computer systems "talk" to each other.

As *Time* magazine tells the story in its cover feature, *How to bring our schools out of the 20th century:* "In 2003, McNealy was up against one of the most vexing challenges of modern life: a third-grade science project. Scott McNealy had spent hours searching the Web for a lively explanation of electricity that his son could understand. 'Finally I found a very nice, animated, educational website showing electrons zooming around and tests after each section. We did this for about an hour and a half—a great father-and-son moment of learning.'" [25] But it happened to be on a site for plumbers, with little more activity on electricity.

For McNealy, says *Time,* that experience provided one of life's aha! moments: "It made me wonder why there isn't a website where I can just go and have anything I want to learn, K to 12, browser-based and free."

His solution: draw on the Wikipedia model to create a collection of online courses that can be updated, improved, vetted and built upon by innovative teachers who, he notes, "are always developing new materials and methods of instruction because they aren't happy with what they have".

And who better to launch such a site than McNealy "whose company has led the way in designing open-source computer software? He quickly raised some money, created a non-profit organization and—voila!—*www.curriki.org* (Curriculum Wiki) made its debut January 2006, and has been growing fast." Some 450 courses are in the works, with over 30,000 registered members. Concludes *Time:* "Curriki, however, isn't meant to replace going to school but to supplement it and offer courses that may not be available locally. It aims to give teachers classroom-tested content materials and assessments that are livelier and more current and multimedia-based than printed textbooks. Ultimately, it could take the Web 2.0 revolution to schools, closing that yawning gap between how kids learn at school and how they do everything else."

Looking with his son for an explanation of electrity, Scott McNealy dreamed up the online Curriki

Shot simulated by innovative photographer.

Globalizing Web 2.0 learning rovolution with the power of co-created ideas

And what do you get if you combine the Web 2.0, browsers, Google, MIT, Prensky, McNealy's Curriki, the Hewlett Foundation OEM Report and many of the concepts promoted in this book and earlier editions of The Learning Revolution? Simply: sensible ways to combine globally, instantly and cheaply, many of the world's best learning methods and interactive tools—including ways to learn anything much faster, more easily and more effectively.

As we'll explore in the remaining chapters, many of those brilliant alternatives are already working in practice to bring that age to fruition. But possibly the biggest spin-off legacy of this new co-creative age comes in inventing *a new way to invent.*

❏ **The second-phase of the industrial revolution**—from the mid-nineteenth century to the mid-twentieth—was in many ways the era of business created by single inventors: Thomas Edison, Alexander Graham Bell, Guglielmo Marconi, Walt Disney and the giants who gave us cars, television and the movies.

Walt Disney's often-quoted concept epitomized the era of the lone innovator: "If you can dream it, you can do it."

❏ **The seventies, eighties and nineties marked the new electronic age:** the new era of small creative teams—epitomized by the innovation and creative ecology of Silicon Valley. Stanford University and Xerox's Palo Alto Research Center provided the lights to guide the new era of group innovation by computer scientists, young "geek" partnerships and in teenage computer hobby clubs.

PARC innovator Allan Kay added to Disney's definition: "The best way to predict the future is to invent it. Figure out where you want to go and that will show you how to get there." [26]

❏ **Now, in the new age of co-creativity,** John Seely Brown, another PARC innovator, sets the tone for the new century, where often the big breakthroughs emerge in the gaps *between* different disciplines.

"Now you don't invent the future," he says. "You unleash it—by leveraging the community mind."[27] Welcome to the new world of co-creative enterprise, where everyone can learn a living: from winner-take-all to all-can-be-winners.

In our view, too, there is an overriding need to simplify the Web 2.0 revolution, and especially to make the new hi-tech tools easy for anyone to use.

Harvard Business School Professor Clayton M. Christensen, in his highly-recommended book—*Disrupting Class: How disruptive innovation will change the way the world learns*—points, correctly, to the need to build simple *platforms* or *templates* so that outstanding teachers can add easy-learning *modules* for anyone to use.

Christensen points to the rise of online "virtual" schools and colleges as one big trend now emerging. The Florida Virtual School is one example. Its motto: "Any time, any place, any path, any pace." Started in 1997 as a trial, by 2005 it was servicing 52,000 online students taking 92,000 separate courses, from algebra to business technology.

Utah's Bringham Young University's online ChemLab is even bigger. It serves some 150,000 students seated at computer terminals around America. It was all started by a chemistry professor who took 2,500 photos and made 220 videos to kick it off. Christensen calls it the classroom of the future, serving 150,000 students instead of twenty to thirty.

Such projects are ideal for learning subject-specific skills: foreign languages at advancing levels; science and computer technology programs available in modules. Also, the skills now needed for the Web 2.0 era are not "age specific". They should be as easy as *Wikipedia's Wiki* platform for anyone to use or add to.

Some of those platforms and programs will be free. Some, like those produced by publicly-owned institutions, such as Britain's BBC, might be free to public schools and by subscription to others.

The biggest free Web-sharing ideas will flower from the platforms suggested by Charles Vest, Mark Prensky and Scott McNealy, with the world's brightest teachers and students co-creating their own learning modules to interlock into those platforms.

And the biggest commercial impact will come from the Web's unequalled ability to allow anyone with a great idea, talent or skill to sell it to millions of others seeking just that expertise.

When Web 2 module techni becomes as simple to use as Lego, creativity flowers

Now you can turn your talents and skills into a global business, run it all from home, and keep learning too

The seven ways entrepreneurship is building the next big growth industry

Cisco Systems' astute CEO John Chambers sums it up in two sentences: "The next big killer application for the Internet is going to be education. Education over the Internet is going to be so big it is going to make email usage look like a rounding error in terms of the Internet capacity it is going to consume." [1]

And a Cisco advertising headline is even more succinct: "One day, training for every job on earth will be available on the Internet. *Are you ready?*" [2]

To MIT MediaLab's co-founder and Director Nicholas Negroponte, that message is so obvious that "I'm convinced our great-grandchildren will look back and wonder why we didn't get it". [3]

The Harvard Business School's leading expert on industry innovation, Dr. Clayton M. Christensen, predicts that, on present trends, 25 percent of all high school courses will be available online for everyone, of all ages, no later than 2014. By 2019, it will be 50 percent. Hundreds of new hi-tech skills courses will be among them. [4]

So, if education is to be The Next Big Thing on the Internet, then the world's best teachers and trainers should be leading experts in creating the innovations to power that change. But are they ready?

In a world where lifelong learning—as you want it, when you want it, where you want it—is about to become the next big growth industry—"the jury is still out" on how many teachers are yet ready for the change.

As *Time* says in *How to bring our schools out of the twentieth century:* "There's a dark little joke exchanged by educators with a dissident streak: Rip Van Winkle awakens in the twenty-first century after a hundred-year snooze and is, of course, utterly bewildered by what he sees. Men and women dash about, talking to small metal devices pinned to their ears. Young people sit at home on sofas, moving miniature athletes around on electronic screens. Older folk defy death and disability with metronomes in their chests and with hips made of metal and plastic. Airports, hospitals, shopping malls—every place Rip goes just baffles him. But when he finally walks into a schoolroom, the old man knows exactly where he is. 'This is a school,' he declares. 'We used to have these back in 1906. Only now the blackboards are green.'" [5]

That's not the case, of course, in business. Great corporations are continually reinventing themselves. And Apple's Steve Jobs is one who not only reinvents companies; he's reinvented three industries:

❏   In the mid-1970s, he and Steve Wozniak were barely out of school when they founded Apple Computer. In 1984, they started the new age of interactive computing with the Apple *Macintosh*. Microsoft was soon to surpass them in sales.

❏   In the 1990s, Jobs reinvented the animated movie industry with Pixar and its seven Academy Award-winning films like *Toy Story, Finding Nemo* and *Cars*. Pixar would eventually turn Jobs into the major shareholder in Disney.

❏   Then, in 2001, Apple i*Pod* and *iTunes* flipped the music industry on its head.

1.   Apple typifies the new Youth Web

Jobs typifies the convergence of the computer, movie and music industries: the marriage of Silicon Valley and Hollywood.

In five years Apple sold 100 million *iPod* units—able to store up to 15,000 music tracks in one mobile device about the size of a pack of playing cards. Now Apple i*Tunes* provides five million music tracks online, for downloading instantly on demand, mainly at 99 cents each. And Apple's new *iPhone*—dubbed by Jobs "the Internet in your pocket"—looks like continuing the Apple innovation leadership. If Google is king of Web 2.0, Apple is queen of the *mass personalization* revolution.

Now Latin American villagers can sell their beautiful blankets on eBay, with no middle man

The Web generation: online, multitasking, mobile, aware and interconnected

Go into the best-led Apple schools in the world and you'll also find even very young children using *iMovie* on their *Macs* to create and edit videos to professional standards. And composing their own music on the free *Garage Band* software that comes with every *Mac*.

Now a developing avalanche of iPod-type concepts is about to turn education upside down—and transform business as well.

It seems as if finally smart marketers have done the arithmetic:

❏ Around 3.3 billion people are under age twenty-five.

❏ That's 133 million in every one-year age-group.

❏ Almost 1.6 billion are aged between thirteen and twenty-four: the high school, college and main university years.

❏ Almost 1.5 billion are of elementary and high school age.

❏ ***School generally takes up no more than one-fifth of their waking hours. They spend four times as much time on other interests as they do at school. And increasingly those interests revolve around this new interactive digital world.***

Even very young children are now taking advantage of the wealth of interactive material available online. Much of it is free for downloading. Like *3D Blender,* the free software program that young New Zealand school teacher and graphic designer Rebecca Merle is using to teach children as young as five to learn computer animation. Thousands of other young children go online to play with other interactive games that she has designed on her Bubbledome site.

"Better get used to it," says *Business Week* in a feature article, *Children Of The Web.* "Millions of digital elite are in the vanguard of a fast-emerging global youth culture. Because of smartphones, blogs, instant messaging, *Fickr, My Space, Skype, YouTube, digg* and *del.icio.us,* young people are instantly aware of what's happening to others like themselves everywhere." [6]

But it's no longer a digital elite. Visit a high school in China and you're likely to find sixty-plus students sitting in rows in a typical English language class, listening to a teacher at a chalkboard. Agree to be photographed, and twenty will take out a mobile phone with camera, another twenty a digital camera and at least ten with a video camera. Visit a nearby cyber cafe after school, and you're likely to find them learning real-life English while singing to the dancing ball on a *karaoke* screen. If many teachers aren't ready yet for the digital age, students are.

Or sit in a coffee bar in a modern business district in India and count the young office employees going to work. At least six or seven out of ten will be talking on a mobile phone or listening to music on earphones.

But visit India in two years' time, and its *Digital Natives* could be buying India's own mobile Internet PC for $100 or leasing it for $10 a month. It's the brainchild of interactive-technology pioneer Rajesh Jain who founded India's first popular browser, IndiaWorld, in 1995, and sold it in 1999 for $115 million. Since then he's invested widely in several hi-tech start-ups, including Novatium and Netcore Solutions, which have pioneered the work into the new low-priced mobile devices, including the new Nova NetPC and NetTV.

As Newsweek puts it in a 2007 cover story: "If Rajesh Jain is successful, the Nova NetTV, which hooks up to any television, could be the first in a family of devices that connect the next billion people to the Internet."[7]

Key to the low-cost mobile devices, which Jain thinks will soon allow the price to drop to $70, is open-source technology, with the operating-system and software not in the set itself but in a network server.

MIT MediaLab's Nicholas Negroponte is also well down the track in producing what started out as a $100 open-source laptop—but has since seen its pre-production price rise to $170—if bought in large quantities. It is also billed as the new computer for the third world.

Whether either or both win out, the era of Web 2.0 low-cost computing is about to unleash Internet power to millions. And the race will be on to find interactive content that matches the unique cultures of Asia and beyond as much as *YouTube* appeals to Americans.

From Laos to Seoul, welcome to the tuned-in, turned on Web 2.0 culture

While ancient tradition abounds, South Korea leads the world in fast broadband and social networking

2. Cyworld leads social networking revolution

As well as DoCoMo in Japan, the most distinctive new Asian Web 2.0 revolution is in South Korea. By 2005, it already had the world's highest fast-broadband penetration, with 76 percent of households signed up, compared with just 30 percent in the United States. And their broadband access was twenty times faster than America.

South Korea is also the home of a modern social-networking phenomena called *Cyworld*. At least a third of families and well over 90 percent of young people, from fifteen to thirty, are enthusiastic users.

"Cyworld is threatening to swallow South Korea," says *Business Week*. "It's an Internet service that lets people create their own home pages—pages that can accommodate an unlimited number of photos, documents and other goodies. It's similar to U.S. social networking sites such as *MySpace* or *Facebook,* but with extra twists that make it more realistic and alluring. Home pages, for example, appear three-dimensional [and every *Cyworld* member has one]. Users decorate their 'rooms' with furniture, art, TVs, even music. Instant messaging is included in the service, so you can chat with visitors. You can even enter *Cyworld* from a mobile phone. An average of 6.2 million photos are uploaded to *Cyworld* each day, many of them directly from mobile phones." [8] Members can store on the site an unlimited number of photos.

But the core reason for *Cyworld's* success is cultural. As in Japan and China, Korea has for centuries been a stratified society, with seniority reflected by age. So—like DoCoMo in Japan— *Cyworld* is seen as "a place of unparallelled and previously unimagined freedom": [9] a new youth culture away from traditional strictures.

3. How to sell your own talent on the Web

But possibly South Korea's biggest business lesson for the world's brightest teachers also comes from the *Cyworld* experience.

Kang Hee Jae is one of thousands of Koreans who have used *Cyworld* to display their talents. At age thirty-one, she was able to quit her job and open her own online shopping site after the collection of dolls and clothes she showed on her 3-D page drew 2.7 million viewers.

Compare that with the world's 59 million K-12 teachers. Most have at least one strong educational talent or skill. Now Web 2.0 makes it easy to pass on that talent to millions: some of it free to attract the crowds to personal websites, and some of it for sale—just like Kang Hee Jae has done with dolls and clothes.

And you don't have to be a giant like Cisco or Google to achieve that—thanks to a new Web 2.0 marketing concept called by *Wired* magazine Editor-in-Chief Chris Anderson *The Long Tail.*

Anderson dubs the last fifty years of the twentieth century as "the age the blockbuster built":[10] the era of radio's hit parades, television's favorite mass-appeal programs, blockbuster movies and best-selling books. While blockbusters are still important— and dominate physical retail stores and movie cinemas—millions of other products can now be sold, profitably, to millions who make up each niche market on the Web.

More than 724,000 Americans report that eBay is their primary or secondary source of income. In Britain more than 68,000 cottage industries depend on eBay for at least a quarter of their income—selling niche items they love to make or collect.[11]

The overwhelming majority of music tracks sold on Apple *iTunes* and *Rhapsody* never even make it to retail stores—because demand locally is low. But on the Web, each piece of *niche music* can sell in millions.

Little wonder that John Battelle, in his 2005 book, *The Search,* could dub the *Google, GoTo* and *Overture* search engines as the producers of billions of dollars in sales "one 5-cent click at a time".*

Amazon provides a similar type of service to sell niche books. They even print them, one copy at a time, on one of America's most efficient on-demand printing systems.

It's in the new online digital world that the biggest potential exists in lifelong learning. Unfortunately, the worlds of schooling and business are so separate that few of the planet's 59 million school teachers—and other specialist teachers and trainers

---

* While most associate Google with the model for linking free search information with adjoining click-through "sponsored sites", Californian innovator Bill Goss came up with the original concept which he introduced as GoTo, then changed the name to Overture, before trying unsuccessfully to sell it to Google and then selling it to Yahoo for $1.6 billion.

One South Korean doll-maker draws 2.7 million viewers to her website to create new global business

Even babies can see colors, shapes and hear words in eight languages with BabyWow

outside school—realize that their talents can now be sold to millions. Yet, according to Harvard's Christensen—in his new book, *Disrupting Class: How disruptive innovation will change the way the world learns*—these talents will be precisely those that can turn the new online skills-training potential into a world-class industry.

Very few qualified teachers have also trained to be creative computer graphics experts, like Bubbledome's Rebecca Merle has done in New Zealand. But she and her team regularly train teachers to learn the introductory basics of individual multimedia programs in under half a day. At Bubbledome seminars, teachers also learn how students can easily personalize digital graphics so that they, too, can dress up as any character in history or fantasy—in the new world of *mass customization.*

Virtually every learning and teaching breakthrough highlighted in this book represents an opportunity to take new methods of learning and turn them into global commercial opportunities. Many innovators have done just that, but not many yet in a total Web 2.0 way:

❏   **Early learning:** In the late 1970s, California kindergarten teacher Jan Davidson wondered why there were no computer products in her specialty: teaching preschoolers to read and count. After trying unsuccessfully to find a multimedia publisher for her idea, Jan's husband Bob suggested setting up their own company, using $6,000 from a family college savings account. In 1982, they launched *Reading Blaster* and *Math Blaster,* first as computer floppy discs, and later as CD-roms. In 1997, they sold Davidson Associates for $1 billion. They now concentrate on their foundation for developing gifted children, the Davidson Talent Development Institute.

❏   **Even younger:** Now infants even as young as six to twelve months can start using the family computer by touching any of the keyboard keys while using *BabyWow!* software. Former Amazon executive Tony Fernandes created *BabyWow!* after the birth of his first child. He now produces it in eight languages: English, French, Spanish, Japanese, German, Italian, Portuguese and Chinese. The software features great photographs of bold content, 2,000 key words and teaches concepts such as near/far, front/back, and in/out: a great way to introduce infants to some new fun.

❑ **Geography:** In 1985, two young Iowa trivia-game fans, Doug and Gary Carlston, turned one of their games into a computer floppy-disc hit called *Where In The World Is Carmen Sandiego?* It was a pioneer in "edutainment": the fusion of education and entertainment. It quickly sold 4.5 million copies in pre-CD-rom floppy discs.

The deluxe CD-rom edition appeared in 1992, and millions more children and their families have learned the basics of geography as they search for Carmen around the world, using 3,200 clues—including 500 in foreign languages—with photographs, animations, and audio excerpts of traditional music. It has even been developed into a movie and TV games show.

❑ **Music:** Great interactive CD-roms have also become teachers to a whole new generation of aspiring singers, songwriters, conductors, composers and musicians.

Thousands of schools already use the *Groovy* range of software, produced by London-based Sibelius company, to teach music: *Groovy Shapes* for five- to seven-year-olds, *Groovy Jungle* for children from seven to nine, and *Groovy City* for children from nine to eleven. While programs like Apple's *Garage Band* allow young students to compose music on their computer, *Groovy* goes further: it can automatically translate their basic composition into written annotated notes. And it lets children manipulate a wide range of instruments.

On Dorling Kindersley's *Musical Instruments* CD-rom, you can hear the tones and timber of about 200 instruments, from Australian *didgeridoos* to Japanese *shakuhachi* flutes. You'll find around 1,500 sound samples, more than 500 high-quality photos and extensive text.

Benjamin Britten's *The Young Person's Guide To The Orchestra* has long been a classic on both audiotape and videotape. The CD-rom version offers musical notation of every melody, lets you know which instruments are playing at all times, and includes 50 audio examples. And you get to play the conductor, too.

❑ **Young painters** can practise with Broderbund's *Kid Pix*. New deluxe editions also provide additional authoring options.

❑ **Montessori for the new century:** Even Maria Montessori's great early childhood

Programs like Groovy and Garage Band make it easier to learn and compose music

New fMRI-enabled brain research helps infants to read better

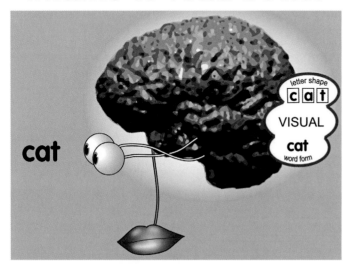

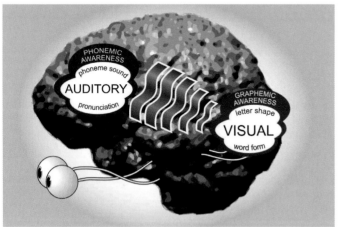

Slides from Duncan Milne's doctoral research showing how infants process different types of visual words through separate pathways in the brain. The slides, based on fMRI brain-scans are fromm his book, Teaching The Brain To Read.

work a hundred years ago has now been brought into the new century by the New Zealand family-owned *SmartKids* group. *SmartKids* also provides a good example of linking new brain-based learning research with older common-sense wisdom. Mother Sue Milne is the former kindergarten teacher who designed the basic new range. Husband David Milne is the manager. Ph.D son Duncan is the educational psychologist—and author of the book, *Teaching the Brain to Read,* based on his doctoral research. His fMRI-scan research proved small children process simple phonic words and sounds, like *cat,* through a different brain-path than words whose sounds are recognized through "whole-word" sight. Other son Fraser is the producer of interactive educational CD-Roms that provide the moving visuals and sounds to back up the hands-on non-digital Montessori-type sensory activities the company markets internationally.

By contrast, many earlier programs to teach infants to read and count are very much first-generation games based on the classroom-instructional method of teaching—with colorful graphics added, but children left simply to click on multiple-choice (or multiple-guess) boxes.

4. The new world of serious learning games

Now the biggest Web 2.0 educational potential lies in what people like John Seely Brown and Marc Prensky call "serious games": games which allow millions of online players to jump outside the classroom "instructional design" box and start creating their own virtual worlds.

Probably the best known are those produced by Will Wright, a native of Atlanta, Georgia, where he was fortunate enough, he recalls, to attend a Montessori school.* "Montessori," he says, "taught me the joys of discovery. It showed me you can become interested in pretty complex theories, like Pythagorean theory, by playing with blocks. It's all about learning on your terms, rather than a teacher explaining stuff to you." His famous *SimCity* multi-player simulation game, he says, "comes right out of Montessori—if you give people this model for building cities, they will abstract from it principles of urban design."[12]

* Both Sergey Brin and Larry Page, the co-founders of Google, also say they were both fortunate to have Montessori early-childhood educations.

Wright started building complex models as a kid. But when he went on to high school he found it completely boring. He later studied architecture, economics, mechanical engineering, computers and robotics before deciding to specialize in serious simulation games. In 1989, he created the game that would evolve into *Sim City,* and later *The Sims,* which extends the concept of planning your own city to actually building your own personal universe. *Sim City* has sold over 100 million copies for well over $2 billion. His latest sequel, *Spore,* lets players control "their life, the Universe, everything". At its preview unveiling, Wright described it as being "about the entire history of life and where life goes in the future." It would, he said, take players "seventy-six years, without any sleep, to explore all of *Spore's* different planets".[13]

But it's much more than a trivial game. "It's a philosophy tool to play with," he says. "I want people to think about the infinite possibilities of life." For example, a climate-change tool allows players to flood their *Spore* world with greenhouse gases, demonstrating the disastrous consequences of that result."

Wright says he believes that this type of game will be a more durable form of entertainment than cinema. "Film directors take you to an end point they create," he says. "Games designers ask: Can you extract an entire world from your imagination?"

But interactive games are not the only new learning tools teachers and companies can provide.

Promethean Ltd., Britain's main seller of interactive digital whiteboards to schools, provides a typical example of Web 2.0 marketing. Not only are its touch-screen *ActivBoards* premier products but the company links satisfied teacher-users into a global *collaborative classrooms* project. In this way, some of the world's most creative teachers can share their best lesson-plans and interactive teaching and learning concepts.

At the high school level, excellent examples of Web 2.0 principles come from the way in which Europe's biggest textbook publisher, Nelson Thornes, now produces online *blended learning* programs to replace old-fashioned textbooks. Starting with math and science subjects, students can access the interactive lessons, with animated models, from home or school. Instant assessment is built-in automatically at every

From Web 1.0 phonics to new pre-school robotics program

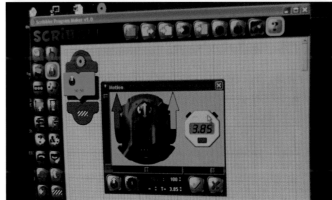

Phonics language games were among the early CD-roms. Now MIT's MediaLab produces a variety of early learning games such as Scribbler, which four-year-olds can use to make robots. Will Wright's new Spore, for release as this book is being printed, is entirely different. It allows students to design a new universe.

More Chinese learning English than the total population of the United States: many of them online

stage. This identifies weaknesses and provides exercises to overcome them.

LEGO—voted as the "Best Game of the Twentieth Century"—is now cited by Chris Anderson as a perfect example for Web 2.0 marketing of non-digital products. At least 90 percent of LEGO products are not available in traditional retail markets, and products sold through LEGO's traditional retail outlets account for no more than 15 percent of its $1.1 billion in sales. LEGO ranks its online club-members from *casual* to *fanatic,* and those classed as *fanatics* have designed 100,000 new models, to be shared and rebuilt by thousands of other members. Many have also been licensed by LEGO, for resale as packaged kits.

Another to seize the opportunities is British innovator Colin Rose. His Accelerated Learning Systems group has specialized for almost twenty years in do-it-yourself, multimedia foreign-language programs. And now it's offering other accelerated learning programs online.

Second-language learning, in fact, is one of the world's big educational Web 2.0 opportunities. China has more people learning English than the entire population of the United States. And now millions outside China are learning to speak Mandarin through a typical Web 2.0 service, Praxis, co-founded by Irish businessman Ken Carroll, Hank Horkorf, a Canadian, and Steve Williams, of Britain. The company provides free Chinese podcasts online. About 250,000 people pay for individual training services, which include daily personal coaching sessions over Skype—personal phone lessons from Mandarin-speaking trainers in China. The customers are everywhere from California to the Vatican.

Rosetta Stone is one of the best interactive CD-rom programs—for thirty-one languages from Arabic to Welsh and all the major ones. In our view, it is typical of the type of program, available for schools and individuals of all age-groups, that Chester Christensen is forecasting will change education so much in the next decade

5. New directions in corporate training

In a world where everyone now needs to be continually retrained to acquire new skills, the traditional corporate training classroom is also rapidly becoming obsolete—

because it is boring and ineffective. In his book, *Digital-Based Games Learning,* Marc Prensky says much online training is even worse. As many have experienced, boring lectures are even more boring when videotaped and viewed in isolation. "The true twenty-first-century learning revolution," says Prensky, "is that learning—training *and* schooling—is finally throwing off the shackles of pain and suffering which have accompanied it for so long. Within most of our lifetimes, pretty much all learning will become truly learning-centered and fun—fun for students, trainers, teachers, parents, supervisors, administrators and executives. The workers of the games generation will no longer accept, attend or do training that they consider boring."

Instead, says Prensky, two seemingly diametrically opposed worlds are coming together: **serious learning** in schools and businesses, and **interactive entertainment.** When we succeed in combining them, he says, "adding fun into the process will not only make learning and training much more enjoyable and compelling, but far more effective as well".

Prensky says online digital learning games can make corporate training as enjoyable as playing *Sim City, Doom* or *Quake.* In the Introduction to his book, available free online,* he cites *The Monkey Wrench Conspiracy* as a highly effective game that not only teaches high-quality 3-D CAD (Computer Aided Design) but, with a demonstration CD-rom given away in trade magazines, effectively sells the product. Like all good Web 2.0 programs, the key is not only to make learning enjoyable, experiential and highly interactive, but to make it available anywhere, anytime.

6. Business lessons for education

Successful modern business, of course, has many other lessons for transforming education. Perhaps its biggest one is to show how business has moved away from the old military-style command-and-control role into new forms of leadership, management and co-creative systems:

❑   **Accenture** now employs 100,000 people in its worldwide consulting business. It spends more than $400 million a year on staff development. And it runs an enor-

* www.marcprensky.com: Digital Games-Based Learning, Chapter one free online.

Put fun and interactive entertainment into business training, and not just at the staff end-of-year party

The innovation lesson from ATMs: banking is still necessary, retail banks are not—so redesign the system

mous database of the world's best "business case studies"—available instantly to all its staff. At a cost of $100 million a year, that works out at $1,000 per staff member: one-twentieth the cost of a year's study at most U.S. business universities, and way below that for the top business MBAs.

❏   **Cisco** no longer has to answer most customer queries through telephone call centers. Its online system puts thousands of networking customers directly in touch with other customers in the same industry who've solved the same problem: a typical global *community of interest*.

❏   **Oracle,** with its automated teller machines, has revolutionized banking—with "relational database" automated-teller systems. Now customers control their own banking: at an ATM kiosk or online. ***The lesson is stark: banking is still necessary; retail banks are not.***

❏   **General Electric** has jumped even further into the co-creative revolution. CEO Jeffrey Immelt believes countries like the United States can maintain high incomes only if they can move from the *Knowledge Economy* to the *Creative Economy*. He's investing $5 billion in eighty GE initiatives that he calls *Imagination Breakthrough*.

Education can also learn greatly from the business model that has produced so many Silicon Valley hi-tech corporate successes—what Geoffrey A. Moore calls "crossing the chasm".[14] He argues that in hi-tech industries:

❏   Under 2 percent of adults are *technology enthusiasts*—the *geeks* who love working long hours to write complex *source code*.

❏   13 percent are *visionaries*—the first to turn hi-tech innovations into break-through products or ideas.

❏   35 percent are *pragmatists*—or "early majority" —who will buy the new products once they are made really simple to use.

❏   35 percent are *conservatives*—or "late majority"—who will come on board when forced by their customers; and

❏   15% are *laggards*—or sceptics—who resist new technology.

The major task of all hi-tech business today, says Moore, is to "cross the chasm" from the first 15 percent to the big majority. From our experiences around the world, school principals and teachers work on a similar bell curve to industry: again with around 2 percent innovators and another 13 percent eager to be first to put those new ideas in practice—the early adopters.

But education generally lacks a system to make those great breakthroughs instantly welcomed and used by the big majority of principals.

Even worse: quite often the 15 percent who create, and are the first to use, new teaching and learning methods know little about information and communications technology. And the 15 percent who lead the interactive-technology revolution generally know little about new teaching and learning methods.

7.　Lifelong learning: the big opportunity

But combine both concepts together—as many of the world's best schools are doing—and the result is both great new learning methods and the outstanding use of interactive technology in education.

That combination also provides the biggest opportunity to cash-in on the new era of lifelong learning and its incredible demand for millions of people to continue learning new skills throughout life. That will often be based around the unique abilities of the world's best teachers, students and often parents or grandparents.

You have only to consider the 30 million *Powerpoint* presentations made every day to glimpse how much greater interactive skills can now be sold instantly to millions every day around the world. And how "keeping it simple" is one of the big keys to success in the new digital age.

Harvard's Christensen says the lesson is simple for learning too: look to change the entire education system so that it becomes as easy to reinvent it as Google, Microsoft, Apple, Cisco, Oracle, eBay and DoCoMo have reinvented business.

Fortunately some leading states, education departments, universities, schools, teachers and students are already showing us how.

Education is no longer for 20% of a year's waking hours at school but a lifetime of family upskilling

Mexico: land of dance, history and music; what a colorful culture to create a learning revolution

How to use interactive technology as the catalyst to reinvent school

If Geoffrey Moore's *crossing the chasm* model is fairly accurate—and we think it is—then only about 15 percent of adults readily welcome major technological change.

In education, that percentage seems to be even lower, except with young students who have grown up in the new digital, interactive age. But, as we've seen throughout this book, school *innovators* and *early adopters* have already shown the way. Fortunately the models are also emerging for the planet's other schools to cross the chasm into a different, more exciting learning world.

From New Zealand: a new system to release the brilliant creativity of trend-setting principals and teachers—specially in public primary or elementary schools—and a chasm-crossing model to spread that change to all schools.[1]

From the north England county of Northumbria: the model to transform public secondary schools inside a standard national curriculum.

From Singapore: how to add interactive school digital networks to the global International Baccalaureate curriculum in an international school catering to 3,500 students from pre-kindergarten to senior high school.

From Canada: a smaller private school, with an outstanding record in achieving "masters' level" results.

From Mexico: a private pre-K-12 school, with three campuses digitally interlinked—and together twice voted the Spanish-speaking world's most visionary schools.

And generally: some models for holistic, balanced schooling.

We've chosen these examples for very specific reasons, and from our personal research and involvement:

❏   All excel in the use of digital technology and instant information, but also use many concepts they have used as the catalysts to reinvent schooling.

❏   All have a vision of how their students and teachers are part of a more holistic, sharing global community of learners and co-creative innovators.

❏   All share a commitment to building an ecology of learning that embraces their communities and families.

❏   And all are leaders in building continuous professional-development programs for teachers.

1. From New Zealand—the innovation begins

Imagine a country the same size as the United Kingdom or the American state of Colorado, around the same population as Singapore: four million people, with 500,000 primary and secondary students at 2,600 schools, and a Government* that has:

❏   Abolished its entire national Department of Education, and replaced it with a scaled-down policy-advising Ministry.

❏   Abolished all its district School Boards.

❏   Turned all its schools—public and private—into charter schools, run by boards elected by parents, teachers and high school students.

❏   Then challenged those boards to reinvent "tomorrow's schools".

❏   Not just to reinvent them: but to set out in their charter how they'll each achieve excellence in any field they chose, over and above minimum national standards.

And to launch this in 1989-90, when, unknown to the Government:

* Former Prime Minister David Lange viewed education as so important he also became Minister of Education, and appointed an independent committee, headed by business leader Brian Picot, to recommend how to organize "Tomorrow's Schools". The Picot Report was delivered in May 1998, and largely implemented over the following two years.

New Zealand is Lord of The Rings country, and sometimes it seems every kid wants to be Peter Jackson

New Zealand's Southern Alps, where Peter Jackson shot a large part of his Lord of the Rings movie trilogy.

What a neat place to reinvent school, using world as a classroom

The Visa visionary who reinvented money also inspires four simple questions to reshape education's goals

Dee Hock was a virtually unknown middle-executive in a small Oregon bank when he played the biggest part in reinventing the way the world shops, with the Visa card and organization. He is sure the original "chaordic" principle provides a simple way to restate the challenge to reinvent education and schooling.

❏   The free World Wide Web, free Internet browsers and free Web search engines were about to be invented—and change the world.

❏   A couple of American university students were seven years away from creating Google and its ability to scan billions of Web pages in half a second to provide answers to any question.

It would be great to report that all 2,600* New Zealand community school boards, elected by parents and teachers, immediately reinvented schooling. They didn't. But the brightest innovators did.

And a chance appointment hastened the process. Because any new schools about to be built had no students and thus no parents to elect the boards, the Minister of Education had to appoint interim ones.

The first new public school was near the country's biggest exporting port: the departure point for New Zealand's giant lumber, pulp and paper export industries. So the new Minister appointed a senior executive from the port company to be the interim board chair.

We suspect the new chair must have studied the writings of Visa International pioneer Dee Hock, with his theories of organization and education. Or maybe he'd also read "the ancient bit of philosophy" that Hock has since quoted in his book, *Birth of The Chaordic Age:* "Understanding requires mastery of four ways of looking at things: as they *were,* as they *are,* as they *might become,* and as *they ought to be.*" For that is what the new chair recommended at the first meeting of the Interim Board: to set up a new primary school where the students would become fully confident and competent globally-minded citizens, able to tackle any challenges in life on the basis of:

❏   **THE PRESENT:** *Where are we now?*

❏   **THE PAST:** *Why do we do it this way?*

❏   **THE OBVIOUS ALTERNATIVES:** *Who else is doing better, anywhere in the world (in business terms: bench-marking)?*

* *At the start of its reforms in the early 1990's, New Zealand had 2,700 schools, many still with only one or two classrooms. Since then many smaller schools have been amalgamated.*

❏　**AND THE FUTURE:** *How can we create even better answers—not just to invent "tomorrow's school", but invent tomorrow's world?*

The new Interim Board of Tahatai Coast Primary School agreed. And that is what they set out to do, in the Papamoa suburb of Tauranga in the Bay of Plenty (Tahatai in Maori means "by the ocean"). That simple aim became the "job specification" for the school's first principal, Mark Beach, in the mid-1990s.

❏　It was to become not only a model school but a prototype for marrying new interactive technology with new methods of learning and teaching.

❏　It was also to become one of the pace-setters for the new national challenge to build tomorrow's schools, with the new interactive technologies as one area of excellence written into the school charter.

❏　The charter also committed the school to providing rich learning experiences for what was then a low-income population with a 35 percent "minority" school roll: from New Zealand's indigenous Maori culture—often failed by traditional learning methods.*

New Zealand has a long history of innovation in schooling, specially at primary-elementary level. From the late 1930s it was one of the first countries to follow John Dewey's educational theories: to learn by doing, with all the senses, to learn by practical discovery, and to involve all children as creators of their own knowledge and future.

New principal Beach was a fan of Dewey, of Gardner's concept of *multiple intelligences,* of Edward de Bono's *lateral thinking* methods, and many of the other innovations already covered in this book. But Beach also sensed the rising tide of global technology and the new era of instant information. So he recommended the new school board should spend all of its NZ$400,000 "establishment grant" on big-ticket items. These included a satellite receiving dish, a full set of orchestral equipment and the first of the school's new Apple *Macintosh* computers. He also agreed with Hock: that "only a fool worships his tools". So no teacher was employed on the basis of any

* For funding, the New Zealand Ministry of Education ranks communities on a decile scale, from 1 to 10—with 1 the lowest incomes and 10 the highest. When it opened, Tahatai was a decile 2 school.

New Zealand started its bold leap to reinvent schooling at the birth of the first Web age

*As New Zealand started to move into the 1990's, it made every school—public or private—a charter school. Each school's charter identified its goal for specific excellence, inside a national curriculum framework. Tahatai Coast Primary School was the first to be built under the new era. It's goal: to develop confident, competent global citizens. Now its competent multimedia students interview hundreds of international visitors for the school's online TV program. **In photo:** a school TV crew interview the Director of Mexico's Thomas Jefferson Institute, Jeanene Carvajal—comparing schooling in Mexico and New Zealand.*

In New Zealand, digital technology does not mean passive gazing at a TV or PC screen

Although it started as a new Web-age school, New Zealand's Tahatai Coast Primary regards itself more as a project-based innovative creative thinking and discovery center. Students are encouraged to use the best possible appropriate tools to become participating global citizens, with the competence and confidence to tackle any challenge. Music, art, drama, video and using the world as a classroom are all in the mix. Each year the entire school's activities revolve around four "inquiry projects", from communications to conservation. By working together, students learn how to blend their on talents into multi-talented teams, like the real world.

hi-tech knowledge. Instead, all were judged on their enthusiasm to introduce change, and to make a real difference to the lives of their students.

The result is history. By 2007, the school had been visited by more than 8,000 teachers, including around 3,000 from all parts of the world. All visitors are struck by the differences between what they see and most other typical school practice:

❏   Students themselves show visitors around. There's a complete sense of democracy: open dialog and partnership between students, teachers and principal.

❏   The school started with fewer classroom computers than many schools elsewhere in the world. But at Tahatai they have been used much more effectively. The school even bars *Powerpoint* in favor of creative *authoring* software, such as *Hyperstudio* basic animation at ages five and six, and up to Macromedia's *Director* series by age twelve.

❏   A sense of happy creativity pervades the place, from the entrance displays right around the corridors and classroom walls.

The New Zealand school-year is divided into four "terms", not two semesters. In each of those terms, all Tahatai students study an overall "global theme". It could be *learning how to learn, learning how to think, communications* or *conservation.* But in all cases the students use it to investigate that topic around the four-basic questions we've outlined.

But walk into any class and you'll finally get the "big Aha!" at what this all means. Instead of "reading for an hour", "math for an hour" and other subject-divided study, students will be using all their varied talents and skills to research and report their findings on the group theme. But not just in the classroom. *Their world has become the classroom.* They could be studying a New Zealand novel or short story on that same theme. And, inside that, they might be using all their different "learning styles" or "intelligences" to both research and report their group findings. So instead of multiple-choice questions about the story, the students would almost certainly be recreating it in a "Stephen Spielberg" or "Peter Jackson" way: producing a multimedia movie-like version of their version of the original story: twenty-first-century literacy.

❏ In producing their multimedia findings: The *mainly visual learners* might be making television storyboards of the finished product, or designing the titles. *The mainly kinesthetic, tactile* learners might be making *Claymation* models of the characters. The video experts might be shooting background scenes. And the animation experts might be producing professional computer graphics.

Innovation abounds. The year even starts a week later than others, and makes it up with an extra fifteen minutes a day. But in that advance week, the entire staff, at a live-in "retreat", plan the year's "learning how to learn, learning how to think" program.

Of course Tahatai was not the only change-making school under the new Government policy. But as the first one built from scratch it was soon seen as a model for the rest. It doesn't even look like a school: more like the kind of buildings you'd find as a Californian gated golf resort. And all this for low-income families.

But Tahatai wasn't the only coincidence. By 1995, when the school was being set up, Apple Computer in America had just completed the first decade of its ACOT program (Apple Classrooms of Tomorrow).[2] And the American company's New Zealand distributor had set up an Apple Education subsidiary to pioneer a similar concept. Tahatai was to be its model. Working in partnership, the two brought Canadian Lane Clark to work with the new school. She had been one of the pioneer teachers at the River Oaks ACOT school near Toronto, Ontario. She spent twelve weeks fulltime at Tahatai, and trained the new staff in how to link the new tools of interactive technology with the Dewey principles of *inquiry, discovery* and *students creating their own future.*

It was the start of a partnership that has continued, between Apple, Tahatai and Clark. Some of its follow-on highlights:

❏ An annual series of two-day Apple weekend teacher retraining conferences, where teachers from other schools would learn to marry great new teaching and learning ideas with Apple's ICT tools.

❏ Apple bus tours, where visiting teachers would spend a week at trend-setting schools who were using interactive technology as the catalyst for change.

At age six, in this digital classroom, every child starts school learning to be a a television journalist

From the first day in grade one at Sherwood Primary School on Auckland's North Shore, New Zealand, children start using digital cameras to video and then edit a classroom movie. In that way, they capture each child's dreams, passions and early talents. It's also the start of twenty-first century multimedia literacy. Within a few days they are also learning compute animation—at New Zealand's first state-owned "digital school".

Working in co-creative multi-talented teams is one key to New Zealand's cooperative school model

Around 1,600 of New Zealand's 2,600 schools have now learned to use interactive technology as part of a national sharing program. It started with twenty-three "cluster-leading" schools each sharing its methods with about eight others. They then all set up other clusters. But inside each school, a similar sharing encourages those with different talents to make up a multimedia team. At Gulf Harbor Primary School students often work like a TV or movie production unit: script-writing, music, acting, costume-design and editing to produce a finished show, all learning from the others. In photo: two of its students studying their weekly project-plan.

❏   The sharing of teacher training methods: what schools like to call "professional development"—but, under the Tahatai model, this is integrated into each day's work Not a static series of lectures, but the collaborative sharing of information on the job. Once a week, for example, the teachers hold a "techie breckie": a breakfast where each one passes on any new technical tips.

❏   A coordinated staff reading program, in which all its teachers share copies of articles recommended by other teachers—and then discuss how to put the best research into practice quickly and then compare notes. By the end of 1997, when a second edition of *The Learning Revolution* appeared, the Tahatai success story started to spread nationally and internationally. The school took pride of place in that new edition, and the trickle of foreign visitors started to become a flood.

By then, too, it was obvious that not all New Zealand's schools were *crossing the chasm* at the same pace—even if they'd ever heard of the term. Of the country's 2,600 schools, many in farming districts are small, often one-teacher or two-teacher schools. And of the total, by the end of the nineties, only between fifty and sixty appeared to be using the new technology well. Amazingly: that validates Geoffrey Moore's 2 percent.

To spread the message of how information and communications technology could be the catalyst for change, the Government appointed an ICT coordinator. And that task went to another creative country school principal, Carol Moffatt, then head of the Oxford Area School in the South Island province of Canterbury. Then Murray Brown, who had coordinated the Freyberg High School's integrated studies program, with its school, university and IBM partnership, became the Ministry's National ICT Manager. In a small, closely-knit community like New Zealand, innovator Moffatt knew the other pace-setters and invited them to a two-day conference to brainstorm how best to make excellence the norm.

They recommended the concept of "ICT clusters", with one "lead school" acting as the coordinator to share the new methods with up to ten other schools. All 2,600 schools were invited to apply for cluster leadership, and twenty-three were chosen for the first two-year contracts. Their only payment: the salary of an extra teacher, with Tahatai being paid the equivalent of two teachers, to act in a broader advisory role. That system has worked wonderfully well. About 60 percent of the country's 2,600 schools have so far been involved.

❏   Two state-owned primary schools, Sherwood and Gulf Harbor, have pioneered "digital classrooms"—with parents wishing to take advantage of this paying NZ$600 per student a year in extra fees (about $US450). Tahatai is also developing similar classrooms with more PCs.

❏   Discovery One, in Christchurch, has become the country's first public primary school to use "the city as a classroom", where students study out in "the real world" but return to their central-city base to collate their findings on computers and in other "show you know" projects. Its associated high school, Unlimited, has a similar policy. The individual learning plan for each student builds in time to study the national basics of literacy and numeracy—generally linked in with their own projects. The parents who inspired both schools wanted to be involved in their children's schooling—and knew each child was bored and under-stretched at traditional schools.

❏   And New Zealand's southern-most region has extended the concept with the Southland Innovator Project. This included two five-day seminars to retrain many of the district's principals and teachers. A follow-up project helped all Southland schools coordinate enterprise and ICT programs with local businesses.

Other similar "ICT cluster models" have been tried elsewhere, noticeably the *Navigator* schools in the Australian state of Victoria and the United Kingdom's *Beacon* schools. But most visitors award top marks to the New Zealand effort. So do we. The Government has also chipped in with grants to provide every New Zealand school principal with a laptop, and to subsidize laptops for teachers.

The Government's Education Ministry also runs two websites to provide online information and share it—at: *www.minedu.govt.nz* and *www.tki.org.nz* (the initials for the Maori words for "three baskets of knowledge: *Te Kete Ipurangi.* That site is in both English and Maori.)

Even the school's name is Unlimited, and at 13 he's already designing an eBusiness program

At Unlimited, a completely new-type public high school in New Zealand, students are encouraged to use their city of Christchurch as a study resource. They often work for days on end in city businesses as they research their own vision of the future. This thirteen-year-old is already designing a highly-interactive website to provide eBusiness planning and costing software for the hospitality segment of the world tourist industry. His 3-D kitchen design is on the computer screen behind him.

The innovations at this United Kingdom high school would be hard to match anywhere in the world

Computerized personal learning plans are only one of the innovations at Cramlington Community High School, on the outskirts of Newcastle-Upon-Tyne in the north of England. England's Ministry for Education and Skills regard it as one of the country's most visionary models for redesigning secondary schools.

2. The United Kingdom high school model

If New Zealand is a model for decentralized schooling, the United Kingdom is proving an equally great one for introducing interactive technology to a national curriculum, specially at secondary level. And just as New Zealand's innovation started off with a business-school partnership, England's was to benefit from the same pattern. But its business partner is a home-grown one: Lancashire's Promethean, designers and manufacturers of *ActivBoard* touch-screen interactive whiteboards. Promethean now has many school partners. But one of the frontrunners has been Cramlington Community High School, on the outskirts of the Northumbrian city of Newcastle-Upon-Tyne: recently redesigned and renamed the Cramlington Learning Village.

Like Tahatai and the other great New Zealand schools, it's almost impossible to do justice to Cramlington solely in writing. Even its informative website can convey only a little of the story *(www.cchsonline.co.uk)* :

❑   The first to provide an accelerated-learning cycle in each class schedule—even fifty-minute ones—and link it with both interactive technology and the Internet.[3]

❑   Among the first to make full use of Promethean's *ActivBoards* and that company's online *collaborative classroom* project, which shares lesson-plans and "learning and teaching tools" through the Internet.

❑   Its own digitized accelerated-lesson plans stored on the Internet— and, in the words of *The Guardian* newspaper: "accessible at lightning speed from all 700 networked computer stations around the school".[3]

❑   Interactive whiteboards in every classroom, and used by fully-trained teachers to provide George Lucas-type dramatic movie effects to stimulate class discussion.

❑   Two-hour weekly planning and training sessions for all staff on ICT and on individualizing learning.

❑   Three fulltime graduate web-designers plus a video technician.

❑   Personalized learning for all students, including free time to study at home and out in the community for all senior students.

❏   A special grant from the U.K. Ministry for Education and Skills to set up a separate training center, fully equipped with digital whiteboards, to share the message with other schools.

❏   An exchange program with schools around the world.

❏   Rave reports from England's OFSTED school-review authority, as the model for training teachers to integrate interactive technology into the national curriculum.

❏   One of only 100 U.K. schools accorded "leading edge" status.

❏   And continuing professional development for all teachers as the key to the school's performance—apart from its excellent leadership.

Innovative head Derek Wise and Deputy Head Mark Lovatt have even written two books on how to create a technology-linked accelerated learning school.[4]   And the school's teachers and students have produced a detailed guide filled with bright ideas as part of upgrading their learning program to the next level. Wise sees that as "a completely personalized curriculum", where every student is helped to identify his or her talents and then develop the skills and abilities to improve them. Cramlington, too, benefits from the U.K. Ministry's excellent online backup for interactive technology, and the British Broadcasting Corporation's world leadership in online services.

Wise and Lovatt wish, however, that all England's primary schools could produce student-graduates at the same level as the best they have visited in New Zealand. They also see the Tahatai and Cramlington examples as a great way to link talent-development, personalized learning and the Promethean *collaborative classroom* concept of sharing great work online.

3.   Singapore's networked global curriculum

Like New Zealand, Singapore has only four million people. But all are crammed into an area the size of New Zealand's biggest lake. And while its public investment in school ICT dwarfs New Zealand, one of Singapore's best educational initiatives also stems from New Zealand leadership.

New Zealand businessman David Perry—a former successful Apple dealer—first

Where every high school student has own personalized learning-styles analysis and plan

Cramlington Community High School Head Derek Wise and his deputy, Derek Lovatt, are joint authors—with England's leading school teacher-trainer Alistair Smith—of a definitive book on Smith's "accelerated learning cycle". And they have worked in closely with his new company, Alite, and its "I Learn2" personalized program to identify individual students' learning styles and build on them.

3,500 students from over 70 countries, with personal learning schedule for each

Designing their own websites is almost second nature now to the international students at Singapore's Overseas Family School. Because many Asian students are brilliant at math but may be less competent at English, all 3,500 students now have personal computer-scheduled learning programs. This enables each student to develop excellence in favorite subjects while increasing competence on others.

visited Singapore in the early 1990s, on a consulting assignment. That involved visits to an international school. And soon afterwards he received a phonecall from one of its key executives, Irene Chee. The Singapore Teachers College had moved, and all its giant central-city campus was empty. Why not set up a model school there?

So together they did: the Overseas Family School, one of several international schools in Singapore licensed to service the island city-state's successful policy of attracting more than 3,000 foreign companies to their country. Like Tahatai and Cramlington, it's impossible to convey its model in mere typescript. But its *chasm-crossing* can be briefly summarized:

❑   The first school in Singapore, and one of the first in the world, to adopt the International Baccalaureate global curriculum for all age groups from early-childhood to senior high school, with 3,500 students from more than seventy nations.

❑   Extensive use of interactive technology as part of that program, and effective staff training in the IB philosophy and methods.

❑   An open-source digital network that links all administrators, teachers, students and their families—so the entire school program becomes a family affair.

❑   And many of its staff now digitizing lesson plans and "curriculum maps", using a wide variety of interactive software, including Macromedia *Flash* and professional animation applications.

But the Overseas Family School example has wider ramifications. The IB curriculum it has embraced is a truly international one—and ideal for every student, not just those who are "academically gifted". It is based around a multicultural, global model: trying to develop students as globally-minded citizens, with an open-minded understanding of what it means to be a participating international and local citizen.

It has both widely-accepted international *academic* assessment standards and its digital network offers all students the facilities to carry through life a digital portfolio of all their individual achievements, talents and strengths.

It sees a "curriculum" not as a narrow set of subjects, but as an interlinked way of becoming both a global-thinking citizen and a personal creator of a talented future.

And it has linked that with its own innovations to build a six-faceted global model for the school of the future, as we return to in the next chapter.

4. The Canadian Master's Academy

Master's Academy in Calgary, Alberta, Canada, is another private K-12 school. Its bold Mission is to develop *Master Learners*. Since it was set up in 1997, it has set out to define that student-centered leadership in seven ways: character, love of learning, independent worker, creative and critical thinker, quality producer, principle-centered leader and collaborative worker.[5]

But the Academy's Vision Statement is much more precise:

❏   To exceed all the current standards and expectations that have been set by Alberta Education.

❏   To equip all students as twenty-first-century knowledge workers with the skill-sets to succeed in an ever-changing world.

On both levels, the achievements are outstanding. Alberta's provincial government compares student performance with two Provincial Achievement Tests: a minimum pass rate and a standard of excellence—rated as around 84 percent.

And here the Academy's results are outstanding, with half of all students achieving 80 or higher and 42 percent scoring excellent[6] *(www.masters.ab.ca).*

Master's is not a big school—fewer than 600 students—but its interactive technology network and equipment would do justice to a school five times its size. And every student is trained not only in computer technology but to use hi-tech tools artistically and creatively.

Like all the other schools in our selection, Master's has committed "an unprecedented amount of time and energy towards teacher training. Over the past ten years we have spent between 150 and 200 hours a year in teacher training and vision development," says founder, Superintendent and CEO Tom Rudmik.[6] It is now combining its own excellent teacher training program and its high emphasis on technology with a view to making this total system available for teacher-development internationally.

In a school plan for a trip to Mars one student made her own planetary craft to take with them

Planning an entire trip to Mars as part of a school-wide space-travel project is typical of the innovative study programs at the Master's Academy in Alberta, Canada. Like all schools in this chapter, its commitment to professional teacher development is phenomenal—and so are the Academy's results.

At this Mexican pre-kindergarten, it starts with lots of fun and a personal learning profile

At age four, all children at the Mexico City campus of the Thomas Jefferson Institute can speak flluently in English as well as Spanish, enjoy each fun-day in a wide variety of learning activities. And trained psychologists work in with parents and teachers to start a personal learning profile that will be updated each year through to high school. The Institute has twice won the award as Latin America's school-of-the-year for vision and innovation.

5. Mexico's Thomas Jefferson Institute

In any review of *the school of the future,* it's hard to know where to start in summarizing Mexico's Thomas Jefferson Institute: truly one of the world's outstanding school systems.

❏   It operates both a 2015 Vision and 2020 Vision program to continually focus on the future—and what that is likely to bring to Mexico and the world the school's student will live in.

❏   It has working partnerships with Harvard University's Business School, the Massachusetts Institute of Technology in IT and creativity, and the Universities of West Florida and San Diego, in English-language training, with each running courses at its K-12 schools.

❏   Its students produce two Broadway musicals each year to professional standard, from *Wicked* to *Chicago* and *Cats* to *Joseph and His Amazing Technicolor Dream Coat.* (The professional cast of *Cats* attended one of the student performances and were amazed at the standard. In 2006, when leaders of Mexico's top private university watched a high-school production of *Wicked,* they immediately offered six fulltime scholarships to the production's main student contributors.)

❏   The school links three campuses and 3,500 students by video-conferencing, with specially-equipped performance centers at each campus and where students in each classroom can participate online.

❏   It was the world's first school whose students work in so closely with NASA (the U.S. National Aeronautical and Space Administration) that they became the first to talk with astronauts in space.

❏   In 2006 and 2007 it was chosen for the supreme school-of-the-year award out of 10,000 schools in Mexico, Central America, South America, Mexico, Portugal and Spain.*

❏   It's even had its student production of *The Disney High School Musical* videoed

* Organized by the Ibero American Council in Honor of Educational Quality (Consejo Iberoamericano en Honor a la Calidad Educativa).

for full reproduction on the Disney Television Channel.

The institute's total philosophy and scope represents the drive of co-founder Ricardo Carvajal, the Institute's CEO, and his American-born wife Jeanene, the group's School Director. They met while Ricardo was finishing his university study in America, married in 1968 and returned to Mexico. But when their three young children were nearing school age, no nearby school met the parents' vision. So they set up their own, in Mexico City, in 1978, with 225 students. Within three years they had 850, and built their present main campus. It now has 1,850.

The other two pre-K-12 campuses have since been opened, at Guadalajara and Queretaro. They were linked with headquarters from the beginning through the online classrooms and video-conference centers.

Virtually every cutting-edge teaching and learning method highlighted in this book has been explored and adapted by the schools' leadership and teachers: with the aim of a totally holistic education.

From kindergarten through elementary, middle and high schools, trained psychologists work with parents and students to compile a personal profile of each child, with strong emphasis on each one's social and emotional development. These profiles are reviewed and updated twice a year and are a vital part of the child's journey through school.

In each well-equipped kindergarten, children have a choice of different *attention centers*—areas where they can choose what to do: reading, writing, science, blocks, sand, costumes, board games and computers. They can also choose individually what projects they would like to work on—as they learn to explore their preferences, to plan ahead, to become responsible for their own work, to share material, to work in teams and clean their work area. Eyesight and hearing are checked regularly. And one of the key features of this pre-school period is the high-quality reporting to parents, with mutual guidance on how to detect and overcome any stress, emotional or social problems—as part of a total program of holistic learning and development.

From kindergarten to high school, the Institute also runs a *Family School* program of

The Mexican high school where students study at the Harvard Business School and partner High Tech High

Harvard has one of the university world's best-known business schools. And when it decided to offer a senior high school version of it methods and content, Mexico's award-winning Thomas Jefferson Institute was one of the first to sign up. The university's high school program is solely on line, with video presentations by its top professors, each backed by a student-involvement program at an appropriate level. The Institute also partners with several other organizations, including San Diego-started High Tech High program, MIT's MediaLab, Microsoft and Apple.

The basic core of interactive technology in education: see it as creative art and how to produce and share it

conferences and workshops, so parents, too, can learn to become better educators. With the importance of English as an international language, each day the class language is split 50-50 between Spanish and English.

Interactive technology tools are a normal part of classroom activities, with the students creating video games, their own blogs, and developing confidence by public presentations, both inside the network that links the Institute's three campuses and on the public stage. The Institute also has its own Special Projects Department, with ten fulltime and twenty-five part-time staff—developing a range of programs from educational technology to *How the mind learns.*

Visit the *2020 Vision* world of the Thomas Jefferson Institute—with its brilliant inter-campus links—online (at *www.itj.edu.mx* —in English or Spanish) and you'll see why we believe teacher-training and retraining should ideally be closely linked to schools which are leading the new revolution—not stuck in a model designed over 300 years ago.

6. Technology leadership joins holistic learning

Significantly, each of the model schools featured in this chapter — for leadership in digital technology — also excels in holistic education: the development of the *whole student* inside a caring, happy community.

Singapore's OFS's "master policy" since it opened in 1991 has been to "provide a happy, safe and effective school for overseas families living in Singapore".

And Mexico's Thomas Jefferson Institute, in its *2015 Vision* lists its aims to develop students who are bilingual, multicultural, creative, flexible, team-workers, happy and successful with strong values, alongside their academic, sporting, lifelong learning, critical thinking and hi-tech skills. Its *2020 Vision* expands these into a bigger, Web 2.0 global plan, based on the new world and Latin America that is emerging in this new century.

Not one of the schools would say that digital technology is their dominant feature. It is one of many tools they use as the catalyst to provide a balanced new-style education for all their students, while linking families into that entire holisic process.

7. The challenge to extend the lessons to all schools

As we near the end of this summary, we are more than aware of the many great schools, and excellent administrations, in "education".

Sweden alone has been an inspiration to both authors, first when co-author Dryden visited it with a television crew and then when co-author Vos spent months on end running seminars the length and breadth of the country.

Although Sweden is well known as one model for "Social Democracy", in education it is also a striking example of public-private partnerships. Its Teachers Union is one of the strongest and most active in the world. Yet Sweden is one country which has welcomed the concept of private companies contracting to run schools on behalf of government.

The Pysslingen group, for example, operates fifty-eight pre-schools, with 4,400 pupils, and twenty primary-secondary schools, with 3,300 students, under such contracts. Like Sweden's public schools and public services, it abounds with innovation. Its teacher development program is excellent. Lemshaga Barnakademi provides a different model of a community as a total learning environment, set up on the initiative of Helena M. Wallenberg of Sweden's most prominent investment families.*

And all the schools—public and private—highlighted in this book are strong advocates of wealthier countries sharing their best educational innovations with nations that, at least financially, are less wealthy—and learning from their cultures in return.

To take one simple possibility: New Zealand, with four million people, has the same-sized population as all the small islands in the vast Pacific Ocean. It has strong government aid and cultural ties with many. Given New Zealand's own history of cooperative enterprise, it seems straight common sense to link its own successful ICT school cluster concept and share it, on a school-to-school basis, with those countries.

And it is to that potential for ***cooperative enterprise*** and ***co-creativity*** that we turn to in our final chapter: how to globalize the Web 2.0 learning revolution.

* Co-author Vos has been involved for many years as a teacher-development consultant and trainer for both organizations.

What if schools leading the IT revolution were to each share with a third-world school?

Many adults confuse computers in education with the passive watching of television at home. But those schools showing the way to introduce interactive technology reverse that. They see students as multimedia authors and producers. The preferred starting point: the digital video cameras and the software that enables students to create their own music, edit their own videos, create their own graphic art, set up their 3D sets. And now to share those skills with others—inside and outside their country. Photo at Tahatai Coast School, New Zealand, during an interview for student TV.

'You may say I'm a dreamer, but I'm not the only one . . .

I hope some day you'll join us and the world will be as one'

From John Lennon's classic song, Imagine.

How to unleash the talents of billions to reinvent the world

Now it's your turn. The challenge: to reinvent the way the whole world learns—and especially the two billion people below the poverty line.

That could be easier than you think.

John Lennon summed up the challenge in a word: ***Imagine.***

Albert Einstein took six: ***Imagination is more important than knowledge.***

And Victor Hugo could have been talking about today's Web 2.0 revolution when he wrote: ***Nothing can resist the power of an idea whose time has come.***

Today the importance of imagination and innovation is even more obvious:

❏ For centuries major progress depended on three drivers: *land, labor, capital.*

❏ In this new twenty-first century, the big three are simply: *knowledge, imagination* and *innovation.*

❏ And, as the Web 2.0's interactive co-creative era flowers, it now becomes possible to use that knowledge, imagination and innovation to reinvent education—in all its forms—so the whole world benefits. And to reinvent almost everything else.

The previous three chapters outline that concept in three dimensions:

❏ The cyberspace and new technology infrastructure.

❏ Wide-ranging new opportunities in business, for everyone, but especially for those with the talent and knowledge to package and sell their skills to millions.

❏ Great existing change-models at schools and universities.

Silicon Valley's ecology of creative innovation also shows how to expand those concepts globally.

Take any great idea to the Valley's best venture-capital funders and they will almost certainly evaluate it on four main criteria:

❏ **How big is the idea?** *How large is the total market?*

❏ **How simple is it?** *How easy is it to "cross the chasm"?*

❏ **How quickly can it scale?** *How fast can it become global?*

❏ **What leadership is needed to achieve that?**

Now what better idea to evaluate than a great education for all? And what leadership is needed to scale that challenge globally? The answer, too, could be much simpler than you think . . .

1. It's YOU

For years we've been taught to believe Thomas Carlyle's theory that "the history of the world is but the biography of great men". But, as Time magazine summarizes it: "That theory has now taken a serious beating. Time's person of the year for 2006 is YOU."

In a year of bloodshed in Iraq, Lebanon and the Sudan—in a decade where celebrity television trivializes almost every issue—*Time* invited us all to view the future through a different lens: to see another, bigger story: "It isn't about conflict or great men. It's a story about community and collaboration on a scale never seen before. It's about the cosmic compendium of knowledge, *Wikipedia,* the million-channel people's network *YouTube,* and the online metropolis, *MySpace.* It's about the many wrestling power from the few and helping one another for nothing, and how that will not only change the world, but also change the way the world changes."[1]

The tool that makes that possible is the new World Wide Web. Not the basic Arpanet conceived in the 1960s as a way for scientists to share research. Nor only the Web that Tim Berners-Lee turned into a mass-information tool in the early 1990s. Certainly not

The history of the world is no longer 'the biography of great men; *Time's* person of the year is YOU'

A personalized learning, health and success plan for everyone?

the over-hyped dot-com, get-rich-quick investment frenzy of 2000.

"The new Web is a different thing," says *Time*. "It's a tool for bringing together the small contributions of millions of people and making them matter. Silicon Valley consultants call it Web 2.0, as if it were a new version of some old software. But it's really a revolution." Not all of it is great. Says *Time* correctly: "Web 2.0 harnesses the stupidity of crowds as well as its wisdom.

"(But) this is an opportunity to build a new kind of international understanding, not politician to politician, great man to great man, but citizen to citizen, person to person."

Marketers call this concept "mass personalization": the ability to personalize information and knowledge so that it is specific and usable to millions:

❏   To collectively share each others' talents so that each of us can construct ***a personal lifelong learning plan*** and ***a personal health plan***—and make it work: just like Dell makes it easy for anyone to design a personal computer from an online choice of components.

❏   But also to provide the online, simple tools for everyone—including the world's poorest people—to sell their talents, products and services on the Internet to the world: ***a personal success plan.***

The basic cyber-infrastructure is already in place. Silicon Valley specialist Kevin Kelly says that achievement will eventually "be recognized as the largest, most complex, most surprising event on the planet. Weaving nerves out of glass and radio waves, our species has begun wiring up all regions, all processes, all facts and notions into a grand network."[2]

In the affluent Western world, the main tools appear as the Web, the personal computer and interactive digital software.

But we agree with Indian innovator Rajesh Jain: Web 2.0 for the world's poorest billions is mobile, digital, personal and multi-faceted.

At its simplest, it's a mobile phone. In developing countries these outnumber personal computers up to ten to one. More than 550 million Chinese use them every day.

Worldwide, more than 3.3 billion people are already walking around with "the same computing power in their pocket as a mid-1990s personal computer—while consuming only one-hundredth of the energy. Even the simplest voice-only phones have more complexity and power than the 1969 on-board computer that landed a spaceship on the moon."[3] And of course few mobile phones are now only that.

In the second quarter of 2008, 302 million cellphones were sold. In the full year the forecast is 1.2 billion So, even allowing for discards, the total in use is expected to reach 4 billion sometime in 2009. That's more than the world has television sets. And around three times as many as personal computers around the globe.

Coastal fishermen in India are linking mobile phones with geo-positional satellites to search for the best fishing grounds. And then to find out which ports and traders are offering the best prices. Millions of students in China, Japan, Korea and the Philippines are using them to learn English.

And if you'd like a quick course on how mobile technology can revolutionize many other aspects of learning, visit *www.marcprensky.com*—Marc Prensky's website—and, in his list of articles, read *What can you learn from a cell phone? Almost anything!*

Read Adam Cohen's book on eBay, *The Perfect Store,* and you will learn how Karin Stahl and the eBay Foundation are already helping Guatemalan villagers to sell their colorful woven handcrafts online. Or check out the Catalog Generator website *(http://www.catgen.org)* to find out how the PEOPLink not-for-profit foundation has won several global excellence awards for its role in helping village artisans in many countries to sell their handcrafts through the Web.

The World Resources Institute report on *The Next Four Billion[4]* also lists mobile telephony as "the strongest success story" in helping to lift the world's poorest people out of poverty.

Now mobile phones have incorporated multimedia technologies: with Internet access, cameras and video screens. Rajesh Jain's Netcore and Novatium groups have designed cheap ones in India to plug into TV screens.

Now add a simple projector into each mobile device, and a global classroom be-

'A simple voice-only phone has more power than the onboard computer that landed a spaceship on moon'

In China's cities families spend 35% of their total income on the education of their one child

comes a reality—lessons projected on to a village wall or screen: an instant source of learning and health programs.

Mexico's school of the year—the Thomas Jefferson Institute—already links its three campuses with video-conferencing technology.

The University of Western Australia has included an online interactive white-board to link in with *Skype*-type free telephony and *Moodle* open-source digital courseware to provide worldwide online schooling through its *DiscoverE* program. The entire system makes it easy to share lessons with students in many countries

And in the foothills of New Zealand's Southern Alps, former British school principal Frances Hill uses that system to run online home-schooling and wide-ranging teacher-retraining programs from her Alpha Educational Consultancy's virtual classroom *(www. alphaed.org.nz)*.

But for graphic proof of the power of spreading educational change by visual and interactive example, the sales success of an earlier edition of *The Learning Revolution* in China is another model. Both the co-authors of this book travel with many accessories to demonstrate how learning can be interactive and fun. These include many video clips of new learning methods in action.

In late 1998, China's then leading educational software group organized thirty simultaneous three-week *Learning Revolution* exhibitions in that country's biggest cities. Each featured giant-screen videos of these new methods. A massive television advertising program promoted the free exhibitions direct to parents, after the co-authors had demonstrated many on a half-hour evening network television show. Well over 250,000 people attended the exhibitions on *the first day*—and 261,000 books were sold: 44,000 in Beijing alone—10 million in seven months. Perhaps that's not surprising in cities where the average family spends 35 percent of its income on the education of its only child.

Ten million watched the half-hour television show which launched that book. Now "streaming video" means hundreds of millions, who can already afford good personal computers and broadband access, can access 83 million *YouTube* TV videos.

2. It's GLOBAL

So if 10 million people in one country can quickly grasp the personal implications through TV, how can the Web 2.0 revolution make it global?

Jeffrey Sachs and his United Nations Millennium Project puts the challenge simply: to end world poverty by 2025, cut it in half by 2015—and provide a primary education for every child in the world. His book, *The End of Poverty,* spells out precisely how this could be achieved for less than one-sixth the world's current military spending of one trillion dollars a year. Every major national government has committed itself to guarantee this money: by contributing each year only seven cents from every $10 of each national income. Most have yet to reach anywhere near that goal. It is beyond the scope of this book to repeat all the detailed, specific and low-cost proposals in Professor Sachs' book. We endorse them.

There is also no need to detail further the concepts summarized in chapter ten of this book for a Cyber Meta-University.[5] That is already unleashing the talents of the world's finest research universities to be freely shared with the rest of the planet. Exactly the same principle can unleash the power to change every other aspect of education for every age group, everywhere. So let's list some challenges and possible answers:

For early childhood and parenting education:

As chapters three and seven summarize, infants before they start school develop more of their brain-based learning ability than in their school years.

That means home and neighborhood combined are the world's most important schools, and parents and grandparents the world's most important teachers. Our own research continually reiterates that lesson:

❏   A century ago, Maria Montessori was proving it in the slums of Rome, by creating a multisensory environment in which tiny infants could learn to read, write, spell and count well before starting school.

❏   Refugee children in Sweden—from more than 100 countries—have even improved on that: learning to speak three language well before age five. Even sharing only Montessori's wisdom online with millions of parents would be a great start.

In India almost 50% of villages don't even have a school, and to many people home is a hovel

7 cents in every $1 of the rich world's income would solve both

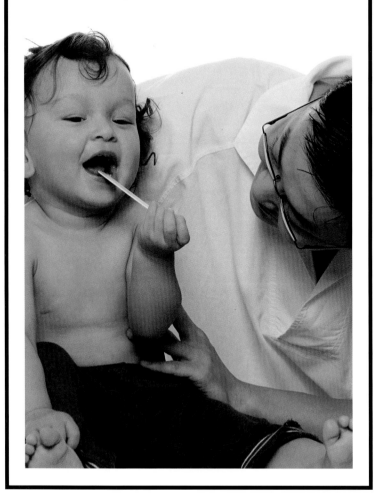

For one-sixth of arms spending, child poverty could be halved; primary school and health care for all

❏   When co-author Dryden and a television crew first visited the Pacific island of Rarotonga thirty years ago to do a program on health, they found the country's Minister of Health and Education, Dr. Joseph Williams, at a Montessori-type combined early-childhood center and parent-training center. Everything at the center was labelled in two languages: English and Cook Island Maori. All pregnant parents who enrolled there learned practical lessons in childcare and nutrition in pregnancy and infancy.

Result: early childhood admissions to Rarotonga Hospital were reduced by 90 percent—by a simple parent-education program. Now share that with the world!

❏   Later detailed research shows how similar nutrition programs impact on educational opportunities. Of the 559 million children under five in the world's poorest countries, 219 million will grow up "intellectually stunted". Poverty and poor nutrition is by far the main combined cause.[6]

Jeffrey Sachs' book abounds with simple examples of how the worst problems of poverty can be solved if all countries join the Netherlands, Norway, Denmark, Sweden and Luxembourg in donating 0.7 percent of their total income to simple aid programs. As he wrote in an article headed *The Weapons of Mass Salvation,* after 2001's terrorist attacks on New York: "Almost 3,000 people died needlessly and tragically at the World Trade Center on September 11. Ten thousand Africans die needlessly and tragically *every single day*—and have died every single day since September 11—of AIDS, tuberculosis and malaria. We need to keep September 11 in perspective, especially because the 10,000 daily deaths *are preventable.*"[7] Of those, 3,000 die every day—over 3 million a year—from malaria: deaths easily preventable by providing long-lasting insecticide-treated bed nets at a total cost of only $1.50 for each child each year.

Parenting education is probably the most neglected aspect of all learning in the world. Very few are ever fully trained to excel in it. Yet that is exactly the kind of on-the-spot, as-needed information that the new Web is geared to deliver. And the world's best early-childhood specialists are geared to mass-personalize it.

A global primary-years curriculum:

At elementary-level, the International Baccalaureate (IB) already provides a global

Primary Years Program (PYP) for children from three to eleven years—introduced briefly in the previous chapter.

It could be easily-scaled as an online program to fit in with Professor Sach's United Nations Millennium project to provide an excellent primary education for every child in the world: through satellite, wireless, computer and low-cost mobile-teleputer-projector technology.

Overall a modern curriculum should involve four interrelated parts:

THE CONTENT: *What information is studied and learned.*

THE PROCESS: *How it is studied, so that lifelong habits are formed to inquire, investigate, probe, analyze, present, reflect and create.*

THE METHOD: *The format, so that every project also involves learning how to learn and learning how to think.*

PERSONAL GROWTH: *What attitudes are "caught"—the lifeskills to create an holistic, well-rounded, fully-participating citizen.*

The International Baccalaureate curriculum aims to achieve all four—while allowing all the other innovations, and many not yet invented, to be included from other great schools, principals, teachers and students:

The content: *Every year, each IB primary class studies six global themes. By using the new networking technologies, the same program can be shared with schools and students everywhere—and their families.*

Those six-weekly topic-themes enable students to absorb the building-blocks of their world: the planets of the universe, continents, minerals, oceans, rivers, inventions, ancient civilizations and technologies of the world, including one's own country and current global issues. Literacy, numeracy, social studies, music and other languages are integrated into each theme for real-life experience.

The process: The whole approach can be built on identifying and developing student's individual talents inside multi-talented teams, so that concepts such as "multiple intelligences" are constantly, and almost automatically, blended and absorbed into the

One possible plan for a global movement to provide primary schooling for every child by 2015

When students are seen as multimedia journalists, the whole world becomes their reporting classroom

learning process. Create the right environment, and children automatically start with their strengths—then share these with others. This process also develops a wide range of multimedia skills: to discover information, turn it into creative knowledge, test it, reflect on it, create with it and apply it.

The method: Singapore's Overseas Family School, a leading IB school, calls this *focused inquiry:* starting with the IB's eight-question method of tackling every possibility. To any non-teacher visiting the school for the first time, all students seem to be developing the combined skills of multimedia investigative journalists. Each teacher is trained NOT to volunteer ready-made answers. Each acts instead as *a guide on the side,* not *a sage on the stage.* By contrast, we've visited many others schools in the world (including Singapore) where teachers say they feel guilty if they are not themselves talking for at least 90 percent of the time.

At IB schools, the students quickly learn to use eight main questions to start their *focused inquiry* into whatever they are studying. This research-discovery and creative process thus becomes second nature:

❏   **Form:** *What is it like?* Everything has a form with recognizable features, which can be observed, identified, described and categorized.

❏   **Function:** *How does it work?* Everything has a purpose, a role or a way of behaving which can be investigated and categorized.

❏   **Cause:** *Why is it like it is?* Things do not just happen. Everything has a cause, and actions have consequences, which need to be considered.

❏   **Change:** *How is it changing?* Everything is in a state of change. Change is universal, and one of the best tests of an educational system is how it develops students' ability to manage change.

❏   **Connection:** *How is it connected to other things?* We live in a world of interacting systems, in which the actions of individuals, communities, nations and elements affect others.

❏   **Perspective:** *What are other points of view?* We all view issues and concepts through different perspectives, and often preconceptions.

❏ ***Responsibility: What is our responsibility?*** We are not passive observers of events. We can and must make choices. By doing so we can make a difference, on a personal, community and global scale.

❏ ***Reflection: How do we know?*** And how do we know when we are correct? Reflection also encourages us to focus on our way of reasoning, and the quality and reliability of the evidence we have considered.

Now many of the other schools highlighted in these pages also have similar inquiry models. But the benefit of the IB Primary Years Program is the way these tie into universal themes, to unlock the building blocks of knowledge—and, at the Singapore school, to record the answers in multimedia ways. It's also available globally.

Personal development: PYP teachers also have to build, into their daily lesson plans, projects to cultivate eleven distinct attitudes, all designed to develop balanced, real-life skills, so that students become:

❏ **Inquirers:** using all the skills needed to find out what they need to know.

❏ **Lifelong learners:** with an active love of learning.

❏ **Thinkers:** skilled in using thinking skills to create better solutions.

❏ **Communicators:** confident and competent to communicate in many ways.

❏ **Risk-takers:** equally confident to explore new ideas, roles and strategies.

❏ **Knowledgable:** with a good basic general knowledge.

❏ **Principled:** with integrity, honesty and a sense of fairness and justice.

❏ **Caring:** with commitment to action and service, sensitive to others' needs.

❏ **Open-minded**: ready to explore a range of views and alternatives.

❏ **Well balanced:** linking physical, mental and lifeskills balance.

❏ **Reflective:** with the ability to reflect wisely and consider all alternatives.

Each International Baccalaureate school employs curriculum coordinators to support teachers. And while classroom teachers are working with students on the current six-week project, the coordinators are helping plan the next six weeks: checking on satel-

The International Baccalaureate's 11 guidelines to develop rounded citizens*

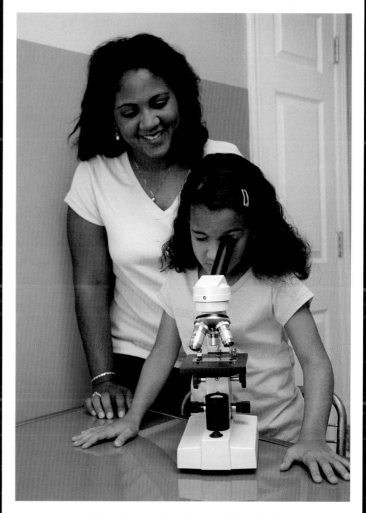

* See eleven points in checklist at left.

When high creativity drops from 92% as infants to 2% as adults, maybe we're debating the wrong 'basics'

lite television programs, confirming the latest research, downloading new videoclips, checking new books. Now that knowledge can easily be shared globally. So the IB PYP curriculum also has the added benefit that all the creative new ways to teach and learn can be incorporated inside a shared framework and structure—and easily added to the global knowledge-pool. IB teacher-retraining, to concentrate on enthusing students themselves to find answers to every challenge, can also be partly done online.

Middle and high school programs

The International Baccalaureate and many of the other model schools already reported in this book, plus Scott McNealy's Global Educational and Learning Network, could easily be combined into a best-of-the-best global program for middle and high schools. All these model schools, and the best of the New Zealand primary programs, also move way beyond the simple standardized-testing-of-memorized-content that seems to be the sole aim of many school systems. Instead, the aim is to develop competent, confident explorers, able to tackle any problem, challenge or opportunity they will face in life with the skills of scientific inquiry, exploration and creative thinking.

Unfortunately, that is exactly the kind of natural ability that so many school systems seem to quickly destroy in children. Yet that creative problem-solving ability is precisely what is needed to provide creative leaders of the future in all countries, especially those that are currently very poor.

❏ *In research on 1,600 three-to-five-year-olds, 98 percent tested at the genius level or higher in divergent thinking: the ability to think creatively in different ways.*[8]

❏ Five years later the same children were checked at age eight to ten. By that stage, 32 percent tested at the genius creative-thinking level.

❏ By the time the children were thirteen it was down to 10 percent.

❏ *When the researchers gave the same test to 2,000 adults only 2 per cent were highly creative. The other 98 percent automatically tried to use yesterday's solutions to today's challenging opportunities. Re-read those figures and weep.*

In reporting the results, former McKinsey management consultant and author Steven

Carden says: "Something eroded in the capacity of those children to think creatively. It might just have had to do with the way modern educational systems teach children to think."[9]

Or don't teach them. Significantly the very abilities that have been used to create much better and thriving national economies are those that seem to disappear in most school systems. Carden identifies three "primary ingredients in a society honed for change and adaptation":

❏ ***Each has creativity in its veins:*** *highly successful in generating new ideas.*

❏ ***A thirst for new ideas:*** *great at seeking out the ideas of others.*

❏ ***A willingness to change:*** *great at applying new ideas.*

We would add a fourth ingredient:

❏ ***The ability to co-create:*** *The ecology typified by Silicon Valley*—the ability to link together co-creative universities, research institutes, young entrepreneurs, venture-capital funders, skilled globally-experienced managers and a total community of innovation.

As a result, Silicon Valley is often said to have produced, in one generation, "the greatest creation of legal wealth in history".[10]

Now China, South Korea, Taiwan, Hong Kong and Singapore could equally make that claim—but using creative methods that combine "the best of the West and the best of rest": including ancient wisdom. China and the new Asian Tigers already lead the world in blending the new-era technologies of mobile phones, digital cameras, wireless and rapid broadband internet connections with their own traditional strengths.

Many critics wrongly identify rote-learning for exam-passing as the sole inheritance from China's most famous philosopher, Confucius *(Kung Fu Tze, or Kung The Master).*[11] Confucius certainly stressed the need for training in *six disciplinary arts:* ritual, music, archery, charioting, writing and mathematics. But China was also centuries ahead of the West in creating educational methods that many would now claim as "accelerated learning": the abacus or *suan pan*—to learn mathematics with all the senses; playing cards; *dominoes; go; mahjong:* and of course paper and (with Korea)

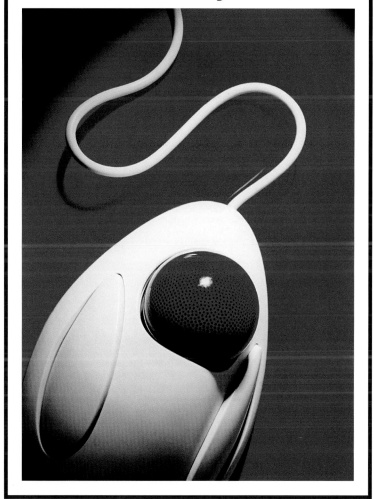

The Silicon Valley creative eco-system: 'The greatest creation of legal wealth in history'

What if Mexico's high school creativity joined with New Zealand's charter system and IB global curriculum?

Photo from Guys and Dolls, professional Broadway musical by students at Mexico's Thomas Jefferson Institute.

printing itself. Confucius was also a strong advocate of *learning by doing* and using the world as a classroom, as summarized in Chen Jinpan's book, *Confucius as Teacher.*

Singapore's new-generation Prime Minister Lee Hsien Loong is one Asian leader strongly in favor of returning to that same balance today. His strongest call: "Teach less—and learn more",[12] with fewer boring lectures and more creative to-learn-it-do-it involvement activities.

So how might the U.N. Millennium program provide not only primary schooling for all the world's poor children by 2015—but the **best** primary education?

How might it involve the Bill and Melinda Gates Foundation, Google, Scott Mc-Nealy's Curriki, the Hewlett Foundation and many similar bodies to fund the search to create an even better new Global Baccalaureate? *Would that not include:*

❏   The best of the present International Baccalaureate programs—but geared to the online retraining of teachers and the global online sharing of lesson plans, so that all schools have the choice of opting in to a proven global success story?

❏   A system similar to the New Zealand two-part charter guidelines[13]—so that schools in poor countries can also develop their own creative innovations and goals, while using the Baccalaureate curriculum guidelines as the second-part choice?

❏   The great models of pre-kindergarten to high school private schools such as Mexico's Thomas Jefferson Institute and Singapore's Overseas Family School—and others only too happy to share their programs with others less fortunate?

❏   And the great public high school models of America's High Tech High and Britain's Cramlington—which has just opened its Cramlington Learning Village to add to its outstanding high school?

But school alternatives are not the only ones. Learning is now lifelong.

3. It's INTERACTIVE

As former Xerox Chief Scientist John Seely Brown keeps stressing, today's students love to learn interactively: to learn by doing, creating, and co-creating.

And, as experience proves at all the schools highlighted in the previous chapter, even very young children can quickly learn to script, shoot and edit videotape, make computer animations, create music, and even invent new digital learning games. So why not develop new methods to develop those skills among the users of low-cost mobile *teleputers?*

Ask any parent in China or India what they'd like to achieve for their children's education and they'll probably list three goals: to speak fluent English—the modern international language; to be competent in using computers and digital technologies: and to gain internationally-accepted qualifications.

Each goal can be partially achieved by the skilled use of cheap mobile phones, with cyberspace access to learning tools—including the development of new projection programs added to cellphones for projecting lessons into village homes and schools.

❏   Millions of Asians are already learning English through mobile phones, texting friends and singing to *karaoke* machines.

❏   Even very young children can learn interactive technology. Many of the digital tools are available free online.

❏   And universities almost everywhere now offer online degrees.

The private University of Phoenix is now America's biggest university, with 280,000 students, 239 campuses and offshoots around the world, including some in India and China. Around 95 percent of its students are working adults. In the early 1990s it became the first U.S. university to offer degrees online—or mainly online.

Another private American University, Pepperdine, runs undergraduate, graduate and doctoral courses in Educational Technology. The big majority of course-work is online—while teachers taking each course have the added benefit of putting each lesson to practical use each day in their own school classrooms.

The late Peter Drucker—probably the most widely read management thinker of the twentieth century—forecast not long before he died that "the continuing professional educational education of adults will be the number one growth industry of the next thirty years". His further forecast: that "in five years we will deliver most of our executive management programs online".[14]

280,000 business people get degrees online from University of Phoenix from 239 global campuses

The private University of Phoenix is the world's biggest, with 285,000 students, including many in China and India. It was America's first university to offer degree courses online, in 1990. Around 95 percent of its students are working adults.

Now great jazz players can train musicians around the world online or on interactive discs

China's Academy of Science is already doing that with an online MBA course to thousands of students.

In India, a computer training company, NIIT, has forty wholly-owned centers and more than 1,000 franchise operations to teach computer training: typical of the type of operation that will soon link on-site and online learning. NIIT has become so popular that some advertisements in the matrimonial pages of the *Times of India* specify NIIT graduates.

Both co-authors of this book have personal experiences of how individual talents can be turned into online digital courses—and interactive classroom and multimedia projects:

❏   As well as her doctoral research into new accelerated methods of learning, co-author Vos has particular expertise in the use of music in all forms of learning and teaching. In 1999 she turned this into a *Music Revolution* book, intending to sell it with six or seven music CDs with 120 selected tracks. Unfortunately right then the world music industry erupted with the soaring growth of free Internet swapping of music tracks through *Napster.* The five giant international music companies then insisted on royalties that would have priced the CDs off the market for reuse in school class-rooms. Now Apple's creative team has thought laterally, and invented both the *iPod* and *iTunes.* So a revamped program on *the seven ways to use music for learning and teaching* will be on sale shortly, with online links to download recommended music.

❏   Co-author Dryden has for years run corporate training courses to teach creativity in business. When the British Government introduced trial courses in *Enterprise Education* at high school level, early this century, he was contracted to run ten one-day seminars on the subject, and adapted his program for high-school teachers. So he created the *Aha!* board game to show teachers how to start with their own talent and turn it into an international business plan. The teachers soon saw how California kindergarten teacher Jan Davidson turned her early-reading and early-math talent into interactive CD-rom programs and a company later sold for $1 billion. The teachers were quickly enthused. Most had never dreamed of turning their teaching talent into a world online business. Now in Mexico that game is being turned into an interactive course to teach creative enterprise skills at school—but it won't stop at Mexico.

4. It's INSTANT

Earlier this book quoted Atomic Learning as an excellent example of a great Web 2.0 concept to provide instant learning-on-demand at an incredibly low price.

Atomic Learning provides schools—and all their teachers and students—with 24/7 access to 35,000 short video tutorials on the most popular interactive-technology programs: from Microsoft *Office* to Adobe *Photoshop,* and their open-source alternatives. Each tutorial provides instant access to demonstrate a specific answer to a specific query: like how to add video-clips, clip-art or clip-simulations to *Powerpoint* color slides. The annual cost to schools for each student: between $1 and $2.

Virtually any of the world's most used Web sites now offer similar instant access: like *Wikipedia, Google, Yahoo, MySpace* and *YouTube.*

And this is the kind of potential that Harvard's Prof. Christensen refers to when he uses detailed graphs to show that, on current trends, 25 percent of high school courses will be available online by 2014 and 50 percent by 2019—for all ages.[15]

5. It's a FREE or NEARLY FREE

This is also a major feature of the Web: give away basic information free—and sell "the extras" for a few-cents-a-click.

Some sites, of course, like Google and Yahoo's *Overture,* use this concept as their major profit earner. Many others give away similar search-information free, but earn their income from banner advertising.

6. It's EASILY SHARED

Go on the Web to MySpace, Facebook, Flickr or similar sites and you'll find millions of people already taking part every day in the rapidly-expanding concept of global social networking and sharing.

❏ Yahoo alone—the biggest online directory—has millions of users in cooperative groups. They can even play games like bridge and chess with strangers online.

'25% of high school courses will be available online by 2014, 50% by 2019—for all ages'

The first global revolution in history where so many people everywhere can co-create the future

If they can produce biggest encyclopedia, with 10 million entries, then what's next?

❏ New Yorker Thomas Friedman, in *The Lexus and The Olive Tree,* includes the story of his seventy-nine-year-old mother phoning him from Minneapolis. She was perturbed, and when he asked why, she replied: "Well, I've been playing bridge on the Internet with three Frenchmen, and they keep speaking French with each other." When Friedman chuckled, she took umbrage. "Don't laugh," she said. "I was playing bridge with someone in Siberia the other day." Friedman adds: "To all those who say that this era of globalization is no different from the previous one, I would simply ask: Was your great-grandmother playing bridge with Frenchmen on the Internet in 1900? I don't think so."[16]

❏ The Global SchoolNet Foundation links schools in more than 100 countries in a similar online *Global Schoolhouse,* with funding from the U.S. National Science Foundation *(http://www.globalschoolnet.org)* .

❏ The ePALS *Classroom Exchange* also links thousands of Western K-12 schools with similar schools in China.

❏ And an international group of educators met in Canada in 2007 to plan how to integrate software technologies to achieve a bold vision: to develop a free education curriculum by 2015. Their first big challenge: to improve *Mediawiki* software—which already powers *Wikipedia* and *WikiEducator*—to widen free access to education around the world. *WikiEducator* is being co-sponsored by the Commonwealth of Learning, an organization now headed by Sir John Daniels.

7. It's CO-CREATIVE

But by far the biggest key to the new Web 2.0 revolution can be stated simply in the compound word: it's co-creative.

For the first time in history: not only can we now store all the world's existing knowledge and make it available, almost instantly, in almost any form, to almost anyone on earth . . . we can also use the entire world as a creative talent pool. Again the examples abound—as we have explored throughout this book.

❏ **Jimmy Wales**, with *Wikipedia,* has shown how to co-create the world's biggest encyclopedia, free, with an army of thousands of talented enthusiasts.

❏ **Linus Torvalds,** a young Finnish student, has done likewise with his Linux movement where thousands of other computer-science students have co-created a free modern computer operating system, for downloading from the Internet.

❏ **Brian Behlendorf,** the American student who co-founded the Apache Software Foundation, has involved thousands of other open-source fans to co-create the Apache software that now powers 70 percent of the world's web-servers.

❏ **The Hewlett Foundation's** 2007 Report on the Open Educational Resources movement includes links to dozens of projects to share university learning tools.

❏ **Marc Prensky** is seeking support to involve the schools, universities, teachers and students of the world in co-creating *serious games* to teach and learn everything.

❏ **Singapore's Overseas Family School** is digitizing all its K-12 lesson plans on open-platform *Java* and *Flash* technology so that they can be easily shared with other schools under open-source licensing.

❏ **Teachers at The New City School,** in St. Louis, Missouri, have already co-written two books on how to teach every subject at every grade level, using Howard Gardner's multiple-intelligence learning concepts. That's an already-researched idea crying out for online digitized and interactive sharing.

❏ **Heritage Publishing** in Hawaii marked the U.S. Bicentenary in 1976 by running a competition for school students to write and illustrate *A Child's History of Hawaii.* The best entries were edited together, and the resulting book would do credit to Hemingway and Picasso.

Now that same concept could easily be combined into a global competition to involve the world's students in co-creating an interactive online history of the world. It would start with their individual countries, cities, villages and communities—with videos they have shot themselves, edited themselves, with music they've composed themselves, and computer animations they have created themselves.

The result could be A Child's Multimedia History of the World—co-created by the kids of the world! Just like those five-to-ten-year-olds at Bubbledome's school holiday classes. Or the five-to-thirteen-year-olds at New Zealand's Tahatai Coast

A world where the longer-living wisdom of grandparents can blend with new-tech skills of the young

Each of us is now a center of the new web of unlimited challenge and possibilities

Primary School, with the two-hour complete CD-rom they created ten years ago with their own videotapes and animations to design their "school of the future".

Simple templates now make such multimedia co-creation easy—for anyone, anywhere. And, as stressed throughout this book, interactive technology is not about passively gazing at a TV screen, but using new tools to showcase your talent.

But the best is yet to come

Both co-authors of this book are convinced that even better innovations are yet to come—when the collective creative brainpower of 59 million teachers and 2 billion students is unleashed. When we first met by accident, sitting next to each other at an international learning conference in 1991, we came from completely different backgrounds, professions and different cultures.

❏ One, the Dutch-born, Canadian-raised, American doctor of education who had just completed a seven-year research program into new methods of effective learning—after many years as a classroom teacher, district resource teacher and doctoral researcher.

❏ The other, the New Zealand-born journalist, radio and TV anchor and producer, then editing 150 hours of globally-shot video into six one-hour, prime-time national television documentaries on the same subject.

When we swapped our results a few months later—a giant doctoral dissertation and six TV programs—the findings coincided completely. A year later we decided to co-create a book. With one author in California, the other in New Zealand, 9,600 kilometers (6,000 miles) apart, that book was co-authored by fax machine. Even then we had never heard of Tim Berners-Lee or the World Wide Web. Who could have forecast that, less than ten years later, the world would be completely changed by the globe-encircling network he created: owned by no one, ready to be used by anyone?

In 1993, when we completed the first edition of *The Learning Revolution,* Amazon, Netscape and Internet *Explorer* were unknown. In 1997 we co-created a second edition—by email while one author was in Sweden, the other in Singapore. Google was a year away from being incorporated. Now John Batelle, in *The Search,* says

Google is tapping no more than 5 percent of what is to come in online "search". What will the next 95 percent make possible? Who could have foreseen even in 2000:

❏   That around 100 million people would today be writing online personal blogs, many of them daily, and sharing them free with millions of others?

❏   That the local flea market would explode into the global eBay?

❏   That it would now be possible to set up a free global online university, or a global interactive network for pre-kindergarten to senior high school learning?

❏   That every movie or TV show ever produced could be available to anyone on demand, just as hundreds are today on international flights?

❏   That it would be possible for everyone to learn new skills throughout life when you need them, where you need them?

❏   That small children could produce professional movies, compose their own music, animate their own graphics—and work together to simulate virtual cities, worlds, civilizations and even the universe?

There is only one time in history when all people start to link together in a shared all-embracing network of unbounded possibilities.

We are now living through the birth of that new era—all of us, interlinked together.

We could also be the first generation to end the extreme, appalling poverty that sees millions of children die needlessly of hunger each year in a world of plenty.

We are also the first generation that can afford to provide a decent education for all—because knowledge, once co-created, can now be freely shared with millions.

But the real answer, of course, is not technology, although it can be the catalyst. The real need is even simpler and much more profound:

❏   The vision and wisdom to see the unbounded possibilities.

❏   The leadership and co-creative drive to unleash them.

For who can resist the power of an idea whose time has come? If not now, when? If not us, who?[17]

Who can resist the power of an idea whose time has come?

Chapter reference notes ∎

When the same reference source is used more than once, later references are abbreviated in this way:

1.2—meaning: See chapter 1, reference source number 2.

GD is Gordon Dryden; JV is Jeannette Vos.

Other page references refer to pages in this book.

Summaries of many sources are now readily available on *www.wikipedia.org*

Preface

1. Pepperdine University, Los Angeles.

Foreword

1. Joseph Stiglitz and Linda Bilmes, *The Three Trillion Dollar War*, Allen Lane (2008).

Introduction

1. Quoted by David A. Wise, *The Google Story*, Bantam Dell (2005).

2. *Time*, cover story, December 25, 2006.

3. Dee Hock, *Birth of the Chaordic Age*, Berrett Kohler (1999).

4. Michio Kaku, *Visions*, Anchor Books (1997).

5. Tim Berners-Lee, *Weaving the Web*, Harper Collins (1999).

6. *A Review of the Open Education Resources Movement, Report to Hewlett Foundation (2007), http://www.oerderves.org*

7. www.ibo.org

8. www.curriki.org

9. www.johnseelybrown.com (Articles in Sandbox).

10. www.atomiclearning.com

11. Chris Anderson, *The Long Tail*, Hyperion (2006).

12. Clayton Christensen, *Disrupting Class*, McGraw-Hill (2008).

13. www.wikipedia.org

14. Quoted in www.wikipedia.org

15. www.markprensky.com (under *Writing: Proposal for Educational Development Software Sites.*

16. Eric S. Raymond, *The Cathedral and the Bazaar*, O'Reilly (1999), basic philosophy of the Open Source movement.

17. www.stuff.co.nz/thepress/4447249a19743.html

18. Gary Hamel, *Leading The Revolution*, HBS Press (2000).

Chapter 1: *The converging revolutions*

1. Peter Drucker, *The New Realities*, Harper & Row (1989)

2. Don Tapscott and Anthony D. Williams, *Wikinomics*, Atlantic (2006).

3. Intel website under Intel Museums/Moore's Law.

4. Margaret Wheatley, *Leadership and The New Science*, Berrett-Koehler (2001).

5. George Gilder, *Telecosm*, Free Press (2000).

6. Kevin Kelly, *New Rules for the Next Society*, *Wired* magazine (September 1997).

7. Peter Drucker, *Managing in the Next Society*, Butterworth Heinemann (2002).

8. Google *world poverty statistics.*

9. 1.8

10. 1.8.

11. 1.7.

12. www.internetretailer.com (2008).

13. Thomas Goetz, *Open Source Everywhere*, *Wired* (November 2003).

14. March 7, 2008, press release.

15. *Business Week* (January 23, 2008).

16. Tapula Digita press release (April 8, 2008).

17. *Business Week* (February 19, 2008).

18. Introduction.15.

Chapter 2: *The network revolution*

1. Seymour Papert, various articles, all available at www.papert.org

2. Graham Nuthall, *The Cultural Myths and Realities of Classroom Teaching and Learning: a Personal Journal*, article in *Teachers College Record*, New Zealand (May 2005).

3. William D. Pflaum, *The Technology Fix*, ASCD (2004).

4. Mark Prensky, *Digital Natives, Digital Immigrants*, www.markprensky.com (2001).

5. Mark Prensky, *Do They Really Think Differently?* www.markprensky.com (2001).

6. Mark Prensky, Introduction.15.

7. www.wisdomquotes.com

8. Quoted by Matt Ridley, *Nature Via Nurture*, Harper Perennial (2004).

9. 2.1.

10. John Holt, *How Children Fail*, Delta (1982).

11. *The Promise and Limitation of Smart Drugs*, *Business Week* (Sept. 26, 2005).

12. Michio Kaku, *Visions*, Anchor (1997).

13. Speech to Edinburgh Television Festival (August 27, 2005).

14. 2.1.

15. Karl Popper, *The Open Society and Its Enemies*, Philosophy Books (1945).

16. 2.8.

17. Quoted by Bryan Magee in *The Story of Philosophy*, Dorling Kindersley (2001).

18. *Celebrating Multiple Intelligences:*

Teaching for Success, New City School (1994).

19. Bruce Nussbaum, *Get Creative*, *Business Week* (August 8/15, 2005).

20. Marcus Buckingham and Curt Coffman, *First, Break All The Rules*, Simon & Schuster (2000).

21. *It's a Wikipedia World*, *Time* magazine (June 6, 2005).

22. 2.21.

Chapter 3: *The talent revolution*

1. Steven Rose, *The 21st-Century Brain*, Vintage (2006).

2. 2.20.

3. 1.1.

4. Bill Bryson, *A Short History of Nearly Everything*, Doubleday (2003).

5. Robert J. Sternberg and Helena L. Grigorenko, *Our Labelled Children*, Perseus (1999).

6. Howard Gardner, *Frames of Mind*, Basic Books (1983).

7. 3.5.

8. Ronald Kotulak, *Inside The Brain*, Andrews and McMeel (1996).

9. 3.8.

10. Steve Hamm, *The Wired Campus*, *Business Week* (December 11, 2000).

11. Douglas R. Fields, *The Other Half of the Brain*, in *Scientific American* (April 2004).

12. Quoted by Daniel Goleman, *Emotional Intelligence*, Bloomsbury (1996).

13. Candice B. Pert, *Molecules of Emotion: why you feel the way you feel*, Simon & Schuster (1997).

14. Todd Risley and Betty Hart, *Meaningful Differences in the Everyday Experiences of American Children*, Paul H. Brooks (1995), summarized well in 1.12.

15. TV interview with GD (1990).

16. 3.5.

17. David Perkins, *Outsmarting IQ*, Simon & Schuster (1995).

18. 2.20.

19. 2.20

20. Interview with GD.

Chapter 4: *Learning-styles revolution*

1. 3.6.

2. Howard Gardner, *Intelligences Reframed: Multiple Intelligences for the 21st Century,* Basic Books (1999).

3. Lloyd Geering, *In The World Today,* Allen & Unwin and Port Nicholson Press (1988).

4. Of many articles by the Dunns: *Learning and Teaching Styles and Brain Behavior,* published by Oklahoma Department of Education Newsletter (1988).

5. Michael Grinder, *Righting The Educational Conveyor Belt,* Metamorphous Press (1989).

6. 4.4.

7. Anthony Gregorc, *An Adult's guide to Style,* Gabriel Systems (1982).

8. See also, Bobbi dePorter with Mike Hernacki, *Quantum Learning,* Dell (1992).

9. 4.8.

10. Howard Gardner, *The Unschooled Mind,* Basic Books (1991).

11. See detailed coverage in Chapter 8, from pages 210 to 213.

Chapter 5: *Learn-a-living revolution*

1. 2.20.

2. Marilyn King, *Dare to Imagine,* in *The Beam,* New Horizons for Learning (1991).

3. *It's a Whole New World, Business Week* cover story (September 26, 2005).

4. Colin Rose, *Accelerated Learning,* Dell (1985).

5. Terry Wyler Webb, with Douglas Webb, *Accelerated Learning With Music—a Trainer's Manual,* Accelerated Learning Systems (Georgia, 1990).

6. Georgi Lozanov, *Suggestology and Outlines of Suggestopedy* Gordon and Breach (1978).

7. Tony Buzan, *Make the Most of Your Mind,* Linden (1984).

8. Marian Diamond, TV interview with GD, Berkeley (1900). Also: Marian Diamond, *Enriching Heredity,* Macmillan (1988).

9. Two-day seminars pioneered by Apple Education; four-day five-day developments coordinated by co-author Dryden.

Chapter 6: *The creative revolution*

1. Thomas Friedman, *The World is Flat,* Penguin/Allen Lane (2005) provides graphic examples of the creative links between the developed world, on the one hand, and India, China and Eastern Europe on the other.

2. *The World Book Encyclopedia.*

3. Frank Rose, *The End of Innocence at Apple Computer,* Arrow (1998).

4. John F. Love, *Underneath the Arches,* Bantam (1986).

5. *The Sunday Times Rich List,* London (1996).

6. Gordon Dryden, *Out of The Red,* William Collins (1978).

7. Adrian J. Slywotsky and David J. Morrison, *the Profit Zone,* Times Books (1998).

8. 6.7.

9. David Ogilvy, *Ogilvy on Advertising,* Crown (1983).

10. Peter Ellyard, speech to New Zealand School Principals Association (1992).

11. James L. Adams, *Conceptual Blockbusting,* Penguin (1987).

12. Peter Evans and Geoff Deeham, *The Keys to Creativity,* Grafton (1998).

13. Alex Osborn, *Applied Imagination,* Charles Schribner & Sons (1953).

14. 6.11.

15. Masaaki Imai, *Kaizen: The Key to Japan's Competitive Success,* Random House (1986).

17. Toshihiko Yamashita, *The Panasonic Way,* Kohansha International (1987).

18. Edward de Bono, *De Bono's Thinking Course,* BBC Books (1982).

19. Roger von Oech, *A Whack on the Side of the Head,* Warner (1983).

20. 6.11.

21. Edward de Bono, *Six Thinking Hats,* Penguin (1977).

Chapter 7: *Early-childhood revolution*

1. Benjamin S. Bloom, *Stability and Change in Human Characteristics,* John Wiley (1964), was the first major book to summarize all the research findings of the previous hundred years on this issue. In the past twenty years many different and specialist research projects have confirmed this. Some are covered in previous editions of our book, *The Learning Revolution.*

2. 2.20.

3. Professor Marian Diamond, TV interview with GD, Berkeley (2000).

4. Ruth Rice, *The Effects of Tactile-Kinesthetic Stimulation on the Subsequent Development of Premature Infants,* University of Texas (1975).

5. Professor Lyelle L. Palmer, *Kindergarten Maxi-Stimulation: Results Over Four Years,* at Westwood School, Irving, Texas (1971-75); *A Chance to Learn: Intensive Neuro-Stimulation in Transition Kindergarten* at Shingle Elementary School, Minneapolis (1990-91); and *Smooth Eye Pursuit Stimulation Readiness in Kindergarten,* at Shingle Creek Elementary School, Minneapolis (1990-91).

6. Palmer interview and correspondence with Lyelle Palmer (1993).

7. Interview with JV (1996).

8. Notes provided by Jerome Hartigan to GD (1995).

9. Interview with GD, Philadelphia (1990).

10. Dorothy Butler, *Babies Need Books,* Penguin (1984).

11. *Oxford English Dictionary.*

12. J.A. van Elk, *Threshold Level for Modern Language Learning,* Longman Paul (1976) for the Council of Europe. The most-used 1,700 words in the English language from the *Extended Ayres List,* are listed by Romalda Bishop Spalding in *The Writing Way To Reading,* Quill/William Morris (1990).

13. Peggy Kaye, *Games For Learning,* Noonday Press (1991).

14. Since 1974, GD has studied the Doman results at first hand in Australia, New Zealand and the United States. He has not yet met a critic of Doman's methods who has actually visited his training headquarters—while many of his critics use identical methods.

15. TV interview with GD, Philadelphia (1990).

16. Dr. Noor Laily dato' Abu Bakar and Mansor Haji Sukaimi, *Child of Excellence,* Nury Institute, Malaysia (1991).

17. Felicity Hughes, *Reading and Writing Before School,* Jonathan Cape (1971).

18. 7.3.

19. All the details of the Missouri Parents as Teachers Program obtained by GD during videotaping visit to Missouri (1990).

20 7.19.

21. Burton L. White, *The First Three Years of Life,* Prentice Hall (1986).

22. Interview in *The Brains Behind the Brain,* in *Educational Leadership* (November 1998).

23. 7.22.

24. The HIPPY Program was introduced into New Zealand in the early 1990s by The Pacific Foundation, jointly pioneered by co-author Dryden and Lesley Max. Lesley Max remains Executive Director today of the Foundation since renamed Great Potentials. Details from Lesley Max.

25. Details from Lesley Max, Great Potentials Foundation.

26. GD television interviews and research in Sweden during 1990 visit.

27. Paula Polk Lillard,, *Montessori: A Modern Approach,* Schocken Books, provides an excellent guide to Montessori's work.

28. Details of the Foundation Center for Phenomenological Research gained on a visit by GD to the Artesia II Montessori Center at French Camp, CA (1990). Information since updated in personal conversations.

29. 7.28.

30. Maria Montessori, *The Montessori Method,* Schocken books (1964), first published in English in 1912.

31. Pauline Pertab interview with GD in Auckland, New Zealand (1990).

Chapter 8: *The teaching revolution*

1. From Glenn Capelli's seminar, SALT Conference in Minneapolis (1991).

2. Tony Stockwell, *Accelerated Learning in Theory and Practice,* EFFECT, Liechtenstein (1992).

3. Television interview with GD, Washington DC (1990).

4. Television interview with GD at Sodertalji High School, Sweden (1990).

5. Television interview with GD in San Francisco (1990).

6. 8.2.

7. *500 Tips for Teachers,* prepared by staff of Cramlington Community High School, and available through their website: www.cchsonline.co.uk

8. 5.5.

9. 8.5.

10. 8.5.

11. The current authors have found no evidence of anyone outside Bulgaria achieving results as high as 1,000 to 2,000 words learned in a day.

12. 5.5.

13. 8.2.

14. 8.5.

15. 5.5.

16. GD had been visiting this school regularly since 1997, and has for many months of that period been a consultant to the school.

17. Copious research notes provided to the authors by the organizers of the SMART program.

18. Thomas R. Hoerr, *Becoming a Multiple Intelligence School,* ASCD (2000).

19. 8.18.

Chapter 9: *The high school revolution*

1. Bill Gates in address to American Governors' National Education Summit on High Schools, February 26, 2005.

2. Introduction.12.

3. Roger C. Schank, *Engines for Learning,* Laurence Erlbaum (1995).

4. Jack O'Connell, quoted by George Lucas Educational Foundation, www.edutopia.org

5. Betsy Hammond and Bill Graves, Road Map to Success, Oregonian (January 13, 2004).

6. 9.5.

7. 9.5

8. www.edutopia.org

9. 9.8.

10. 9.8.

11. 9.8.

12. 9.8.

13. www.papert.org for an excellent collection of Dr. Seymour Papert's writings

14. Introduction.12.

15. Our thanks to The Management Edge Ltd., Wellington, New Zealand, and especially to Ross Peddler, Director, for assembling various reports on Mt. Edgecumbe High School.

16. Ken Jones and Paul Ongtooguk, *High Stakes Testing in Alaska,* article filed at www.edst.edu.abc

17. Myron Tribus, *The Application of Quality Management Principles in Education at Mt. Edgecumbe High School,*

Sitka, Alaska, (1990), reprinted in *An Introduction to Total Quality for Schools,* American Association of School Administrators (1991).

18. 9.1.

Chapter 10: *The co-creative revolution*

1. Sir John Daniels, quoted by Daniel E. Atkins, John Seely Brown and Allen E. Hammond in *A Review of the Open Education Resources Movement,* Report to Hewlett Foundation (February 2007). http://www.oerderves.org

2. 10.1.

3. *Time* magazine, *How to bring our schools into the 20th century,* cover story (December 10, 2006).

4. Unicef 2006 World Hunger Report.

5. George Gilder, in *Telecosm: How infinite bandwidth will revolutionize our world,* The Free Press (2000)

6. 10.5.

7. Li Lanqing, former Chinese Vice Premier, in *Education for 1.3 Billion,* Pearsons (English-language edition, 2005), with satellite data updated from Li Kaishing Foundation website.

8. 10.1.

9. 10.1.

10. Quoted by David A. Wise, *The Google Story,* Bantam Dell (2005).

11. 10.5.

12. John Battelle, *The Search: How Google and its rivals rewrote the rules of business and transformed our culture,* Nicholas Brealey (2005), by far the best book to date on the history and future of online "search".

13. John Seely Brown, *New Learning Environments for the 21st Century,* address to Forum for the Future of Higher Education's 2005 Aspen Symposium. Available with many other speeches, interviews and presentations at Brown's website: *www.johnseelybrown.com*

14. 10.13.

15. 10.3.

16. Michael W. Hiltzik, *Dealers of Lightning (XEROX PARC and the dawn of the computer age),* Harper Business (1999).

17. 10.1.

18. www.bubbledome.com

19. 10.1.

20. Charles M. Vest, President Emeritus of Massachusetts Institute of Technology, in *Open Content and the Emerging Global Meta-University,* article in *Educause Review* (May-June 2006).

21. Full details at *http://www.eol.org*

22. Mark Thompson, BBC Director-General, to Edinburgh International Television Festival (August 27, 2005).

23. Marc Prensky, *Proposal for Educational Software Development Sites,* article at www.marcprensky.com, then *Writing* and select article by title. Several other excellent background articles on similar subjects on same site.

24. 10.23.

25. 10.3.

26. Quoted in 10.16.

27. 10.13.

Chapter 11: *The innovation revolution*

1. Marc J. Rosenberg in *e-Learning,* McGraw-Hill (2001).

2. 11.1.

3. Nicholas Negroponte, *Being Digital,* Alfred Knopf (1995).

4. Introduction.12.

5. 10.3.

6. *Children of The Web,* Business Week (July 2, 2007).

7. *The $100 Un-PC, Newsweek* cover story (February 12, 2007, Asian edition).

8. *E-Society: My World is Cyworld, Business Week* (September 26, 2005).

9. 11.8.

10. Chris Anderson, *The Long Tail,* Hyperion (2006).

11. 11.10.
12. Adam Sherwin, *Sims Guru Will Wright unveils Spore to rapt audience*, article in *The Times*, United Kingdom (March 16, 2007).
13. 11.12.
14. Geoffrey A. Moore published his first *Crossing The Chasm* book in 1991, and has revised it under various titles since. See www.wikipedia.org under *Crossing the chasm*.

Chapter 12: *The digital revolution*

1. Co-author Dryden has been closely involved with the New Zealand, Singapore, British and Mexican models in this chapter, and co-author Vos in Canada and Sweden.
2. Charles Fisher, David C. Dwyer and Keith Yocam (editors), *Education & Technology,*, jointly published by Jossey-Bass and Apple Press (1996).
3. *In a class of their own, The Guardian* online newspaper (September 23, 2003).
4. Derek Wise and Mark Lovatt, *Creating an Accelerated Learning School* (2001); Alistair Smith, Mark Lovatt and Derek Wise, *Accelerated Learning: a user's guide* (2003), Network Educational Press, England.
5. Summary of Master's Academy results from both their website—www.masters.ab.ca—and personal correspondence with JV.
6. 12.5.

Chapter 13: *The global revolution*

1. *Time's* 2006 Person of the Year: *You*, in *Time* magazine, December 25, 2006.
2. Kevin Kelly, *We are the Web*, *Wired* magazine (August, 2005).
3. Desmond Keegan, *Mobile Learning: the next generation of learning*, Distance Learning International (2005).
4. *The Next Four Billion (Development through enterprise)*, published by the World Resources Institute (2007).

5. 10.8.
5. 10.14.
6. 10.4.
7. Jeffrey Sachs, *The End of Poverty*, Penguin (2006).
8. George Land and Beth Jarman, *Breakpoint and Beyond: Mastering the future today*, Harper Business (*1992*).
9. Steven Carden, *New Zealand Unleashed*, Random House (New Zealand, 2007).
10. John Doerr, leading venture capitalist in Silicon Valley: a recurring phrase used by him.
11. Chen Jingpan, *Confucius as a Teacher*, Foreign Language Press, Beijing, China (various editions).
12. Lee Hsieng Loong, son of Singapore's first Prime Minister Lee Kuan Yew, when sworn in as new PM in 2004 almost immediately announced *"Teach Less—and learn more"* as the basis of a new creativity-building education policy.
13. New New Zealand curriculum comes into force in 2009. See *nzcurriculum.tki. org.nz/new_notices*
14. A continuing theme stressed by Peter Drucker in his last books before his death in November 2005, at the age of ninety-five: *Managing in a Time of Great Change* (1995) and *Managing in The Next Society* (2002), both published by Butterworth Heinemann.
15. Introduction.12.
16. Thomas Friedman, *The Lexus and the Olive Tree*, Harper Collins (2000).
15. Paraphrased from Rabbi Hillel's Hebrew writings of 2,000 years ago: *If I am not for myself, who will be for me? If I am for myself alone, what am I? If not now, when?* From *Ethics of the Fathers (Pilke Avot)* 1.14: : the precept that one should not separate oneself from the community. This is normally closely linked with Rabbi Hillel's Hebrew version of the Golden Rule. Versions of this are found in nearly all religions.

Authors' sincere thanks

❏ ***Both authors thank:*** All the authors and researchers in so many fields on whose shoulders we have stood in completing this book, including those quoted in it and in our recommended reading list. Also to those schools who generously supplied us with photos, including those which could not be used for space or other reasons.

❏ ***Our thanks, in particular, to:*** Bradley and Cathy Winch (our international agents), Bobbi dePorter (co-founder of SuperCamp), Eric Jensen, Colin Rose, Tony Buzan, Dee Dickinson, Marian Diamond, Lyelle Palmer, Tom Hoerr, Glenn Capelli, Glenn Doman, Peter and Anne Kenyon, Derek Wise, Mark Lovatt, David Perry, Irene Chee, Pat Keenan, Mark Beach, Warren Patterson, John Petrie, Viki Laurence, Vicki Buck, Noel Ferguson, Monica Lundberg, Helena Wallenberg, Tom Rudmik, Dick and Kathy DeBoer, Mats and Irene Niklasson, Ulla Eriksson, Daniel Lundquist, Johanna Gagner, and all the others around the world, too numerous to mention, who have shared their experiences with us.

❏ ***Special thanks to:*** Jeanene and Ricardo Carvajal, Mariana Cortes, Cristina Osorno, Masahiro Saito, and the incredible team at Mexico's Thomas Jefferson Institute, who with us have pioneered the simultaneous production of this edition in two languages—and together planned a truly multinational revolution.

❏ ***Jeannette Vos thanks:*** John Green for his incredible support while taking on a book project yet another time. And especially my immediate family members, Leisha and Summer Groenendal, and Elly Van Barneveld. Also, a special thanks to the many personal friends who have supported my work. And to Gordon Dryden, for all the areas of content that he contributed, plus his journalistic ability to make the book so readable, and his cooperation and joint effort in making *The Learning Revolution* concept such a best-seller internationally.

❏ ***Gordon Dryden thanks:*** Margaret Dryden, for 52 years of love, wisdom, tolerance, patience, support, great parenting and good fun. And Jeannette Vos, for suggesting the original *Learning Revolution* book, for the excellent teaching experience distilled into various editions, and for tolerance (and sometimes despair) at seeing volumes of her research slashed and simplified in an editor's drive to make academic research understandable to general readers.

The Unlimited Library ▬

To start learning any subject (if you're a print-oriented learner) the co-authors recommend you first read three or four simple books on that subject by practical achievers. Then try more depth. Here are our recommended starter books on each subject:

THE FUTURE

Tapscott, Don, and Anthony D. Williams, *Wikinomics: How mass collaboration changes everything,* Portfolio/Penguin, New York (2006).

Laszlo, Ervin, *The Chaos Point, London (2006).*

Friedman, Thomas, *The Earth is Flat,* Penguin/Allen Lane (2005).

Hock, Dee, *Birth of the Chaordic Age,* Berrett-Koehler, San Francisco (1999).

Kaku, Michio, *Visions: How science will revolutionise the 21st century,* Anchor, New York (1997).

LeGrain, Philippe, *Open World: The truth about globalization,*Abacus, London (2002).

THE DIGITAL ECONOMY

Kelly, Kevin, *New Rules For The New Economy,* Viking, New York (1998).

Tapscott, Don; Ticholl, David; and Lowy, Alex, *Digital Capital,* Harvard Business School, Boston (2000).

Tapscott, Don (Editor), *Blueprint to the Digital Economy,* McGraw-Hill, New York (1998).

Martin, Chuck, *The Digital Estate,* McGraw-Hill, New York (1996).

Tapscott, Don, *Growing Up Digital,* McGraw-Hill, New York (1998).

Downes, Larry; and Mui, Chunka, *Unleashing The Killer App.,* Harvard Business School Press, Boston, Mass (1998).

LEADERSHIP

Buckingham, Marcus, and Coffman, Curt, *First, Break All The Rules,* Simon & Schuster, New York (1999).

Covey, Stephen, *The 7 Habits Of Highly Effective People,* Simon & Schuster, New York (1989).

Goleman, Daniel, *The New Leaders: Transforming the Art of Leadership Into The Science of Results,* Little Brown Book,UK (2002).

Drucker, Peter, *Managing in the Next Society,* Butterworth Heinemann, Oxford (2002).

Cowan, Christopher C., & Todorovic, Natasha, *The Never Ending Quest,* ECLET Publishing, Santa Barbara, California (2005).

TO START SCHOOL REFORM

Christensen, Clayton, with Michael B. Horn and Curtis W Johnson, *Disrupting Class: How disruptive innovation will change the way the world learns,* McGraw-Hill, New York (2008).

Smith, Alistair, *Accelerated Learning In Practice,* Network Educational Press, UK (1998); see their catalog for other Alistair Smith books in series.

Lovatt, Mark; and Wise, Derek, *Creating an Accelerated Learning School,* Network Educational Press, UK (2001): the Cramlington experience.

Smith, Alistair; Lovatt, Mark; and Wise, Derek, *Accelerated Learning: a user's guide,* Network Educational Press, UK (2004): the Cramlington Accelerated Learning Cycle.

George Lucas Educational Foundation, *Learn & Live,* kit includes book and one-hour videotape hosted by Robin Williams, covering U.S. breakthrough school models, direct from: *www.edutopia.org*

Hoerr, Thomas R., *Becoming a Multiple Intelligence School,* ASCD, Alexandra, VA (2000).

Faculty of New City School, *Celebrating Multiple Intelligences in the Classroom,* New City School, St. Louis (1994).

GETTING STARTED: THE BRAIN

Winston, Robert, *The Human Mind— and how to make the most of it,* Bantam, London (2003), in conjunction with BBC TV series.

Rose, Steven, *The 21st-Century Brain,*Vintage, London (2005).

Restak, Richard, *The New Brain: How The Modern Age Is Rewiring Your Mind,* Rodale Ltd., UK (2001).

Pink, Daniel H., *A Whole New Mind,* Riverhead, New York, (2006).

Bragdon, Allen D; Gamon, David, *Use it or Lose it,* Bragdon Publishers, San Francisco (2000).

Le Doux, Joseph, *The Emotional Brain: The Mysterious Underpinnings of Emotional Life,* Simon and Schuster, New York (1996).

Ornstein, Robert; *The Amazing Brain,* Houghton Mifflin, Boston (1984).

Robert Kotulak, *Inside The Brain,* Andrews and McMeel, Kansas City, Mo. (1997).

Sylwester, Robert, *A Celebration of Neurons,* ASCD, Alexandria, VA (1995).

Diamond, Marian; and Hopson, Janet, *Magic Trees of the Mind: How to Nurture Your Child's Intelligence, Creativity, and Healthy Emotions from Birth Through Adolescence,* Plume, New York (1998).

BRAIN SYSTEMS

Purves, Dale and others, *Neuroscience,* Sinauer Associates, Sunderland, Mass. (2007) .

Givern, Barbara, *Teaching To The Brain's Natural Learning Systems,* ASCD, Alexandria, VA (2002).

GETTING STARTED: DNA

Ridley, Matt, *Nature Via Nurture: Genes, Experience and What Makes Us Human,* Harper Perennial, London (2003).

Ridley, Matt, *Genome: the autobiography of a species,* Fourth Estate, London (1999).

Sulston, John, & Georgina Ferry, *The Common Thread,* Bantam, UK (2002)

ACCELERATED LEARNING

Meier, Dave, *The Accelerated Learning Handbook,* McGraw Hill, New York (2000).

Rose, Colin, *Master It Faster,* Accelerated Learning Systems, UK (1999).

GETTING STARTED: TEACHERS

Loomans, Diane; and Kohlberg, Karen, *The Laughing Classroom,* Kramer, Tiburon, CA (1993).

DePorter, Bobbi; Reardon, Mark; and Singer-Nourie, Sarah, *Quantum Teaching,* Allyn & Bacon, Boston (1999).

Grinder, Michael, *A Healthy Classroom,* Michael Grinder & Associates WA,

GETTING STARTED: MUSIC

Campbell, Don, *The Mozart Effect,* Avon Books, New York (1997).

Barzakov, Ivan and Associates, *Essence & Impact* (includes *How to Use Music*), Barzac Institute, Novata, CA (1995).

Andersen, Ole; Marsh, Marcy; and Harvey, Arthur, *Learn with the Classics,* LIND Institute, San Francisco (1999).

MIND MAPPING

Mukerjea, Dilip, *Superbrain: Train Your*

Brain To Unleash the Genius Within By Using Memory Building, Mind Mapping, Speed Reading, Oxford University Press, Singapore (1996).

Buzan, Tony, *The Mind Map Book—Radiant Thinking,* BBC , London (1993).

Margulies, Nancy, *Mapping Inner Space,* Zephyr Press, Tucson, AZ. (1991).

ACCELERATED LEARNING

Rose, Colin; and Goll, Louise, *Accelerate Your Learning,* Accelerated Learning Systems, UK (1993): a kit.

DePorter, Bobbi, *Quantum Learning,* Dell, New York (1992).

Rose, Colin; and Nicholl, Malcolm. J., *Accelerated Learning For the 21st Century,* Accelerated Learning Systems, UK (1997).

CREATING NEW IDEAS

Michalko, Michael, *Cracking Creativity,* Ten Speed Press, Berkeley, CA (1998).

von Oech, Roger, *A Whack On The Side Of The Head,* Warner, New York (1990).

Adams, James L., *Conceptual Blockbusting,* Penguin, New York (1987).

von Oech, Roger, *Creative Whack Pack* (playing cards), U.S. Games Systems, Stamford, CT.

Michalko, Michael, *Thinkertoys,* Ten Speed Press, Berkeley, CA (1991).

MEMORY

Squire, Larry; and Kandel, Eric, *Memory: From Mind to Molecules,* Scientific American Library, New York (1999).

Higbee, Kenneth L., *Your Memory: How it Works and How to Improve it,* Piatkus, London (1989).

Buzan, Tony, *Use Your Perfect Memory,* Plume-Penguin, New York (1991).

INTELLIGENCE

Goleman, Daniel, *Emotional Intelligence,* Bloomsbury, London (1996).

Siler, Todd, *Think Like a Genius,* Bantam, New York (1997).

Gardner, Howard, *Frames Of Mind,* Basic Books, New York (1983).

Gardner, Howard, *The Unschooled Mind,* Basic Books, New York (1991).

PERSONAL DEVELOPMENT

Rosenberg, Marshall B., *Nonviolent Communciation: A Language of Compassion,* Puddle Dancer Press, CA (1999).

Demartini, John F., *The Breakthrough Experience: A Revolutionary New Approach to Personal Transformation,* Hay House, UK (2002).

FOR STUDENTS

Rose, Colin; and Civardi, Anne, *Champs,* Accelerated Learning Systems, UK (2001).

Martel, Laurence, *School Success,* Learning Matters, Arlington, VA (1992).

Ellis, David B., *Becoming a Master Student,* College Survival, Rapid City, SD (1985).

FOR PARENTS

Kline, Peter, *The Everyday Genius,* Great Ocean Publishers, Arlington, VA (1988).

Armstrong, Thomas, *In Their Own Way,* Jeremy Tarcher, LA (1987).

Clark, Faith and Cecil, *Hassle-Free Homework,* Doubleday, NY (1989).

FOR TEACHERS

Nicholson, Tom, *Reading The Writing On The Wall,* Dunmore, New Zealand (2000). Excellent to teach reading.

Capelli, Glenn: and Brealey, Sean, *The Thinking Learning Classroom,* The True Learning Centre, Perth, Western Australia (2000).

Campbell, Linda and Bruce; Dickinson, Dee, *Teaching and Learning Through*

Multiple Intelligences, Allyn and Bacon, Boston (1999).

Jensen, Eric, *SuperTeaching,* Kendall/Hunt, Dubuque, Iowa (1988).

Caine, Renate Nummela and Geoffrey, *Unleashing the Power of Perpetual Change,* ASCD, Alexandria, VA (1997).

PARENTING FOR INFANTS

Eliot, Lise, *What's Going On In There? How the Brain and Mind Develop in the First Five Years of Life*, Bantam Books, New York, (1999).

Dryden, Gordon; and Rose, Colin, *FUNdamentals,* Accelerated Learning Systems, UK (1996): complete kit; and as book, HarperCollins, UK (2000).

Beck, Joan, *How To Raise a Brighter Child,* Fontana, London (1985).

Marzolla, Jean; and Lloyd, Janice, *Learning Through Play,* Harper & Row (1972).

White, Burton L., *The First Three Years of Life,* Prentice, Hall, New York (1986).

EARLY READING

Milne, Duncan, *Teaching The Brain To Read,* SK (SmartKids) , Auckland (2005).

Hughes, Felicity, *Reading And Writing Before School,* Jonathan Cape (1971).

Young, Peter; and Tyre, Colin, *Teach Your Child To Read,* Fontana (1985).

Doman, Glenn, *Teach Your Baby to Read,* Better Baby Press, Philadelphia (1979).

EARLY WRITING

Martin, John Henry; and Friedberg, Andy, *Writing To Read,* Warner (1986).

Spalding, Romalda Bishop and Walter T., *The Writing Road To Reading,* Quill/William Morrow, New York (1990).

CREATIVE WRITING

Stein, Sol, *Stein on Writing,* St. Martin's Griffin, New York (1995).

Rico, Gabriel, *Writing The Natural Way,* J.P. Tarcher, Los Angeles, CA.

SPELLING

Cripps, Charles; and Peters, Margaret L., *Catchwords,* Collins, London (1993).

Hornsby, Beve; and Shear, Frula, *Alpha to Omega,* Heinemann, UK (1993).

MATHEMATICS

Help Your Child With Maths (the book of the BBC TV series), BBC Books, London.

Johnson, Virginia, *Hands-On Math,* Creative Teaching Press (1994).

Doman, Glenn, *Teach Your Baby Math,* Better Baby Press, Philadelphia (1979).

GAMES FOR LEARNING

Kaye, Peggy, *Games for Reading,* Pantheon Books (1994).

Kaye, Peggy, *Games for Learning,* The Noonday Press (1991).

Perry, Susan K, *Playing Smart (four to 14 years),* Free Spirit (1990).

GAMES FOR TEACHERS AND TRAINERS

Thiagarajan, Sivasailam (Thiagi), *Diversity Stimulation Games* (1994);*Teamwork Games* (1994); *Cash Games* (1994); *More Cash Games* (1995); *Matrix Games* (1995); *Lecture Games* (1994); *Instructional Puzzles* (1995); *Creativity Games* (1996), all published by HRD Press.

LEARNING DIFFICULTIES

Levine, Mel, *A Mind At A Time,* Simon & Schuster, New York (2003).

Bluestone, Judith, *The Fabric of Autism: Weaving the Threads Into A Cogent Theory*, Handle Institute, Washington, USA (2004).

Reichenberg-Ullman, Judyth; Ullman, Robert, *Ritalin Free Kids,* New York, (2000).

Sternberg, Robert J.; and Grigorenko, Elena L., *Our Labelled Children,* Perseus, New York (1999).

Block, Mary Ann, *No More ADHD: 10 Steps to Help Improve Your Child's Attention and Behaviour Without Drugs,* Block Books, Texas, USA (2001).

Doman, Glenn, *What To Do About Your Brain-Injured Child,* Better Baby Press, Philadelphia (1974).

Armstrong, Thomas, *The Myth of the ADDS. Child,* Dutton, NY (1995).

Vitale, Barbara Meister, *Unicorns Are Real: A Right-Brained Approach to Learning,* Jalmar Press, Torrance, CA (1982).

MUSIC FOR LEARNING

Brewer, Chris Boyd; and Campbell, Don, *Rhythms of Learning,* Zephyr Press, Tucson, AZ (1990).

Campbell, Don, *100 Ways to Improve Teaching with Your Voice and Music,* Zephyr Press, Tucson (1992).

Merritt, Stephanie, *Mind, Music and Imagery,* Asian Publishing, Santa Rosa, CA (1996).

Barzakov, Ivan, *How to Read with Music,* Barzak Educational Institute, Novato, CA (1995).

MONTESSORI

Elizabeth G. Hainstock, *The Essential Montessori,* Plume, New York (1997).

Britton, Lesley, *Montessori: Play And Learn,* Vermilion (1992).

Lillard, Paula Polk, *Montessori: A Modern Approach,* Schoken Books, New York.

LOZANOV METHOD

Lozanov, Georgi; and Gateva, Evalina, *The Foreign Language Teacher's Suggestopedia Manual,* Gordon and Breach, New York (1988).

Lozanov, Georgi, *Suggestology and Outlines of Suggestopedy,* Gordon and Breach, New York, (1978).

Stockwell, Tony, *Accelerated learning in Theory and Practice,* EFFECT, Liechtenstein (1992).

DIET, ECOLOGY & LEARNING

Hills, Sandra; Wyman, Pat, *What's Food got to do with it?* Windsor, CA (1998).

Boutenko, Victoria, *Green for Life, Raw Family Publishing, www.rawfamily.com (2005).*

Rapp, Doris J., *Our Toxic World: A Wake Up Call,* Environmental Medical Research Foundation, Buffalo, New York (2003).

Robbins, John, *May All Be Fed: Diet For A New World,* Avon Books, New York (1992).

Roberts, Gwilym, *Boost Your Child's Brain Power: How To Use Good Nutrition,* Thorsons, England (1988).

Ausubel, Kenny, Harpignies, J.P., *Nature's Operating Instructions: The True Biotechnologies,* Sierra Club Books, San Francisco (2004).

FOREIGN LANGUAGE TEACHING

Dhority, Freeman Lynn; and Jensen, Eric, *Joyful Fluency: Brain-Compatible Second Language Acquisition,* The Brain Store, San Diego, CA (1998).

Dhority, Lynn, *The ACT approach: The Artful Use of Suggestion for Integrative Learning,* Gordon & Breach, New York (1991, expanded edition).

FOREIGN LANGUAGE LEARNING

Colin Rose, *Accelerated French, Accelerated Spanish, Accelerated Italian, Accelerated German,* Accelerated Learning Systems, Aston Clinton, Bucks, U.K. (full programs).

LEARNING & WORKING STYLES

Prashnig, Barbara, *The Power Of Di-*

versity, Network Educational Press, UK (2002).

Markova, Dawna, *How Your Child Is Smart,* Concari (1992).

Carbo, Marie; Dunn, Rita and Ken, *Teaching Students to Learn Through Their Individual Learning Styles,* Allyn and Bacon, Boston (1991).

Keirsey, David; Bates, Marilyn, *Please Understand Me,* Prometheus, Del Mar, CA. (1984).

TEACHING THINKING

De Bono, Edward, *Teaching Thinking,* Penguin, London (1977).

De Bono, Edward, *Edward de Bono's Thinking Course,* BBC Books, London (1982).

EDUCATIONAL KINESIOLOGY

Dennison, Paul E. and Gail E., *Edu-K for Kids! The Basic Manual on Educational Kinesiology for Parents and Teachers of Kids of All Ages,* Edu-Kinesthetics, Ventura, CA (1987)..

Dennison, Gail E. and Paul E; and Teplitz, Jerry V., *Brain Gym for Business,* Edu-Kinesthetics, Ventura CA (1994).

MIND-BODY CONNECTION

Pert, Candace, *Molecules of Emotion: Why You Feel the Way You Feel,* Simon & Schuster, New York (1997).

Hannaford, Carla, *The Dominance Factor: How Knowing Your Dominant Eye, Ear, Brain, Hand & Foot Can Improve Your Learning,* Great Ocean Publishers, Arlington, VA (1997).

Promislow, Sharon, *Making The Brain Body Conection,* Kinetic Publishing, West Vancouver, BC, Canada (1998).

Hannaford, Carla, *Smart Moves: Why Learning is Not All in Your Head,* Great Ocean Publishers, Arlington, VA (1995).

Hartley, Linda, *Wisdom of the Body Moving: an introduction to body-mind center-*

ing, North Atlantic Books, Berkeley, CA (1995).

TOMATIS METHOD

Tomatis, Alfred, *The Ear of Language,* Stoddard, New York (1997).

Gilmor, Timothy M.; Madaule, Paul; and Thompson, Billie (Editors); with Wilson, Tim, *About The Tomatis Method,* Listening Center Press, Toronto, Ont., Canada (1989).

TEACHING VALUES

Eyre, Linda and Richard, *Teaching Your Children Values,* Simon & Schuster, New York (1993).

Glenn, H. Stephen; and Nelson, Jane, *Raising Self-Reliant Children in a Self-Indulgent World,* Prime Publishing (1989).

BUSINESS TRAINING

Rylatt, Alastair; and Lohan, Kevin, *Creating Training Miracles,* Jolley-Bass, San Francisco, CA (1997).

Gutherie, Richard L.,*Working With Spirit: to replace control with trust,* Integrated Systems Thinking Press, Walled Lake (2000).

LEARNING ORGANIZATIONS

Senge, Peter M., *The Fifth Discipline,* Random House, Sydney (1992).

Senge, Peter M.; Roberts, Charlotte; Ross, Richard B.; Smith, Bryan J.; and Kleiner, Art, *The Fifth Discipline Fieldbook,* Nicholas Brealey, London (1994).

TOTAL QUALITY MANAGEMENT

Imai, Masaaki, *Kaizen: The Key to Japan's Competitive Success ,* Random House, New York (1986).

NEW ZEALAND INNOVATION

Treadwell, Mark, *Whatever: The conceptual eta and the evolution of school 2.0,* online at www.schoolv2.net (2008), with many linked support and back-up networks.

Index ▬▬▬▬▬

Publisher, publishing agent and author details

International publisher:

The Learning Web Ltd.
P.O. Box 87209
Auckland
New Zealand 1742
Phone: + 649 5210729
Contact: Publisher, Gordon Dryden: gordon@learningweb.co.nz
Website: www.thelearningweb.net

International translation and publishing rights:

For all foreign publishing rights:

The B.L. Winch Group, Inc.
dba Jalmar Press
International agent for The Learning Web Ltd.
www.jalmarpress.com <http://www.jalmarpress.com>
jalmarpress@att.net or blwjalmar@att.net

Bulk copies of the book for schools, businesses, gifts:

Contact publishers, through website or email (addresses above) for special bulk-purchase rates. Books are packed in cartons of 12.

Note: For previous editions of *The Learning Revolution,* many schools bought a book for each teacher, and then used each chapter as part of their weekly reading and professional development programs. See publisher's website for CD-roms for such programs.

To contact authors:

Jeannette Vos:

Website: www.learning-revolution.com
email: vos@learning-revolution.com or drjvos@mac.com

Gordon Dryden:

email: gordon@learningweb.co.nz